Muslims in Motion

Muslims in Motion

*Islam and National Identity
in the Bangladeshi Diaspora*

Nazli Kibria

RUTGERS UNIVERSITY PRESS
NEW BRUNSWICK, NEW JERSEY, AND LONDON

Library of Congress Cataloging-in-Publication Data

Kibria, Nazli.
  Muslims in motion : Islam and national identity in the Bangladeshi diaspora / Nazli
Kibria.
      p. cm. — Includes bibliographical references and index.
  ISBN 978–0–8135–5055–8 (hardcover : alk. paper) — ISBN 978–0–8135–5056–5
(pbk. : alk. paper)
    1. Bangladeshis—United States.   2. Bangladeshis—Great Britain.   3. Bangladesh—
Emigration and immigration.   I. Title.
  E184.B13K53   2011
  973′.004914126—dc22

                                                                                  2010045580

A British Cataloging-in-Publication record for this book is available from the British
Library.

Visit our Web site: http://rutgerspress.rutgers.edu

Manufactured in the United States of America

For the million and more Bengalis who were killed in 1971, during the birth of Bangladesh—may we never forget your sacrifice.

Freedom, you are
the arbour in the garden, the koel's song,
glistening leaves on ancient banyan trees,
the poetry notebook, to scribble as I please

—From "Freedom You Are" by Shamsur Rahman, translated by Kaiser Haq. Published December 15, 2007, in The Daily Star

Contents

Figures and Tables

Preface and Acknowledgments

On January 27, 2005, my father, Shah AMS Kibria, was assassinated. A member of the Parliament of Bangladesh, he had gone to his parliamentary constituency in Habiganj, Sylhet, to address a public meeting. As he was leaving, several grenades were hurled at him. Four others, including my cousin Shah Manzur Huda, were killed, and over eighty persons were injured. His murder followed a whole string of deadly terrorist attacks in Bangladesh at the time, many targeting progressive intellectuals and artists and members of the political opposition.

My father has been an important presence in this book for me in many different ways. To explain this, let me offer a brief background. Shah AMS Kibria was born in Sylhet in 1931. He was an exceptional student, gaining top marks in every countrywide university examination in which he appeared. In 1954 he joined the elite Foreign Service of Pakistan. And in March 1971, when the Bangladesh war of independence began, we (my parents, brother, and I) were living in Washington, D.C., where my father was serving as political counselor in the Pakistan embassy. My father had been a passionate Bengali nationalist since his days as a university student. He had participated in the Bengali Language Movement of 1952, when he had been jailed by the Pakistani authorities for six weeks. And so after the war began, with the unconditional support of my mother, my father declared allegiance to Bangladesh, quit the Pakistan embassy, and began organizing the Bangladesh Mission to the United States. We requested political asylum. I was a ten-year-old child at the time. But my memories of 1971 are sharp and vivid, from the terrifying images on TV of the violence taking place back home to the demonstrations in front of the White House that we helped to organize in order to protest the U.S. government's support of Pakistan in the war. In December 1971, with military intervention from India, the war ended with victory for Bangladesh. The next month we packed up and left Washington, D.C., to go back home, to a newly independent Bangladesh. In the ensuing period my father worked closely with the leaders of the country, including the first prime minister, Sheikh Mujibur Rahman, to set up the country's Ministry of Foreign Affairs.

In 1981, Shah AMS Kibria joined the United Nations as undersecretary general, taking up leadership of the Economic and Social Commission for Asia and the Pacific (ESCAP). After retiring from this post in 1992, he and my mother returned to Bangladesh. My father began to write newspaper columns and eventually entered the political arena. He joined the Awami League, the political party that had led Bangladesh to independence. And from 1996 to 2001 he served as the country's minister of finance. During his tenure as finance minister, the country was able to achieve relatively fast economic growth even as the prices of rice and other necessities remained stable. His other accomplishments included the introduction of old-age and widows' pensions and innovative youth employment programs, as well as the expansion of lending to small farmers.

In 2001, the Bangladesh Nationalist Party (BNP), in alliance with the Jamaat-e-Islami, came into power in Bangladesh. My father assumed his position as a member of the opposition in the Bangladesh Parliament. He also wrote vigorously, producing a steady stream of editorial pieces for the press. In these he expressed concern about the rise of political violence and religious extremism in the country. He wrote with dismay about the attacks on Hindu communities. He wrote with horror about the spate of bomb and grenade attacks in the country. And then he, too, became the victim of such an attack.

At the time of my father's assassination in 2005, I was completing data collection for this book and preparing to write a draft of it. The assassination plunged me away from these tasks and into worlds that I had only heard and read about before. This was a world in which I often spent all night wondering about what it felt like to have over one hundred splinters gouged in one's body. It was also a world in which my frail mother took to the streets, leading a peaceful campaign for justice, for an end to the climate of impunity for political violence in Bangladesh. Our family also sought international assistance for a complete, impartial, and transparent investigation and trial into the assassination of Shah AMS Kibria. Many public figures in the United States, including the late Senator Ted Kennedy, Congressman Barney Frank, and the then Senator Barack Obama, signed letters urging the Bangladesh government to undertake a complete and impartial investigation. But it is with great sorrow that I report, as I write these words in 2010, that the assassination of my father remains to be fully investigated and its perpetrators brought to justice.

Both before and after his death, Shah AMS Kibria has been a well-known name in Bangladesh. As I gathered data for this book, I did not always choose to reveal my connection to him. Nonetheless, with the exception of those who had grown up abroad and had relatively weak ties with Bangladesh, it was a connection that was almost always known or at least later discovered by those I interviewed. In a culture where family connections are understood to largely determine social identity and status as well as political affiliation and loyalty, it was a connection that carried powerful meanings. For the most part, I believe that my father's name opened doors to people and places that would otherwise have been difficult to access. I found that even those whose political sympathies were different from or even contrary to those of my father were willing to talk to me, perhaps just out of curiosity. Also, what is often described by Bengalis themselves as the Bengali penchant for vigorous political discussion turned out to be extremely useful for me as a researcher. Regardless of where they stood on the political spectrum of Bangladesh, with few exceptions those whom I or my research assistants approached seemed to welcome the opportunity to air their opinions.

I generally refrained from actively engaging in partisan political debates with my informants. Nonetheless, I have little doubt that I was identified with a particular political tradition of Bangladesh, by virtue of my family lineage, if nothing else. This is a tradition defined by the nationalist ideals that guided the 1971 war of liberation for Bangladesh, including the vision of a state that is secular in its commitment to religious neutrality. It is also a tradition that has faced mounting challenge since the 1980s from those who propose an Islamic identity for Bangladesh. My father was an important and well-recognized advocate of the secular nationalist ideals of 1971. Because of this, for some in Bangladesh, his tragic and violent death has symbolized the ongoing struggle to hold on to these ideals in the face of those who would have a different kind of Bangladesh, and who in some cases even resort to violent means in order to achieve it. Sadly, successive Bangladeshi governments since 2005 have failed to deliver justice, to find and prosecute those who planned and funded the brutal murder of Shah AMS Kibria. And so his assassination, along with other unresolved incidents of political violence, has also come to be a source of national disillusionment. It has been a symbol of disenchantment about the nationalist dreams that drove the country in 1971—of a just, harmonious, and prosperous Bangladesh.

But disillusionment about Bangladesh is perhaps the one thing that Shah AMS Kibria would never have accepted if he were alive today. Among the many gifts that my father gave me was a deep appreciation and respect for the struggles and achievements of Bangladesh and its people. He always had hope—that whatever problems his beloved Bangladesh was facing, they would eventually be overcome. It is his spirit, of determination, integrity, and optimism that has sustained me through the course of writing this book.

I am highly privileged in many respects, but especially in having family, friends, and colleagues who never hesitate in their generous support of me and my lengthy writing projects. As a parent of a child with autism, I have developed a keen appreciation for just how much difference this can make in one's life. James Littlefield (or "Allen," as I call him) has cheerfully looked after our children Shomik and Shumita on those many weekends when I have rushed out to the library in order to work on this book. I am also grateful to my in-laws, Jim and Joan Littlefield, for helping out with the children when I have been conducting research away from home. My mother, Asma Kibria, the artist whose painting appears on the cover of this book, furnished all kinds of practical support for my many research trips to Asia. Above all, her graceful courage and unfailing spirit has been a source of inspiration for me. I am grateful to Madhuri Kibria and Abu Taher ("Taher Bhai") for being there for her every day in my absence. My brother, Dr. Reza Kibria, who is an international economist by training and profession, has helped and encouraged me through every phase of this book, from planning and data collection to writing. Reflecting our different disciplinary backgrounds, we have often had lively debates about the theoretical and methodological traditions that inform this project. The book has been greatly enriched by the sharp and intelligent comments on it that he has given me over the years.

Despite the fact that we have not lived in the same city for many years, Sue Chow and Greg Brooks have remained an important part of my life; I am very lucky to have them as friends. Steve Gold, Habibul Khondker, Peggy Levitt and John Stone did not hesitate when I requested them on short notice to give me comments on various chapters. John furthermore took the time to muse with me about appropriate titles for the book. With her tremendous warmth, generosity, and intelligence, Pat Rieker has been a great friend and colleague. I also thank Brigitte Berger and Dan Monti for their loyal support of me.

In conducting a study that spans several continents, I have relied on many wonderful assistants. In gathering data on Bangladeshi labor migrants, I was assisted by Moniza Biswas, Paritosh Biswas, Muntasir Chaudhury, Cashfya Kazi, Shovon Kibria, Shima Mahvish, Golaam Murtaza, Rajeeb Sarkar, and Sakiba Zeba. In the United States and Britain, I was fortunate to have the help of Shamsul Alam, Nehrir Khan, Madhuparna Roy, Moshahida Sultana, and Sonali Jain. Kristi Trevino provided much-needed assistance in the final stages of manuscript preparation. I thank Rutgers University Press for patiently waiting for a manuscript that was too long in coming, and particularly Adi Hovav and Peter Mickulas for guiding it through the various stages of the publication process.

I gratefully acknowledge the funding that I have received for this project from the Fund for the Advancement of the Discipline of the American Sociological Association and the Small Grants Program of the MIT-Mellon Program on Forced Migration. An Albert Morris Faculty Research Grant from the Department of Sociology at Boston University gave me much-needed time off from teaching to complete the writing of this book.

All author proceeds from this book will go to the Shah AMS Kibria Foundation-USA (www.kibria.org). This is a nonprofit organization that is dedicated to enhancing educational opportunities for underprivileged children and adults, including those with special needs, in Bangladesh and in Bangladeshi diaspora communities around the world.

Muslims in Motion

CHAPTER 1

Muslim Migrants,
Bangladeshis Abroad

I trace the beginnings of this book to an informal conversation I remember having in the late 1990s. This was during a trip to Bangladesh, the country of my birth. I was at my parents' house in a middle-class neighborhood of Dhanmondi in Dhaka, the capital city, having tea with friends, a group that included academics, lawyers, and NGO leaders. Eager for their feedback, I expressed an interest in studying the rising prominence in the social and political life of Bangladesh of Islam, in particular an Islam that emphasizes a return to basic principles and the significance of Islamic thought for all aspects of life. I sought their advice on how I should go about conducting this study. In the vigorous discussions that ensued, all agreed that the topic was an important one. But why focus simply on those in Bangladesh? Why not look at those abroad—at Bangladeshis in Abu Dhabi, Kuala Lumpur, London, and New York? My friends spoke of noticing how Bangladeshis who went abroad often became highly religious, indeed "fundamentalist" in their orientation. They found it puzzling and counterintuitive. It was, moreover, a trend that held true across class lines, among not only the rural impoverished Bangladeshis who traveled to Saudi Arabia and Kuwait on labor contracts but also the urban, middle-class Bangladeshis who were going to Australia, Canada, and the United States. For all these reasons, as one friend put it, "Why not look abroad for what is happening at home?"

Among the notable global trends of the late twentieth and early twenty-first centuries is an Islamic revival. Across the Muslim world, there has been a surge of religiosity coupled with the expansion of Islamic movements that advocate a greater and renewed focus on religion in the lives of Muslims. This book is about the relationship of global migrations to these religious developments. My particular window into this topic is a study of movements from the Muslim-majority country of Bangladesh to different parts of the world—to Britain, the United States, the Arab Gulf states, and Malaysia. I look at how, in relation to these quite different settings, Bangladeshi Muslim migrants and their families come to organize their community life and make sense of their place in the world. In my investigations, I pay particular attention to the dynamics of Muslim identity among Bangladeshis abroad, and their implications for the religious landscape of Bangladesh today.

POLITICS AND THE STUDY OF MUSLIM MIGRANTS

The opening of the twenty-first century has seen an explosion of interest in Western societies about the Muslim world. Global political events, most notably the September 11, 2001, terrorist attacks by extremist Islamists on New York and the subsequent U.S.-led military invasion of Iraq, have fueled this interest, infusing it with a sense of urgency and anxiety. As interest in Muslims has surged around the world, the growing Muslim presence within North America and Europe has also attracted attention. This is particularly so in light of such catastrophic events as the July 7, 2005, London bombings (also known as "7/7"), which were carried out by four British Muslim men, three of Pakistani and one of Jamaican descent. Such incidents have raised fears about Muslim communities in the West as breeding grounds for violent extremism.

Reflecting these political currents, this has been a time of vigorous expansion in research and writing in North America and Europe about Islam and Muslims. Many conferences have been convened, research reports commissioned, surveys administered, and monographs written about Muslims. Among other things, these efforts have brought attention to the widespread hostility faced by Muslims in the West. Many post-9/11 analysts have further identified these conditions of stigmatization to be an important reason for the apparent growth of religious identification and practice among Muslims. That is, faced with intensive and largely negative scrutiny, Muslims have come together in a dynamic of reactive solidarity. They have responded to stigmatization by developing a stronger and more self-conscious collective identity coupled with high levels of involvement in pan-national Muslim groups and organizations (Cainkar 2004; Peek 2005; Roy 2004). These trends are reported to be operating in an especially powerful way among Muslim youth—the children and grandchildren of Muslim migrants to North America and Europe.

In this religious resurgence among Muslims, an ethos of what may be described as "revivalist Islam" has been prominent. Revivalist Islam refers broadly to a model of Muslim identity and practice that has also been described as "fundamentalist Islam," "reformist Islam," "resurgent Islam," and the "new Islam." At its heart is the goal of "bringing ... religious beliefs and practices [into line] with the core foundations of Islam, by avoiding and purging out innovation, accretion and the intrusion of local customs" (Osella and Osella 2008: 247–248). Revivalist Islam is multifarious, with a variety of groups that take different positions on many issues, such as that of whether Muslims should actively engage with the political sphere or detach themselves from it. But across these differences, from Wahhabism to the Jamaat-al-Tabligh movement, the common goal is to revive an original Islam based on literalist interpretations of the Qu'ran as well as emulation of the recorded life of the Prophet and his Companions. There is a deep-seated emphasis on the significance of Islamic thought for all aspects of life (see Sutton and Vertigans 2005; Turner 2004).

There is little doubt that the post-9/11 scholarship on Islam and Muslims has expanded our knowledge of the Muslim experience. But in taking on this task, this body of work has also participated in the production of "flattened" understandings of Muslims. There has been a tendency to homogenize Muslims, to present one-dimensional views of who they are and how they organize and understand their place in the world and the role of religion within it. By making this point, I do not mean to suggest that the post-9/11 scholarship has been devoid of diverse portrayals. In fact, many studies do note and indeed try to highlight the vast and complex differences among those they are investigating. But certainly in the West, these efforts tend to be overshadowed, obscured in their visibility by the larger political environment. In a world riven by the Anglo-American–led "war on terror" along with pervasive fears in the West about Islam, it is difficult to get across the simple but important message that not all Muslims are the same. These are conditions that have nurtured the sensational, favoring simplified images of Muslims over more complex ones (Mamdani 2002).

Much post-9/11 scholarship on Muslims has taken a top-down approach toward its subject matter. Texts, official discourses, and the views of Islamic leaders and elites have framed the dominant investigative window into the Muslim experience. Even when researchers have, in fact, taken a broader and more inclusive approach, it has often been to study those Muslims who are active participants in Islamic groups and organizations. The perspectives and experiences of those Muslims who are marginal to these organized forums have received little attention. If only in indirect ways, this too has nurtured the image of homogeneity by reducing the visibility of an important dimension of the Muslim experience.

All of this is not to say that Muslims have nothing in common. At the most basic level, what Muslims share, of course, is an affiliation with the religion of Islam. Even as the meaning of this affiliation for the lives of those who are part of it is highly varied, fluid, and contested, it also offers some common threads of experience. This is especially true in light of globalization, a time of the "intensification of worldwide social relations which link distant localities in such a way that local happenings are shaped by events occurring many miles away and vice-versa" (Giddens 1991: 64). Globalization has given added significance to the notion of the Islamic Ummah—a transnational supra-geographical community of fellow Muslims that transcends nationality and other bases of community. Globalized media and communication technologies have opened up transnational cultural spaces that offer new opportunities for community building among Muslims through the exchange of information and ideas (Mandaville 2001; Sutton and Vertigans 2005). These developments are among the interconnecting conditions that have fostered the growth of revivalist Islam around the world.

But if globalization has expanded the scope and intensity of the shared canvas on which Muslims negotiate their identity today, it has by no means erased the divisions of community and identity that unfold on it. Indeed, at the core of globalization is a fundamental duality. This is that its interconnectivity fosters a self-conscious sense not only of what is shared but also of what is not—of what is, in fact, quite different. Thus even as globalization can enhance for Muslims their sense of membership and belonging in the global Ummah, it may also nurture their sense of being distinguished in important respects from many other Muslims.

TRANSNATIONAL CONTEXT, GLOBAL NATIONAL IMAGE, AND RACE

Among the many axes that organize and give meaning to the dynamics of differentiation among Muslims is that of nationality. International migration describes the crossing of borders—the movements of people from one nation-state to another. These are movements in which nation matters, movements in which the histories and conditions of specific countries and their relationships with each other exert influence. The flows of people across borders are an arena of dynamic interactions among nations, especially among those from which migrants originate (national origins) and those to which they direct themselves (national receptions). International migration is thus a transnational phenomenon, part of an emergent sphere of linkages between specific countries. As highlighted by the burgeoning field of transnational studies (see Basch, Schiller, and Szanton Blanc 2008; Levitt and Jaworsky 2007), migration processes are embedded in a nexus between national origins and national reception—a cultural, economic, and political bundle of fluid connections between the societies of origin and reception. And migrant lives unfold on the canvas of this nexus, of dynamic and cross-cutting histories, ties, networks, and institutions that stretch across the societies of origin and reception. It is against the backdrop of these transnational contexts that migrants confront challenges and develop strategies of global migration. As these strategies emerge, they become part of the nexus of transnationalism, entering into its ongoing development. In short, migrants both shape and are shaped by the transnational contexts of their lives.

A better understanding of the Muslim migrant experience calls, I suggest, for greater attention to transnational contexts—to the varied forms and character of the national origins–national receptions nexus that undergirds migrant lives. Such an approach is quite different from one that takes the primacy of Muslim identity as given, and relegates matters of national differentiation to secondary consideration. It rather begins from the assumption that Muslim migrants are anchored in transnational contexts that inform their strategies of identity and community. Thus in order to understand such trends as the popularity of revivalist Islam among Muslim migrants, we need to look at its appeal in relation to the specific transnational contexts of their lives. It is not enough, for example, to ask the question of why Muslims in Europe are increasingly attracted to revivalist Islam. Instead we might consider how revivalist Islam appeals to British Muslims of Pakistani descent or German Muslims of Turkish descent, speaking effectively to the transnational histories and conditions of these communities.

Studies of migrant transnationalism highlight the significance of political histories between migrant sending and receiving states (see Espiritu 2003; Kim 2008). As in the case of Algerian settlers in France or of Filipino immigrants to the United States, migration flows are often embedded in the histories of colonialism and military engagements that have defined the relations of sending and receiving states. More generally, the transnational contexts of migration reflect the dynamics of interstate power and global national hierarchy. Thus how migrants are received in the destination society reflects the position and status of the state from which they originate within the world political and economic order (Patterson 2006). When there are wide gaps of power and location between the two states involved, the significance of global national hierarchy for migrant life tends to be starkly visible, certainly to the migrants themselves. That is, especially for migrants who originate from a society that is less powerful than the one to where they move, the transnational context is vitally defined by this condition of global national hierarchy.

For migrants, the dynamics of inequality between the state of national origins and the state of national receptions may be felt in many different ways. It may become evident, for example, in the relatively weak position of the sending state government when it tries to negotiate and lobby with the receiving state government on behalf of its expatriates, on such matters as entry laws and labor protection. But it is perhaps most immediately felt in the arena of social reception, in how the migrants find themselves being viewed and understood in the destination society, especially with respect to their perceived potential for effective incorporation into it. More specifically, I suggest that the context of interstate inequality shapes the production and character of globalized national images about the society from which the migrants originate. These images offer naturalized notions of the background and character of those of particular national origins—what they look like, how they live, how they relate to each other, and so forth. They thus serve to racialize the migrant group, constructing it as essentially different and inferior within the receiving society, especially from its dominant members. As Howard Winant has observed in his writings on the historical sociology of race, the current global racial order is one in which racial differences have been reinterpreted "as matters of culture and nationality, rather than as fundamental human attributes somehow linked to phenotype" (2008: 200). The significance of global national image to racialization processes is thus reflective of the shifting meanings of "race" in the world.

Even as they simplify those whom they portray, global national images are clearly complicated matters—fluid, multidimensional, and deeply contested in form and character. Thus they often encompass and negotiate contradictions of various sorts. For example, among the global national images of India in the early twenty-first century is that of "the new Indian," an image that has been actively fostered in various advertising campaigns (Brosius 2009; Fernandes 2006). The image here is that of a middle-class Indian, one who is technically savvy, culturally hip, and in step with the world of global brand consumerism. But "the new Indian" is also grounded in tradition, continuing to adhere to Indian family values such as respect for elders. As further suggested by this example, global national images are far from static, but rather subject to ongoing development. As has occurred in India with its programs of economic liberalization since the 1990s, image changes may reflect the deliberate campaigns of governments to redesign their global national persona as a way of effectively wooing global capital into the country.

The significance of global national image to the effective positioning of nations within the global market economy is also highlighted by the contemporary marketing discourse of "national branding" (see Dinnie 2007; Jaffe and Nebenzahl 2006). This concept sees products and services as gaining their value in part from the global national image of the country in which they are understood to be produced and derived. Besides creating an image that has positive connotations, national branding campaigns are also driven by the general goal of national name recognition. Especially for countries that are relatively unknown and struggling to integrate themselves into the world economy, a big part of the challenge may be simply to be known, to be familiar to consumers and investors around the world. Thus among the complexities of global national image is that it varies not only in the character of its specific portrayals but also in the relative strength of its presence. In *Imperial Citizens (2008)*, Nadia Kim argues that Korean Americans are marginalized in the United States by their relative social and political invisibility in the American public imagination.

But even as migrants struggle with the global images of where they are from and the social and political spaces that these create for them, ties of origin remain important, a focal point of coping strategies. Indeed, an extensive body of literature shows these ties to be an important source of social capital or trust networks on which migrants can draw for social support. For example, in her study of West Indian migrants in London and New York, Vilna Bashi (2007) describes how transnational social networks can successfully organize the migration process, providing access to employment and housing as well as legalized immigration status. Besides the critical material resources of jobs and visas, there are other types of benefits, such as emotional support. Active engagement in transnational networks and institutions can sustain the meaning and significance of the society of origin—the "homeland"—as a point of social reference for migrants. As scholars of migration have often noted, a dual frame of social reference is what helps many migrants to cope with the challenges that they may face as racialized, low-wage workers in the receiving society (see Waldinger and Lichter 2003; Waters 1999). That is, they are able to resist the dehumanizing effects of race and class stigma in the receiving society by turning to another social context—the "homeland"—to understand themselves. Under these conditions, considerable energy and resources may be directed toward maintaining transnational ties, especially in ways that strengthen one's sense of self-worth. Hung Cam Thai's (2008) study of Vietnamese migrant men and remittances vividly illustrates this point. Toiling in low-wage jobs in the United States, these men remit money to kin in Vietnam, often at considerable material hardship to themselves. The remittances are, however, what enable them to cope with the degradations of their life in the United States, offering as they do a means for claiming and valorizing social worth in the community of origin.

Increasingly, as well, the transnational ties of migrants have attracted the attention of sending states, which have sought to actively nurture them in order to promote economic growth. International migrant remittances are critical sources of foreign exchange for many developing countries, often vastly exceeding official aid in their volume (Cohen 2005; Kapur 2005). Development analysts also note the potential role of diasporas in fostering the integration of their "homeland" countries into the global economy. In the case of China, for example, the investments of overseas Chinese have been a vital source of foreign direct investment (FDI), fueling industrial developments in the country.

To summarize, I have argued for the need to examine the transnational contexts of Muslim international migration. Among the conditions that inform
these contexts are those of political histories and relations between sending and
receiving countries and the global national images that are a part of them. These
images can be a vehicle of racialization, or the ongoing construction of migrants
as different and inferior in an intrinsic sense to those of the receiving society,
especially its dominant members. However, if the national origins of migrants
are important, they are certainly not the only way in which migrants are marginalized in the receiving society. Indeed, studies of Muslim life in North
America and Western Europe suggest that the racialization of Muslim migrants
may involve not only their national origins but their identity as Muslim, as well.
The pernicious persistence of racial difference derives at least in part from the
fluidity and multiplicity of its reference points. Depending on the circumstances, racial difference shifts back and forth between various features of
human difference, naturalizing and legitimizing them as bases of social and
political inequality. In short, the analysis of migrant racialization requires us to
consider the stigma that confronts migrants in relation not to just one element of
difference but also to "bundles" that are both in motion and intertwined.

STUDYING BANGLADESHI MUSLIMS ABROAD

In this book I look at the lives of Bangladeshi Muslim migrants and their
families in several parts of the world—Britain, the United States, the GCC
(Gulf Cooperation Council) states, and Malaysia.[1] It is important to note that
although Muslims constitute a large majority (an estimated 85 to 90 percent) of
the population of Bangladesh, the country is also home to many other religious
groups, including Buddhists, Christians, and Hindus. However, because of
my particular interest in the dynamics of Muslim identities, I chose not to
explore the experiences of Bangladeshi migrants from these other religious
backgrounds. It is my hope that other scholars will take up this important task
in the future.

In my analysis of Bangladeshi Muslim experiences, I draw on data gathered
over a span of some six years, from 2001 to 2007. During this time I gathered
over two hundred in-depth interviews with Bangladeshi Muslim migrants and
their families. Although I conducted over half of these interviews myself, I also
enlisted research assistants to gather data. We asked informants to talk about
their migration history and experience, including the impacts of migration on
their family life, participation in civic groups, political views, and religious
practice. Whenever it was possible, to supplement the interviews I also conducted participant-observation at community and family gatherings. Almost

all of the interviews were tape-recorded and then transcribed. They lasted from one to three hours and were conducted in Bangla and/or English, depending on the wishes of the informant.[2] All of the Bangla transcripts were eventually translated into English, either by myself or a research assistant. In many cases, then, the interview excerpts that appear in the book are taken from translations of the Bangla interviews. At times I have included the actual phrases or words that appeared in them. In doing so, I have relied on phonetic translations of the spoken Bengali as used in the interview.

In order to generate informants, I usually began by tapping into my own personal contacts. We then expanded the sample through snowball methods, whereby those interviewed were asked for referrals to other potential informants. In doing so, I made an effort to avoid over-sampling from a particular social network by limiting the number of referrals from any one snowball chain and continuing to recruit participants from other sources. I particularly sought referrals to persons who would expand the range of the sample across such variables as age, gender, levels of education, and time spent abroad. I also sought a variety of political and religious orientations.

But if my methodological strategies were consistent in these basic respects, they did also vary across the targeted settings, incorporating the particular circumstances and research challenges posed by each. For example, reflecting the permanent settlement that is often a part of these migration contexts, in both Britain and the United States I collected data not only from first-generation migrants but from second- and third-generation Bangladeshis as well. In the British sample, nineteen of the forty-four informants were first-generation migrants and twenty-five were either second- or third-generation British Bangladeshis. In the U.S. sample, forty-six of the seventy-two interviewees were first-generation migrants. Twenty-six were either one-and-a-half- or second-generation Bangladeshi Americans who had come to the United States before the age of eighteen or had been born in the United States. The vast majority of these interviews occurred in Britain and the United States, although in six cases they took place in Bangladesh, either because the migrant had returned to the country permanently or because he or she was on a trip there. Most, in fact, took place in London and New York, two important centers of Bangladeshi settlement in the West. But I also gathered data in a number of other cities, such as Boston and Detroit in the United States and Manchester in Britain. Although, for the most part, the interviews were conducted with individuals who were not part of the same household and unrelated to each other, I did also engage in intensive study of three households in Britain and five households in the United States. In these cases, I interviewed several members of the same household and also observed household gatherings in an effort to gain a better understanding of family dynamics, especially across the generations.

Reflecting the character of Bangladeshi movements to these regions, my research on migration to the GCC states and Malaysia focused largely on labor migrants or persons with work contracts and visas of limited duration in the receiving society. I began data collection for this segment of the project in 2003, when I conducted interviews in Bangladesh with international labor migrants who had returned home after working abroad. With the assistance of the Welfare Association of Repatriated Bangladesh Employees (WARBE), an NGO that is dedicated to the welfare of Bangladeshi labor migrants, as well as a team of research assistants, I gathered data with a nonrandom sample of returned labor migrants in the Dhaka, Chittagong, and Sylhet regions of Bangladesh (see Kibria 2004). Between 2005 and 2007, I engaged in another round of data collection. During this period I gathered data in the United Arab Emirates and in Malaysia, conducting interviews with Bangladeshis working in these countries. I also continued to gather data in Bangladesh, speaking to those who had worked in the GCC states and Malaysia and had returned home, either permanently or on temporary leave from their jobs there. My analysis of Bangladeshi experiences in the GCC states and Malaysia is based then on a cumulative total of eighty-five interviews, sixty involving migration to the GCC states and twenty-five to Malaysia. Reflecting once again the socioeconomic character of Bangladeshi migration to these regions, the vast majority of these informants had relatively low levels of education and had worked in unskilled or semi-skilled jobs while abroad. However, fourteen of the eighty-five interviews involved Bangladeshi professionals and highly skilled workers. In addition, reflecting the predominance of men in labor migration flows out of Bangladesh, women were a small minority (eleven out of eighty-five) of the GCC and Malaysia migrants we interviewed.

As we will see in the chapters to follow, the circumstances and experiences of Bangladeshi Muslim international migrants are extremely diverse and challenge facile generalizations. There is, for example, much that separates an impoverished rural Bangladeshi man who goes to Saudi Arabia on a labor contract from an upper-middle-class, urban Bangladeshi woman who goes to the United States for a university degree and then obtains employment in a bank that is based there. But what, then, is the relevance of what these migrants do share? How can we think about the meanings of their common affiliation with the religion of Islam in tandem with shared roots in the country of Bangladesh? I turn next to consider the history and politics of Islam in Bangladesh with an eye to unraveling its significance in the experiences of Bangladeshis abroad.

CHAPTER 2

Bangladesh

NATIONALISM, ISLAM, AND
INTERNATIONAL MIGRATION

Bangladesh, meaning "Bengal nation," is a low-lying country formed by the alluvial plain of the Ganges-Brahmaputra river system—the largest delta in the world. Located on the Bay of Bengal, between Burma and India, it has a territory of 147,570 square kilometers and a population of over 150 million persons, making it the eighth most populous country in the world and also one of the most densely populated (National Web Portal of Bangladesh n.d.). With a majority Muslim Sunni population (85 to 90 percent) it is also one of the largest Muslim-majority countries in the world, after Indonesia and Pakistan. In their accounts of the history of East Bengal, Rafiuddin Ahmed (2001) and Richard Eaton (2001) have described how Muslim rulers, later remembered as "Sufis," brought Islam to the region in the fourteenth century. The religious culture that emerged from their conquests was one in which Islam came to intermingle with local indigenous rituals and beliefs, including those of Hindu and Buddhist origin. This "folk" religion, with its harvest festivals, reverence of popular saints, and tolerance of different faiths, has remained a prominent if increasingly contested feature of the country's social and cultural landscape.

During the era of colonized British India, the area that is currently Bangladesh was known as "East Bengal"—the eastern part of the provincial region of Bengal. With the departure of the British in 1947 and the partition of India, East Bengal became integrated as the province of "East Pakistan" in the newly created state of Pakistan. Accompanied by tragic Hindu-Muslim violence, the 1947 partition spurred the enormous migration of an estimated 12 to 18 million people between India and Pakistan. The basis for the national formation of Pakistan was Islam—the religion of the majority of those within the territory. But this bond soon showed itself to be insufficient for keeping together the geographically and culturally disparate East and West wings of the country, particularly given the position of political and economic dominance assumed by West Pakistan. In 1971, after nine months of bitter conflict in which

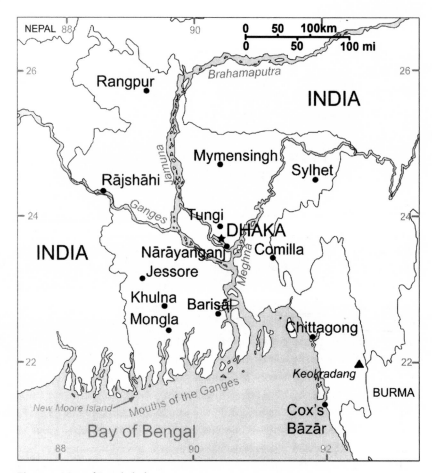

Figure 1. Map of Bangladesh

an estimated 1 to 3 million Bengalis died at the hands of the Pakistani military junta and its allies, Bangladesh emerged as an independent state.

Since its independence on December 16, 1971, Bangladesh has made important development strides, especially in the areas of primary education, population control, and the reduction of hunger. The country remains largely agrarian; almost three-quarters of the population is engaged in agricultural pursuits, in particular the production of rice. But since independence, the rural economy has changed in important ways with the revolution in biotechnological crops and the growth of industrial agricultural practices (Ito 2004). There has also been a proliferation of developmental organizations such as the renowned Grameen Bank, which offers small loans to poor rural women. Indeed, NGOs have become a dominant feature of the rural economy, not only in the area of credit but also in telecommunications and primary education. As far as industrial development, the country has seen the growth since the late 1980s of a large export garment manufacturing sector. The garment industry has been an important source of employment for the displaced rural poor who move to the cities in search of employment. It has been especially important for women, who constitute a large proportion of its workers (BGMEA 2009). Along with migrant remittances from abroad, the garment sector has been a primary source of foreign currency earnings for the country.

Along with these developments, Bangladesh has registered an economic growth rate of 5 to 6 percent since the 1990s. This has led to its identification by the international investment firm Goldman Sachs as a potentially important player in the global economy of the twenty-first century, one that may follow the trajectory of the BRIC countries—the emerging economies of Brazil, Russia, India, and China—in the growth of the country's middle class (*Daily Star* 2009e). With the independence of Bangladesh in 1971 came a rise of employment opportunities for Bengalis in the public administration sector, resulting in an expansion in the ranks of the middle class (Hossain 2005; Islam 2004). Since that time, the Bangladeshi middle class, estimated at 9 to 10 percent of the population, has grown and stratified to include professionals, business owners, and white-collar workers in the financial and retail industries as well as the burgeoning NGO sector.

Notwithstanding these positive signals, the country continues to face major obstacles to development. Poverty remains widespread, affecting the lives of perhaps half the population. The country suffers from the direct fallouts of global environmental degradation and climate change, as glacial melting in the Himalayas leads to more frequent cyclones in the Bay of Bengal as well as a rise in the severity and duration of annual flooding (Huq and Asaduzzaman 2007). Development efforts have also been weakened by poor governance and weak public institutions. The country's system of parliamentary democracy has been undermined by chronic political instability, infighting, and corruption.

Nationalism, Colonialism, and "Race" in Bangladesh

The complex history of colonialism and nationalism in Bangladesh is a critical piece of the puzzle of understanding the strategies of Bangladeshis abroad. British imperialism in India was accompanied by ideologies of racialized difference, of the intrinsic inferiority of the colonized in relation to their colonizers. If these ideologies asserted the central axis of difference to be between British rulers and their Indian subjects, they also provided the basis for discrimination among Indians. Regional origin, religion, and caste were

among the social distinctions used to categorize Indians into groups, to affirm
the presence of "peoples" who were separated by innate and given characteristics and predispositions. Bengalis, for example, were labeled by the British as a
people unfit for military service due to their weak, effeminate, and cowardly
nature (Chowdhury-Sengupta 1995). For Indian nationalists, the racial ideologies of British imperialism were a key point of resistance, a core feature of
their struggle against colonial oppression. As Partha Chatterjee (1993) has
described, for middle-class nationalists in nineteenth- and early twentieth-
century Bengal, the cultivation of an explicitly Bengali cultural sphere emerged
as a core strategy against the denigrations of colonialism. Often described as a
Bengali cultural renaissance, this was a time of great expansion in Bengali
vernacular works in literature, philosophy, drama, and the arts. Bankim Chandra
Chatterjee, Michael Madhusudan Dutt, the Nobel Laureate Rabindranath
Tagore, and Kazi Nazrul Islam are among the distinguished literary names that
have come to epitomize this period. However, the sense of shared Bengali community and identity that emerged from these developments was not enough to
stem the tide of growing political division between Hindus and Muslims in the
region. These divisions gained steady ground, encouraged by British policies
that treated Muslims as a distinct community, separate in all respects from
Hindus and other religious groups (Ahmed 2001).

When British rule of India ended in 1947, Bengal was divided and the
eastern part of the region was incorporated into Pakistan. The two wings of
Pakistan—the East and West—were not only geographically separated by a
thousand miles of Indian territory but culturally distant as well. While those
in the East spoke Bangla or Bengali, the dominant language in the West was
Urdu. These differences were accompanied by the political and economic
dominance of West over East Pakistan. The West Pakistani elite controlled
the military and through it, the central government of Pakistan. In essence,
East Pakistan came to operate as an "internal colony," providing raw materials
such as jute, tea, and paper to West Pakistan–controlled corporations and
receiving little investment in its own infrastructure. In tragic continuity with
British colonial strategies of rule, political and economic dominance was also
accompanied by a racialized ideology in which Bengalis were understood to
be inherently inferior to their fellow Pakistanis in the West. Marked by their
typically darker complexions and shorter stature, Bengalis were said to be a
lesser people, certainly unfit to assume leadership of the country. Furthermore,
Bengalis were scorned for being less devout in their devotion to Islam. The
failure to purge their own culture of its various Hindu and other non-Islamic
elements was a source of pollution, threatening the identity of Pakistan as an
Islamic Republic.

For East Bengal, then, incorporation into Pakistan did not bring about an end to its colonized status. As this became increasingly clear, a Bengali nationalist movement also began to take shape. On February 21, 1952, the Pakistani army fired on Bengali university students who were protesting the efforts of the central government to establish Urdu as the sole official language of the country. The deaths of several students, accompanied by widespread arrests, sparked massive popular protest. The events now commemorated as Shohid Dibosh (Martyrs' Day) and International Mother Language Day signaled a pivotal point in the development of a self-consciously Bengali national identity.[1] Echoing an earlier time, for the middle class of what was then East Pakistan, cultivation of the literature and music of the Bengali cultural renaissance, as described earlier, became an important act of resistance to the forces of political oppression. And so when the songs of Tagore, deemed "un-Islamic" by the authorities, were banned in the 1950s from the state radio of Pakistan, for Bengalis their symbolic significance only deepened. Indeed, in 1971 when Bangladesh became independent it was a Tagore song—"My Golden Bengal" (Amar Shonar Bangla)—that was chosen as the national anthem of the new nation.

The crisis of conflict between East and West Pakistan reached a climax in 1970 when the largest political party in East Pakistan, the Awami League, won a landslide victory in the national elections, thus giving them the constitutional right to form a government. Tensions grew as West Pakistani leaders refused to accept the results. On March 7, 1971, the charismatic leader of the Awami League, Sheikh Mujibur Rahman, delivered a speech to a gathering of 2 million people. He called on Bengalis to launch a major campaign of civil disobedience against West Pakistani rule. And he ended his speech in a thunderous voice with the famous words: "This time the struggle is for our freedom; this time the struggle is for our independence." The retaliation that followed was swift. Army troops were flown in from the West for a military pacification campaign and all foreign journalists were systematically deported from East Pakistan. The killing spree that followed systematically targeted Hindus, the Bengali intelligentsia, university students, and all able-bodied Bengali men and boys, who were simply picked up and shot. Large numbers of women were raped and violated (Mascarenhas 1971). As Rummel has observed, the mass killings were informed by deep-seated racism: "Bengalis were often compared with monkeys and chickens. Said Pakistan General Niazi, 'It [Bengal] was a low lying land of low lying people'" (1997: 335).

Throughout the course of the conflict, the U.S. government, under the leadership of President Richard Nixon and Secretary of State Henry Kissinger, remained steadfast in its support of the West Pakistani government and its policies, and unapologetic for the "tilt" toward a murderous military regime. Indeed, in late April 1971, at the very height of the mass killings, Kissinger sent a message to Pakistani General Yahya Khan, thanking him for his "delicacy and tact" (Hitchens 2001: 21). But in his reports to the U.S. State Department, Archer Blood, the American consul general in Dhaka in 1971, offered detailed and systematic accounts of the atrocities taking place around him. On April 6, 1971, the Blood Telegram, signed by twenty-nine Americans, was sent through to the U.S. State Department to express dissent with U.S. policy:

> Our government has failed to denounce the suppression of democracy. Our government has failed to denounce atrocities. . . . Our government has evidenced what many will consider moral bankruptcy. . . . But we have chosen not to intervene, even morally, on the grounds that the Awami conflict, in which unfortunately the overworked term "genocide" is applicable, is purely an internal matter of a sovereign state. Private Americans have expressed disgust. We, as professional civil servants, express our dissent with current policy and fervently hope that our true and lasting interests here can be defined and our policies redirected in order to salvage our nation's position as a moral leader of the free world. (Blood 2002: 245)

In December 1971, following the military intervention of India, the war ended with victory for Bangladesh. Exactly how many people died in the course of the conflict remains a disputed matter. But most estimates suggest that at least 1 million and perhaps as many as 3 million Bengalis were killed from March to December 1971. Despite its enormity, it is, as Alamgir and Sajjad (2010) have observed, "a tragedy that has become largely invisible in the world's public discourse about genocide . . . in an extraordinary act of forgetting." For Bangladeshis, the absence of acknowledgment from the world for the tragedy of 1971 affirms a larger pattern of the global invisibility of Bangladesh.

In Bangladesh itself, however, the events of 1971 are deeply ingrained in collective memories, forming the heart of a nationalist narrative that highlights Bengali sacrifice, heroism, and the sanctity of the motherland. Thus for Bangladeshis abroad, Bengali nationalism may be an important strategy of affirmation, self-consciously deployed to resist the stings of stigma and alienation experienced in the receiving society. But it is also the case that this nationalist strategy is a deeply conflicted one. Among the conditions that can challenge its ability to be an effective source of pride is the global national image of Bangladesh. As described earlier, since its independence in 1971, the country has made important social and economic progress. Yet Henry Kissinger's mean-spirited labeling in 1974 of the country as "an international basket case" is one that continues to shadow its international reputation. And so for Bangladeshis abroad, being "from Bangladesh" can be a double-edged sword. Informed by a potent nationalist narrative in which Bengalis struggle and prevail over foreign oppression, Bangladeshi identity may be an important source of pride, a way of brushing off belittling encounters and circumstances abroad. Yet this same identity can also be a source of stigma. The global image of Bangladesh as a poor, corrupt, and hapless country is one that haunts those abroad, creating a lens through which they find themselves being assessed in the receiving society.

Besides the dynamics of global national image, strategies of nationalism are also embedded for Bangladeshis abroad in the political contests that surround it in Bangladesh. The core nationalist narrative of 1971 has been a focus of political contention in the country on many different levels. For example, the two major political parties of the country—the Awami League (AL) and the BNP (Bangladesh Nationalist Party) have waged a heated symbolic battle over the question of who precisely first proclaimed the independence of the country in 1971—whether it was AL leader Sheikh Mujibur Rahman or Ziaur Rahman, founder of the BNP.[2] The question of relations with India, the powerful neighboring country that played an important role in the 1971 war of independence, has also been a bone of contention. In the country's volatile political scene, the Awami League is often described by the BNP and Jamaat-e-Islami political parties to be "pro-India" or allied with Indian interests. Invoking the region's history of Hindu-Muslim conflicts, detractors of the Awami League have accused it of compromising the identity of Bangladesh as a Muslim majority country with its allegedly close relations with India. Indeed, it is on the matter of religion—the place of Islam in the nation-state of Bangladesh—that the sharpest fault lines have emerged in the politics of the country.

THE POLITICS OF ISLAM IN BANGLADESH

The leaders of the newly independent country of Bangladesh articulated a nationalist narrative based on the history of the 1971 war of independence and the notion of a national ethnic "Bangalee" identity.[3] These ideas were codified in the constitution passed by the Constituent Assembly in 1972, as follows: "The unity and solidarity of the Bangalee nation, which, deriving its identity from its language and culture, attained sovereign and independent Bangladesh through a united and determined struggle in the war of independence, shall be the basis of Bangalee nationalism."[4]

The Constitution of 1972 also embraced secularism. This was defined as protection against religious discrimination and persecution as well as maintenance of the religious neutrality of the state. The constitution reads, "The principles of secularism shall be realized by the elimination of . . . the granting of the State of political status in favour of any religion."[5] Under these provisions, religion-based political parties such as the Jamaat-e-Islami were excluded from the realm of formal electoral politics. Indeed, in the aftermath of the war, Jamaat was deeply stigmatized for its support of West Pakistan in the 1971 war. Armed and trained by the Pakistani army, it had formed the brutal al-Badr and al-Shams death squads that had engaged in mass killings of Bengalis. But by the late 1970s, following the 1975 assassination of the Awami League leader and Prime Minister Sheikh Mujibur Rahman, the political tides seemed to shift in Jamaat's favor. Under the military regime of General Ziaur Rahman (1975–1982), Islam assumed an increasingly prominent place in the official institutions of the country. Ziaur Rahman removed "secularism" from the constitution and instead inserted, by presidential proclamation, the words "absolute trust and faith in Almighty Allah." He asserted the notion of "Bangladeshi" instead of "Bangalee" identity, in an attempt to highlight the distinction between the country's citizens from the Bengalis (largely Hindu) who lived across the border in neighboring India. And he actively encouraged the growth of Islamic banks, mosques, and schools with funding from the Middle East. Although there were no attempts to curtail the civil rights of non-Muslims or to install *Shar'ia* (Islamic law) in place of modern civil and criminal law, several state-sponsored initiatives of the late 1970s asserted the country's Islamic identity. As Ali Riaz writes, this period saw:

> the introduction of Islamiat—a course on Islamic studies—at primary and secondary levels. This course was made mandatory for all Muslim students. The government established a new Ministry of Religious Affairs. Soon afterward, Eid-e-miladunabi—the Prophet Muhammad's birthday—was declared a national holiday. The state controlled electronic media began broadcasting Azan—the call for prayers—five times a day and to carry programs on Islam's role in daily life. (2004: 36)

The growing role of Islam in the public life of the country was accompanied by the rehabilitation and integration of Jamaat-e-Islami into the formal political arena. Under the leadership of Ziaur Rahman, the ban on religion-based political parties was rescinded, and in 1978, the Jamaat leader Ghulam Azam was allowed to return to the country from exile. While maintaining its commitment to the goal of establishing an Islamic state with *Shar'ia* law, Jamaat also engaged in a wide range of activities to consolidate its position in the country. These included the building of an elaborate and widespread network of institutions—banks, hospitals, schools, and NGOs—with support from Saudi Arabia and other Arab Gulf states. Noting the success of these institution-building efforts, Maneeza Hossain describes Jamaat as "function[ing] as an alternative system in its own right. With its educational, economic, and medical services, it has created in Bangladesh a kind of state-within-a-state" (2007: 25). In the course of the 1990s, Jamaat also became an important player in the electoral politics of the country. It played the role of a kingmaker as the two major political parties (AL and BNP) formed alliances with it in order to achieve power. Indeed, following the 2001 national elections, the project of Jamaat rehabilitation seemed to have reached a pinnacle. At this time a BNP-Jamaat coalition formed a national government in which Jamaat leaders held important ministerial posts.

But by 2008, the political pendulum seemed to have swung once again, this time against Jamaat. In the December 2008 national elections, Jamaat-e-Islami suffered a crushing defeat at the polls, winning only 2 out of 300 parliamentary seats, in comparison to the 17 it had gained in the 2001 elections. The BNP-Jamaat regime of 2001–2006 had been marked by highly visible and widespread corruption as well as a spate of terrorist bombings and attacks. Besides members of the Awami League opposition and the secular intelligentsia, the targets of these onslaughts included such Bengali cultural festivals as Pahela Baishak (Bengali New Year), attacked due to their allegedly "un-Islamic" character (Ali 2006). The 2008 backlash against Jamaat reflected not only the public outcry against these developments but also the efforts of a nationwide movement spearheaded by the Ghatok Dalal Nirmul Committee, founded by the charismatic Jahanara Imam to reignite collective memories of Jamaat's role in the atrocities of 1971.[6] As part of this movement, several private television channels of the country showed widely viewed documentaries on the 1971 war that included graphic newsreels from that time. Thus the landslide victory of the Awami League in the 2008 election included a manifesto pledge to prosecute the war criminals of 1971. As the outcome of this pledge takes shape in the constantly shifting political sands of Bangladesh, the nationalist narrative of 1971 also comes under scrutiny and debate.

But if the history and politics of Jamaat are a critical piece of the contests of nationalism and Islam in Bangladesh today, the strains go far beyond it to encompass a broader set of social conditions. As Robert Hefner (2005) has observed, the 1970s and 1980s were a time of religious resurgence throughout the Muslim world. The ideologies of secular nationalism that had guided many of the postcolonial national projects of the 1950s and 1960s lost support, reflecting widespread disenchantment with the state and its inability to meet rising public expectations. As national policies became increasingly subject to international financial regimes, the principles of state-centered development were replaced by those of integration into the global market economy. As a paradigm for national development, secular nationalism lost relevance, thus generating an ideological vacuum into which religious movements could enter. The resulting environment was ripe for the growth of political Islam, an approach in which "Islam becomes a medium for the expression and practice of politics" (Kamrava 2006: 6).

Across much of the Muslim world, including Bangladesh, the last quarter of the twentieth century was also a time of rapid social change, with such developments as urbanization, the entry of women into the formal labor force, and the spread of global mass media and information technologies. In a variety of ways, these changes produced fertile territory for the growth of popular religious movements, including those of revivalist Islam. For those coping with the social upheavals of modernity, a renewed emphasis on religion can offer moorings, a means of gaining a sense of stability in an uncertain world. The expansion of the market economy in these societies also created new paths of economic mobility for some citizens. For the new middle class that emerged from these opportunities, intensified religious involvements could be an important means by which to enhance and consolidate their gains of social status. In other words, the religious sphere could serve as a vehicle of cultural legitimation for their newfound wealth.

Informed, then, by the unfolding forces of modernity and globalization, Islam has assumed an increasingly self-conscious and visible place in the political and social landscape of Bangladesh and the ongoing contests that mark it. In this book, I consider the relationship of international migration flows from Bangladesh to this religious resurgence, especially to the growing influence of revivalist Islam in the country. As I discuss in the section that follows, the movements of people abroad are an increasingly important feature of Bangladesh today. Although the economic consequences of these movements have been extensively analyzed, their social impacts have received less attention.

INTERNATIONAL MIGRATION FROM BANGLADESH

International migration, especially voluntary migration beyond South Asia, has been an important feature of the landscape of Bangladesh only since the 1980s. Prior to this time, such movements were limited in scope, fettered by the area's colonized status and related circumstances of underdevelopment. But since the 1980s, national and global forces have converged to usher in an era of expanded international migration for Bangladesh. Two major streams of migration have developed since this time.

International Labor Migrants

The first migration stream involves labor migration from Bangladesh to other parts of the world. The primary destinations here have been the Arab Gulf states—members of the GCC or Gulf Cooperation Council. The GCC, also known as Cooperation Council for the Arab States of the Gulf (CCASG), is a trade bloc that was formed in 1981 among the six oil-producing states of Bahrain, Kuwait, Oman, Qatar, Saudi Arabia, and the United Arab Emirates. According to the official figures of the Bureau of Manpower, Employment, and Training (BMET) of the Government of Bangladesh, during the 1976–2009 period over 5 million Bangladeshis had gone to work in the GCC states; Saudi Arabia and United Arab Emirates were the top country destinations (see figure 2). Since the 1980s, international labor migration from Bangladesh has expanded beyond the GCC states to include a wider range of countries, including Japan, Lebanon, Malaysia, Mauritius, Singapore, and South Korea. Of these destinations, Malaysia has been the most important, officially receiving 698,736 Bangladeshi workers from 1976 to 2009 (BMET 2007) (see figure 3).

Although professional and skilled Bangladeshis have participated in these labor migrations, semi-skilled and unskilled workers have predominated within them. According to BMET figures, of the total outflow from 1976 to 2008, 2.9 percent were professionals, 31 percent skilled, 16 percent semi-skilled, and 50 percent unskilled workers (BMET 2005). Recruited for low-level jobs in

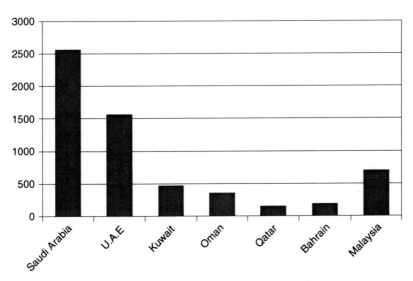

Figure 2. Total Labor Migration from Bangladesh by Major Destinations, 1980–2009
Source: Government of Bangladesh, Bureau of Manpower, Employment, and Training.

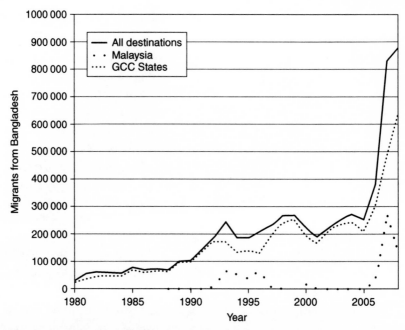

Figure 3. Annual Labor Migration from Bangladesh by Major Destinations, 1980–2005
Source: Government of Bangladesh, Bureau of Manpower, Employment, and Training.

such sectors as construction, food services, and transportation, this stream of
labor migration has largely involved Bangladeshis with low levels of schooling
from the small towns and villages of Bangladesh. Rather than the poorest segments of rural society, these migrants are more likely to be from economically
moderate circumstances, given the expenses of obtaining visas, tickets, and
contracts to work (Buchenau 2008). In addition, the overwhelming majority of
Bangladeshi labor migrants have been men; from 1997 to 2003, women made
up less than 1 percent of the worker outflow from Bangladesh. There are,
however, signs of a slight shift away from this gender imbalance; in 2008,
women migrants constituted 5 percent of those going abroad to work that
year (Siddiqui 2008). This change has been supported by the 2007 removal of
government bans on the labor migration of women, restrictions that had been
periodically imposed by the government of Bangladesh in the 1980s and 1990s.[7]

Long-Term Family Migration

The second stream of international migration from Bangladesh has involved
movements toward the developed world, to the United States as well as to
Australia, Britain, Canada, and Italy. These movements are distinguished from
the first stream by the available opportunities in the destination societies for

TABLE 2.1

GROWTH OF BANGLADESHI-ORIGIN POPULATION OF GREAT BRITAIN, 1951–2001

Year	Bangladeshi	South Asian	Bangladeshi pop. as % of overall South Asian pop. in Great Britain
1951	2,000	43,000	4.65
1961	6,000	112,000	5.35
1971	22,000	516,000	4.26
1981	65,000	1,037,000	6.26
1991	163,000	1,480,000	11.01
2001	280,000	2,027,000	13.81

Source: Figures are taken from Ceri Peach, "South Asian Migration and Settlement in Great Britain," *Contemporary South Asia* 15(2) (2006): 133–146.

family migration and permanent settlement. Of these migration flows, the one to Britain has the longest history as well as perhaps the most distinctive character. As I discuss in more detail in chapter 5, the post–World War II years were an important period of growth in South Asian migration to and settlement in Britain. The 1948 Nationality Act in Britain, passed at a time of labor shortages for the country, allowed unrestricted entry to the citizens of its former colonies. The Bengalis who went to Britain at this time tended to be young men from rural backgrounds with relatively low levels of education. They were also largely from Sylhet (in northeastern Bangladesh), a fact that has given the community a distinct regional identity that remains prominent to the present day. As shown in table 2.1, the 1960s and 1970s were important periods of growth for the British Bengali population as migrant men began to settle their families in Britain. According to 2007 estimates, there are over 350,000 persons of Bangladeshi origin in Britain (Office for National Statistics 2009).

In comparison to Britain, Bangladeshi migration to the United States has a more recent history. According to the U.S. census, in 1980 there were 5,880 foreign-born Bangladeshis in the United States. The numbers rose rapidly in the 1980s and 1990s, from 21,749 in 1990 to 92,237 by 2000 (Kibria 2007). Besides taking advantage of employment-based immigration entry laws, Bangladeshi migration to the United States has also involved family sponsorship and the Diversity Program.[8] Popularly known as the Green Card Lottery, the Diversity Program offers a certain number of U.S. entry slots to citizens (randomly selected) of countries that have sent fewer than 50,000 people to the United States in the previous five years. For groups such as Bangladeshis who have not had an established history of migration to the United States, the Diversity Program has clearly played an important part in creating a community of settlement. Although a precise count of the Bangladeshi American population will be available only after the 2010 census is published, 2008 estimates suggest over 200,000 persons of Bangladeshi origin to be living in the United States.

Besides its more recent history, Bangladeshi migration to the United States is also distinguished from that to Britain by its greater diversity of regional origins as well as a larger proportion of persons from urban and middle-class backgrounds.[9] Indeed, the second stream of international migration from Bangladesh has included an important segment of highly educated persons. In a "brain drain" that is widespread in the developing world, Bangladeshis holding professional credentials and skills that are valued in the global market have migrated in response to lucrative and attractive employment opportunities in the developed world that are far superior to what is available to them in Bangladesh. Unlike the situation during the era of Pakistani rule, these efforts have not been stymied by state efforts to discourage these movements through the denial of passports and thus the right to travel. Besides the possibility of better employment opportunities for themselves abroad, family migration to the developed world has also been driven by the goal of acquiring valued educational credentials and skills for one's children. That is, for middle-class Bangladeshis, family migration to the developed world, especially to Anglophone countries such as Australia, Britain, Canada, and the United States, is valued for its access, especially for the younger generation, to opportunities for education and globally recognized professional credentials. Last but not least, the early years of the twenty-first century have seen the visible growth of middle-class consumption in Bangladesh, along with signs of an emerging personal credit market. As is the case in neighboring India as well as in other parts of the world, this "new middle class," as it is often called, is defined by its taste for globally branded goods, whether electronics or fast food. Under these circumstances, migration to the developed world may be driven by the goal of upward mobility through a lifestyle that satisfies emergent consumption standards.

Bangladesh State Policies and International Migration

Since the 1990s, successive Bangladeshi governments have actively encouraged labor migration flows out of the country. This reflects the growing significance of remittances—the money sent back by Bangladeshis abroad—for the

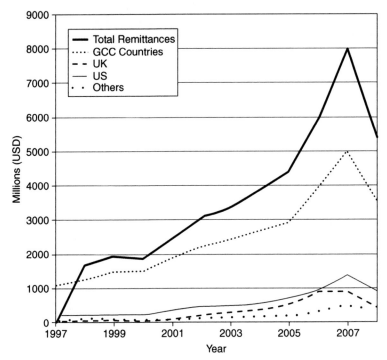

Figure 4. Remittance Flows into Bangladesh from Selected Countries, 1997–2009
Source: Government of Bangladesh, Central Bank of Bangladesh.

national economy. As shown in figure 4, remittances into Bangladesh grew steadily in the opening years of the twenty-first century, peaking in 2007 before declining in response to the 2008 global recession. In the 2008–2009 financial year, official remittances into Bangladesh were nine billion and six hundred thousand dollars, making it the largest source of foreign exchange in the country.

Given the importance of remittances, it is not surprising that international labor migration or "manpower export" has become an increasingly important focus of government policy in Bangladesh. In 1990, the Bangladesh government established the Wage Earners Welfare Fund. The fund, which requires contributions from each migrant worker, was set up to help migrant workers and their families in emergency situations such as illness, death, or legal problems in the receiving countries. And in 2002, the Ministry of Expatriates Welfare and Overseas Employment was created with the goal of facilitating labor migration, exploring new labor markets, and ensuring the welfare of Bangladeshi migrant workers. Since the 1980s, successive governments in

Bangladesh have tried to secure and expand outflows of labor migrants through diplomatic negotiations with labor receiving countries. There have also been efforts to create more effective official channels of remittance to Bangladesh.

Increasingly, as well, the Bangladesh state has faced questions of how best to leverage the resources and energies of the growing numbers of Bangladeshis settled abroad in service of the development of the country. This concern has drawn inspiration from the much-heralded diaspora role in two of the world's most important growing economies—China and India. Like NRI (Non-Resident Indian) in India, NRB or Non-Resident Bangladeshi has emerged as an official category of identification, suggesting a particular connection and attendant privileges with respect to the Bangladesh state. These include special NRB eligibility for certain kinds of foreign currency bank accounts in Bangladesh as well as the official waiver of Bangladesh visa fees and require-ments for NRBs who are traveling to Bangladesh on a foreign passport. The official designation of Commercially Important Person (CIP) has been awarded to some highly prominent NRBs, giving them public recognition as well as access to the privileges that are normally reserved for high-level government officials in Bangladesh, such as police protection. The Dual Nationality policy of Bangladesh, which allows those who are foreign citizens of Bangladeshi origin (as well as the children born to them) to gain or to affirm their citizenship, has also institutionalized NRB status. Here it is important to note that many of these developments have stemmed from the demands of NRBs themselves. As the Bangladeshi presence abroad has grown, so too have expatriate demands for greater, easier, and more meaningful involvements with Bangladesh. For example, since the early 2000s, segments of the diaspora have vigorously lobbied for the extension of voting rights to expatriates for elections in Bangladesh. As of 2009, these claims remained unmet. But dual nationals were eligible to vote in elections in Bangladesh, provided they were physically present there during the preparation of the voting rolls and during the elections.

In this chapter I have offered a brief overview of the history and politics of Bangladesh. In doing so, I have drawn attention to several conditions that are of importance to understanding the migration experiences that I take up in the chapters that follow. These include, for example, a powerful nationalist narra-tive in which the relationship of religion to the state has been a focus of politi-cal contest. There has also been an Islamic resurgence since the 1980s. Informed by the basic tenets of revivalist Islam, this resurgence has emphasized the notion of an Islamic identity for Bangladesh, along with the greater integration of Islam into public life.

In what follows, I explore the experiences of Bangladeshi international migrants and their families in several national settings. As we will see, the story of Bangladeshi Muslims in the United States is in many respects very different from that of Bangladeshi Muslims in Britain or the GCC states. But there are also many common themes. These reflect the collective memories and understandings that are part of being from Bangladesh as well as the ongoing impact of the global national image of Bangladesh on the lives of migrants and diaspora communities around the world. The significance of these commonalities becomes apparent as Bangladeshi Muslims around the world also grapple with the shared dilemmas of what it means to be Muslim in the world today.

CHAPTER 3

Bangladeshi American Dreams

In 2004, I interviewed Dr. Niaz, a Bangladeshi American cardiologist with a thriving medical practice in a suburb of New York.[1] It was three years after the terrorist attacks of September 11, 2001. After coming to the United States with a medical degree from Bangladesh in the late 1970s, Dr. Niaz had successfully taken the U.S. medical licensing exam and completed training in cardiology. Everything around Dr. Niaz signaled prosperity and success, from the spacious and luxurious house in which he lived with his wife and three children to the custom-built imported car that he drove with great confidence. In the home office where I interviewed him, I noted the various award plaques that lined the walls, some for professional achievement and others for community service. The doctor talked of the need for immigrants from Bangladesh to turn away from politics in Bangladesh and to give their attention to American politics. In his own case, he and his wife had been active members of the Republican Party throughout the 1980s and 1990s, although they were rethinking their party affiliation due to discontent with the George W. Bush administration's foreign policies. As we chatted, Dr. Niaz talked of feeling anti-Muslim sentiment after 9/11, the stings of which had spurred in him a newfound consciousness of the significance of being a minority in his adopted country. Despite these experiences, Dr. Niaz repeatedly affirmed his belief in the fairness of American society, often drawing comparisons with his native Bangladesh that were unfavorable to the latter:

> DR. N: 9/11 has made us feel insecure about our place in this country, in a
> way that we never did before. I cannot say that I was ever a victim of
> racism before 9/11. I did not have to explain my religion. But that has
> changed. For example, until recently, I was known as "Dr. Niaz Hussain"
> or "Dr. Hussain." After 9/11, this became a problem, because of the asso-
> ciation with Saddam Hussein. There were hate messages sent to the office

and patients refusing to be treated or being uncomfortable with me. I decided to change how the name is listed for the practice. I am now "Dr. Niaz" or "Dr. H. Niaz." A small change, but it seems to make a difference. Still [laughing], it takes me more time than my colleagues to get through airport customs. But, when I think about it, the reaction from the American government and public after 9/11 was not so bad, when I consider what might have happened in Bangladesh under similar circumstances.

NK: How has it made you feel about being here, in this country?

Dr. N: This is a great country that gives opportunities to those who work hard. I see this in my own life. That has not changed with 9/11. The system is fair here, you play by the rules and do well. This is unlike in our country [i.e., Bangladesh], where it is a corrupt system. I have always told the Bangalis here to become involved in American politics and to not waste their time on Awami League-BNP [Bangladesh political parties] nonsense. Well, they have actually become much more involved in American politics since 9/11, that is one of the good things that has happened. If I had remained in Bangladesh, I would not have had the same opportunities that I have had here. But with 9/11 we are more conscious of the problems of racism . . . we practice a different religion, we are foreigners with a different culture, we are dark-skinned. These things create suspicions toward us.

For Dr. Niaz, as for many other Bangladeshi Americans with whom I spoke, 9/11 and its aftermath had resulted in a heightened self-consciousness of their minority status in the United States. The theme of "racialization" is an important one in the scholarship on Muslims in North America and Europe in the post-9/11 era (see Grewal 2009; Masood 2005). Muslim Americans are a profoundly diverse population, encompassing persons of African, Asian, European, and Middle Eastern descent who have varied histories and cultural traditions. On the basis of such markers as skin color, Muslims quite clearly violate conventional American notions of what constitutes a racial group. Yet much like a racial minority, they have found themselves to be stigmatized on the basis of a presumption of intrinsic difference and inferiority as Muslims in relation to other Americans. Their exclusions then have had a naturalized and racial cast to them. Recognizing these conditions, Muslim Americans themselves may draw on the language of race and perhaps the history of antiracist struggles in the United States to describe and respond to their predicament. In fact, we see this in the above account of Dr. Niaz, who describes his post-9/11 experiences of discrimination as "racism." But we should note that in doing so he also self-consciously affirms the multiple dimensions of this racism—of religious difference, a dark skin color, and cultural "foreignness." "Racism" refers here to a complex bundle of exclusions in which the stigmas of Muslim affiliation are tightly interwoven with other dimensions of disadvantage, such as to make them virtually indistinguishable from each other.

As suggested by Dr. Niaz, the terrorist attacks of September 11, 2001, ushered in an era of transformation in the legal and political environment faced by immigrants and Muslims in the United States. Strengthening a trend that began in the mid-1990s, in the first decade of the twenty-first century there was a growing movement toward exclusionary immigration policies and laws that restricted the rights of immigrants and their families (Hagan, Eschbach, and Rodriguez 2008). A month after the 9/11 attacks, George W. Bush approved the USA-Patriot Act, which gave expanded legal powers to government agencies to implement special measures to address terrorism, both domestically and abroad.[2] These measures included a special registration program in 2002 for non-immigrant men aged sixteen to sixty-four from selected countries— Eritrea, North Korea, and twenty-three Muslim-majority states, including Bangladesh. The program required these persons to register with the U.S. immigration authorities and to undergo interviews with them. As Louise Cainkar (2004) observes, while of questionable value in terms of actually identifying terrorists, special registration did allow the U.S. government to deport thousands of immigrants, largely Muslim, for visa violations.

Although the special registration program was phased out in 2003, the U.S. government's use of "extraordinary measures" to monitor and in some cases to remove noncitizen immigrants deemed possible threats to national security continued throughout the decade. The Patriot Act allowed for immigrants who were not citizens to be arrested on alleged suspicion, to be secretly and indefinitely detained, and also to be forcibly deported. For the purposes of protecting national security interests, the act also authorized government agencies to use surveillance and wiretapping without showing probable cause, and to secretly obtain and search private records and property. If these policies have had consequences for immigrants in general, they have been especially important for Muslims, who have found themselves vulnerable to suspicions of terrorism simply by virtue of their religious affiliation. These policies have derived support from powerful waves of popular anger in the United States toward Muslims. In the years following 9/11, growing numbers of Muslim Americans reported assaults and attacks as well as discrimination in the workplace on the basis of their religion (Council on American-Islamic Relations 2008).

Bangladeshi Americans, a largely foreign-born and predominantly Muslim population, have been profoundly affected by these post-9/11 developments.

Like Dr. Niaz, many of those I spoke to described a heightened sense of marginality in America. Yet they remained optimistic about the possibilities of America and spoke of the American Dream. In 2007, the PEW Center issued a widely cited report on a national survey of 1,050 Muslims in the United States. According to the survey, 71 percent of Muslims agree with the idea that "in America, you can get ahead with hard work" (PEW Research Center 2007). Muslim Americans thus widely subscribe to the notion of America as a land of opportunity—a core element of U.S. nationalist ideology.

But what of the many Bangladeshi Americans in less privileged circumstances, those who do not have access to the protections and resources enjoyed by Dr. Niaz by virtue of his professional status? What did they make of the American Dream in the wake of 9/11? In many ways Belal, another Bangladeshi American I interviewed in 2004, could not have been more different from Dr. Niaz. If Dr. Niaz spoke of the 9/11 aftermath as giving rise to a minority consciousness that he did not have before, Belal, a cabdriver in New York City, spoke of added intensity and complexity rather than novelty. The events of 9/11 had simply added flames to the already smoldering fire of anger that he felt about the doors that had been closed to him in the United States. Ever since his arrival in the early 1980s, Belal had been trying, to no avail, to regularize his legal status in the United States. As a result, he had not been back to Bangladesh and seen his parents and sisters in twenty years, ever since he had left home as a young man in his early twenties. Belal was not married, although unbeknownst to his family he had for several years now been in a turbulent romantic relationship with a Jamaican immigrant woman who was also, like himself, an undocumented immigrant.

As I talked to Belal, I became increasingly puzzled about just what kept him in the United States, given that life here seemed to hold few pleasures or rewards for him. Unlike many other migrants who labor abroad under difficult circumstances in order to support their families back home, Belal had no such responsibilities. His father was a retired military officer and his family lived in modest but secure middle-class circumstances in the city of Chittagong. Indeed, for the past fifteen years, his family had been begging him to come back home. And there were actually times when Belal had come close to doing just that. But he always turned back from that path, burdened by a sense of shame for having nothing to show for all his years in the United States. With a faith that reminded me of the lottery player who buys again and again, blinded by the hope that the next ticket would be the winning one, he held on to the prospect of "making it in America." During our interview, Belal bristled with pent-up anger at the ill treatment that he had suffered in the United States.

Yet ultimately he, too, like Dr. Niaz, also affirmed the idea of America as a place of opportunity:

> B: Since 9/11, I have to be on constant alert. It was easier before, life was more relaxed. Now Homeland Security is everywhere, the spies, the people who betray you, are everywhere. You never know who will come after you. I have friends who have been picked up, they turn up in jail or they get deported. If you're not in the right part of town, you might be attacked.
>
> NK: Has anything like that happened to you?
>
> B: No, I am very careful. Sometimes I get the stupid customers in the taxi. Just yesterday, these guys in Manhattan got in and they were drunk. They started calling me "Osama," saying things like, "Hey Osama, what's up, Osama?" I was quiet because I'm very careful, I don't want trouble. But I was thinking, why do they see me as Osama? I don't wear anything like that, I don't have a beard, I don't display the Qu'ran in the taxi. Even my name, it's not that easy to tell that it's a Muslim name. But they somehow see me as Muslim. I get the stupid questions: [in a mocking tone] "Are you Mo.oh.slem [i.e., Moslem]? Are you Arabic? Do you have three wives?"
>
> NK: Has 9/11 changed the way you feel about this country?
>
> B: No, I have driven a taxi in New York for almost eighteen years. I have seen this type of behavior from Americans for a long time. I have always known about the way this country treats people who are dark-skinned. The whites tolerate us because they need us but in their hearts they would like nothing better than to see us leave. They are clever about it, they pretend to be kind, but I see how they use people and then throw them away like the trash.
>
> NK: Why then do you stay, why not go back?
>
> B: I feel ashamed, after all these years, I would go back with nothing. What would I do there? I am now in my forties . . . would I find a position there? I feel that there are still more opportunities here than in Bangladesh. I am trying to make it and *Inshallah* [God willing], I will do it. I am trying to get a green card [i.e., legal permanent resident status] and start my own web design company.

If for Belal, a single man with no children, making it in America was about what he himself could potentially achieve, for those with families in the United States, the American Dream was likely to center on their children. As is true for many immigrant parents, it was the access to education—to the opportunity for their children to acquire globally valued educational credentials that lay at the heart of the American Dream. I spoke to Azad and Laila, the father and mother of two young children. The Bangladeshi migrant couple operated a business in which they held partial ownership—a twenty-four-hour convenience store in the Boston area. In the immediate aftermath of 9/11 they had faced harassment from customers and passers-by, especially during the late hours of the night and early mornings in the store. Although these attacks had waned over time, they had left behind a powerful residue of vulnerability. The young couple described becoming more attentive to religious practice and actively involved in local Islamic groups since 9/11. Yet even as they expressed considerable anger and frustration with the treatment they had received, they also believed that America was a place of opportunity, particularly for their children:

> L: We know that we are not truly accepted in this country.
>
> NK: Why do you feel that way? How have you been treated?
>
> A: I remember when we first came here, in the early 1990s, we were trying to rent an apartment in Somerville [a city in Greater Boston]. The housing market for rentals was tight then. And we would go and look at the apartment and fill out applications, but we were always turned down. They preferred to rent to white Americans.
>
> L: After 9/11, there were many bad incidents at the store . . . name-calling, spitting. To protect me, my husband told me to take off my head covering, but I said, "No, America is supposed to be about freedom. I want the freedom to cover my head."
>
> A: The very bad time was in 2002; that was the first year that we had the store. Now it is not so bad. But we have to remind ourselves constantly about what this country gives us. My sons are going to have opportunity. They are going to school here, they have the opportunity to be doctors, lawyers. We are also raising our sons to be good Muslims. They are learning Arabic, they are reading the Qu'ran. America allows us to do these things.
>
> L: America has a bad name around the world because of what they do to Muslims in other countries. George Bush is killing Muslims everywhere. But there are still good things about this country. As my husband said, our children can make a good life for themselves here.

The post-9/11 environment was one in which Bangladeshi Americans gained a sharp sense of their marginality. Yet they also saw America as a land of opportunity, whatever its problems. The ideology of the American Dream was a shock absorber, helping them to cope with the indignities of the post-9/11 environment without developing a sense of absolute exclusion from the United

States. As for other migrants from developing countries, the contours of the American Dream gained meaning for them through a process of national comparison whereby American national prosperity came to be highlighted in relation to the relative poverty of the country of origin.

"HERE WE ARE NO ONE, NOTHING": FAMILY SOCIAL CAPITAL AND MIDDLE-CLASS DECLINE

Even as Bangladeshi migrants described America as a land of opportunity, they also often spoke of certain socioeconomic losses that coming to the United States had carried for them. Let us turn briefly to 2000 U.S. census data on the economic situation of Bangladeshis. Table 3.1 offers information on foreign-born Bangladeshis and, for purposes of comparison, on two other South Asian–origin groups in the United States, Indians and Pakistanis. In 2000, median household income for the general U.S. population was $42,148 and for non-Hispanic whites $45,904. We can see that in comparison to these figures, median household income among Bangladeshis was slightly lower, a pattern that was reversed in the case of Pakistanis. The median household income of $70,000 for foreign-born Indians was dramatically higher than that of Bangladeshis. The relatively favorable socioeconomic position of foreign-born Indians in the United States was also confirmed by poverty rates. As shown in table 3.1, 5 percent of Indians in 2000 fell below the poverty line, a figure that was less than that reported for the general U.S. population (9.4 percent) as well as Bangladeshis (16.3 percent) and Pakistanis (11.2 percent).

As presented in table 3.2, with respect to occupational status in the United States in 2000, the foreign-born Bangladeshi-origin population contained significant proportions of both professionals and low-income workers. About one-third of Bangladeshis worked in managerial and professional occupations. Another 29.6 percent were in white-collar jobs in sales and office work. Concurrently, a significant percentage of foreign-born Bangladeshis held jobs in the service sector (18.1 percent) as well as in such industries as production and transportation (15.5 percent). In New York City, for example, reports show Bangladesh to have replaced Pakistan in the early 2000s as the number one country of origin for first-time cab drivers (Schaller Consulting 2004).

To summarize, 2000 census data show Bangladeshi migrants to the United States to be disadvantaged in comparison to foreign-born Indians and Pakistanis. The pattern is similar to that in Britain, as I will discuss in chapter 5, where levels of income and education are lower among Bangladeshis than those of Indians and Pakistanis. However, if one compares Bangladeshis in the United States to Bangladeshis in Britain, the former seem to be faring better, as

TABLE 3.1

ECONOMIC INDICATORS OF FOREIGN-BORN BANGLADESHIS, PAKISTANIS, AND
INDIANS IN THE UNITED STATES FROM 2000 CENSUS

National origin	Median household income (USD)	% of persons below poverty line*	% of persons who have a college degree or higher
Bangladesh	40,000	16.3	48.4
India	47,400	5	71.9
Pakistan	70,000	11.2	51.6

*Persons in labor force, ages 25–64.

Source: U.S. Bureau of the Census, "Foreign-Born Profiles (STP-159)," Washington,
D.C.: U.S. Census Bureau, Population Division, 2000.
http://www.census.gov/population/ www/socdemo/foreign/STP-159–2000tl.html.

TABLE 3.2

OCCUPATION OF EMPLOYED FOREIGN-BORN BANGLADESHIS, PAKISTANIS, AND
INDIANS IN THE UNITED STATES FROM 2000 CENSUS

National origin	% Management, professional, and related	% Service	% Sales and office	% Construction, maintenance, and related	% Production and transportation
Bangladesh	32.9	18.1	29.6	3.9	15.5
India	64.6	5.5	19.2	1.6	8.9
Pakistan	41.2	8.5	30.8	3.5	15.7

Source: U.S. Bureau of the Census, "Foreign-Born Profiles (STP-159)." Washington,
D.C.: U.S. Census Bureau, Population Division, 2000.
http://www.census.gov/population/www/socdemo/foreign/STP-159–2000tl.html.

suggested by a higher percentage of persons in professional and managerial
occupations in the United States. Among the many explanations for this gap is
the larger proportion of highly educated persons from urban backgrounds in
the migration stream to the United States. As we see in table 3.1, the 2000 census shows almost half of all foreign-born Bangladeshis to be college graduates.

These figures make sense, given the generally high costs and difficulties of movement to the United States for Bangladeshis. Whether it is the expense of the plane fare or the difficulties of obtaining a U.S. visa, coming to the United States has largely been an option only for the relatively privileged segments of the Bangladeshi population.

Scholars of migration have noted the importance of class and educational background to understanding the economic adaptation of migrants in the receiving society (e.g., see Portes and Rumbaut 2006). Those migrants with higher levels of human capital are at a distinct advantage, with resources that enable them to more effectively negotiate the available paths to socioeconomic mobility in the receiving society. It is not surprising that these dynamics of class advantage were also an important part of the Bangladeshi American experience. They were reflected, for example, in how families often worked to ensure the academic achievements of their children, drawing on strategies that they had acquired in Bangladesh. These ranged from sitting down every evening with children to help them with homework to paying for expensive tutoring courses for them. But in the course of considering the experiences of Bangladeshi Americans, I also became aware of another potential consequence of the middle-class background of migrants, one that has not been so closely scrutinized by scholars. This is an experience of class decline, of a waning of middle-class identity and its attendant privileges as enjoyed prior to migration.

For some Bangladeshi Americans, the decline was clearly tied to the downward occupational decline that migration had brought for them. Whereas in Bangladesh they had been in managerial and professional positions, in the United States they found themselves in menial and low-paid jobs in the service and manufacturing sectors. Indeed, in the course of my fieldwork I encountered many former professionals from Bangladesh who had experienced such an occupational trajectory. This included, to name just a few, an architect waiting restaurant tables, a doctor at the check-in desk of a motel, a college professor driving a taxi, and an attorney working as a cashier. Weak English-language skills, the devaluation by U.S. employers of educational credentials from Bangladesh, employment discrimination, and unauthorized legal status were among the factors that had not allowed them to effectively convert their skills and experience in the U.S. labor market.

Besides occupational loss, movement to the United States was also seen to carry class decline through a loss of what I would describe as "family social capital" or the status and resources available to them through membership in a family network. Among my informants, this loss was understood to reflect the reduced value in the United States of family social capital that was rooted in and tied to the social and political context of Bangladesh. Several features of the

Bangladeshi middle class are relevant to understanding this context and the dynamics of family social capital within it. In Bangladesh, the state has historically played a critical role in the formation and development of the middle class by creating administrative jobs in the government sector (Hossain 2005; Islam 2004). Since the 1970s, there has been an expansion and diversification of the middle class beyond government officials to include professionals working in the private sector as well as a burgeoning business class. Nonetheless, the middle class remains relatively small—an estimated 9 to 10 percent of the population, compared to 18 percent in Pakistan and 30 percent in India (see AsiaPulse News 2006). And it also continues to be heavily dependent on political connections for state patronage and resources. Thus the Bangladeshi middle class, especially in its upper, elite tiers, has a highly insular character, organized as it is around deeply interwoven social networks: "the national elite remains close-knit, multiply and personally connected through tightly interwoven social relationships. Individuals and families straddle economic and social sectors, and interact a great deal. Any member will have friends, relatives, and friends of friends and relatives who sit in Parliament, own factories, direct NGOs, edit newspapers, and preside over ministries" (Hossain 2005: 967).

Given the significance of family connections for access to resources in Bangladesh, it is perhaps not surprising that Bangladeshi migrants to the United States, especially those from middle-class backgrounds, were deeply aware of how these connections mattered somewhat less in the United States. Of course it is not as if they did not matter at all. Within the arena of Bangladeshi American community life and its activities, from the formation of business partnerships to the search for good marriage partners, family social capital was a meaningful and valued social currency. But outside of the community, in settings where Bangladeshis did not predominate, such capital tended to have relatively little visibility and value. Especially among those who felt themselves to have been disadvantaged in Bangladesh by virtue of their limited family connections, this shift could be welcomed. But for others it was a troubling aspect of the migration experience, bringing a loss of resources and privileges that had been a taken-for-granted feature of their life in Bangladesh.

For Mainul, a migrant in his forties, settlement in America had produced an experience of middle-class loss so profound as to make him seemingly unable to make peace with his life in the United States. I spoke to Mainul in the neat and compact living room of his Astoria, New York, townhouse that he had recently purchased. Mainul showed me many photographs of family members from Bangladesh, prominently displayed on the walls of the living room. He told me that he was from a well-positioned family of the Tangail region; his family members were educated and well positioned in many fields, such as banking, education, business, and politics. Pointing to specific people in the photos, he noted their political and economic connections with such statements as: "His brother-in-law is an MP (Member of Parliament) and her cousin is the owner of __ company."

Turning to his own migration story, Mainul told me that he had been in the United States for almost twenty years, since his mid-twenties. He and his wife Ila, an American-born Bangladeshi woman, had four children. By his own account, as a young man Mainul had been a drifter and less-than-stellar student. Rather than face the shame of failing the college entrance exams, he had chosen to take his chances and go abroad to New York, where he had some relatives. According to the Asian American Federation Census Information Center (2005), New York City is home to the largest Bangladeshi-origin population of any metropolitan region in America, with pockets of concentration in Brooklyn and Queens. The neighborhoods of Astoria and Jamaica in New York City have become important centers of Bangladeshi American life, replete with Bangladeshi stores, restaurants, real estate agents, tax and immigration attorneys, banks, mosques, and schools.

After several difficult years of getting by with odd jobs in Bangladeshi restaurants in New York City, Mainul moved into a stable position, a shift that was facilitated by the legal documentation that he acquired through marriage to Ila, a U.S. citizen and child of Bangladeshi immigrants. When I talked to him, Mainul had been working in the maintenance department of a Manhattan office complex for almost fifteen years. Through careful planning and thrift, he and Ila had managed to purchase a home and even send their oldest child to private school. He was proud of these accomplishments and hopeful that his children would move into professional occupations in the future, thereby fulfilling his dreams. But on a more immediate level, he felt unhappy with his life in the United States. Much of his leisure time was spent on the activities of an HTA (Hometown Association) that he had formed with some friends in New York who originated from the same locality in Bangladesh. He and Ila were engaged in an ongoing battle, sometimes amicable and at other times somewhat less so, over his desire to return home.

M: I would like to return to home. My wife says to me, why do you want to go back? New York is becoming more like home all the time. This is true. Now you can watch ATN Bangla [cable channel] all day. We get hilsa fish from Bangladesh. There are Bangali mosques everywhere. And there are of course the many many associations. I am the president of one of them, the ___ Upazilla Association. It is just a few of us from that area who live around here. We meet every so often to talk about how we can help our

country. We try to do good works. For example, we have been supporting
a local clinic and school in our area. I have traveled a few times there,
to my ancestral village, to oversee their activities.

NK: Tell me then what you are missing from life here.

M: [Long pause.] Life is easier and more comfortable here. But in the end,
we are no one, nothing (*keo na, keechoo na*) in this country. At home you
can hold your head up high because of your family name. People know
that you are part of a well-known family lineage (*nam kora bongsho*).

Besides occupational loss and disconnect from family social capital, as I have
described thus far, the widespread sense of class decline among Bangladeshi
Americans reflected differences between the United States and Bangladesh in
the symbolic meanings of middle-class identity. As Lamont and Molnár (2002)
have observed, the boundaries of social class include a powerful symbolic
dimension of "conceptual distinctions, interpretive strategies and cultural
traditions . . . [used to] separate people into groups and generate feelings of
similarity and group membership" (168). Here it is important to note that in
Bangladesh, as in many other developing countries, the boundaries that mark
the relatively small middle class are notable for their explicit and sharply visible
character. To put it simply, the middle class stands out from the vast numbers
of less privileged persons in these societies, in certain ways more starkly than is
the case in industrialized democratic societies. Thus in Bangladesh, middle-
class identity is informed by a sharp if unspoken sense of elite distinction, of
being special and "above the masses," in terms of resources, lifestyle, knowledge, and outlook. In the United States, this particular sense of elite distinction
generally diminishes for Bangladeshis, regardless of their socioeconomic
location in America. What can be left behind is a feeling of being "just like
everybody else." Or, as an informant from a background of involvement in
left-wing politics in Bangladesh put it with a hint of dry humor, "just one of the
proletariat." To be sure, a complex mixture of sentiments accompanied this
sense of loss. Many Bangladeshi Americans, including those from elite backgrounds, spoke of how the perceived leveling of symbolic class distinctions was
something that they valued and admired about the United States. Indeed, these
were democratic and progressive attitudes that they wished to transmit back to
Bangladesh. But such a stance did not necessarily preclude a sense of personal
loss or at least of disruption to a way of life that had been enjoyed before.

For many Bangladeshi Americans, especially (but not exclusively) for women,
the issue of household work, specifically the necessity for hands-on involvement in it in the United States, was a potent symbol of the elite distinction lost
with migration. In Bangladesh, because of low labor costs, even families of

quite modest means are able to hire domestic servants to perform such household tasks as cooking, cleaning, laundry, and childcare. This access to domestic workers is at least one of the conditions that has facilitated the entry since the 1980s of middle-class women into the labor force in Bangladesh without causing serious disruption to an established gender division of household labor in which women hold primary responsibility for the care and running of the household. In fact, idealized notions of elite femininity affirm the centrality of women to the domestic sphere through their supervisory role—of directing and monitoring paid domestic workers. Elite masculinity, in contrast, is idealized as one of unfettered entitlement with respect to household work, without supervisory or other responsibilities. In the United States these notions are challenged, as the strategy of hiring servants to perform household tasks is generally less accessible and feasible. Household work thus emerges as a focus of considerable frustration for migrants. Indeed, I was struck by how often my informants cited household work as one of the primary disadvantages of living in America.

Along with its challenges to idealized conceptions of masculinity and femininity, the "problem of housework" also signaled a loss of middle-class identity for Bangladeshi Americans. Thus Rumana, an informant in her forties, referring to all the housework she did, told me with wry sarcasm of how she had "become a domestic servant" in the United States. She spoke of how migration to the United States had brought privileges and opportunities for her young adult daughters who were free in the United States to go out and pursue their education and careers. But for her it had resulted in an insular and limited life. Her daughters, as she put it, had become "memsahibs." Deriving from "ma'am" and "sahib," "memsahib" is a term that was used during British colonial times by Indians to deferentially refer to European women. Today it continues to be used by Bengalis, often tongue-in-cheek, at times to refer to white women and at other times to Bengali women who adopt European culture and perhaps resemble the white colonial women of the past in their sense of elite distinction and entitlement. Among other things, Rumana's account underlines the problematic character of analyses that assume the homogeneity of the migration experience and its rewards for members of the same family:

> At home I had my own life, my own car, driver, cook. . . . I had a small business, a tailoring shop that I owned. Now in this country I stay at home all day. I have become the family's domestic servant, cooking and cleaning for them, taking care of their clothes, cleaning their toilets. You know at home I used to cook maybe once in ten years, and here I cook three times a day. I never cleaned a toilet before in my life. My daughters have become

memsahibs and I have become a domestic servant. They get dressed up in
their *bideshi* [foreign, Western] clothes in the morning and say, "Bye, *Amma*
[mother], see you later." When they come back, I have washed their clothes
and cooked their dinner.

As we have seen, for Bangladeshis abroad as for other migrants, the
challenges of global movement include the task of coming to terms with the
attendant shifts in one's class location. In this regard, many of my Bangladeshi
American informants, especially those who were first-generation migrants,
spoke of a sense of class decline, of losing the particular configuration of class
privileges and resources that they had enjoyed in Bangladesh. This experience
could strengthen their resolve to fortify ties to Bangladesh and to draw attention to them, thereby ensuring the continued pertinence of these advantages.
Such strategies were complicated, however, by another condition—the relative
invisibility of Bangladesh as a country in America.

"Bangladesh? Where's That?": The Dilemmas of Invisibility

Among the conditions that differentiate the Bangladeshi American transnational context from the British Bengali one is the absence in the former of a
history of direct colonial ties. As a result, in the United States, certainly in
comparison to Britain, Bangladesh is a generally unknown national entity.
Thus many of my U.S. informants described a pattern of social encounters with
non-Bangladeshis in which their assertion of "I'm from Bangladesh" was
typically greeted with blank stares and ill-informed queries. Although these
were common experiences for Bangladeshi Americans in general, they seemed
especially troubling and thus memorable to the younger generation, especially
those born and/or raised in the United States. Joi, a gregarious twenty-year-old
college student, spoke with both good humor and frustration about such an
encounter with a close white American friend:

J: If you say Bangladesh, the average American says, "Oh, that's the place
with all the floods." Or maybe: "Hey, George Harrison and the Concert
for Bangladesh."[3] Even a close friend of mine the other day, he asked me
where I was from and I said Bangladesh. He said: "Oh, isn't that a city in
India?" I was pretty disgusted, I said: "City in India? Are you crazy?" He
said: "Dude, are you sure it's a country? How come I haven't heard about
it?" I said: "Dude, educate yourself. We were part of India a long time ago."
NK: Does that kind of thing make any difference to how you feel about
being Bangladeshi?

J: Umm . . . Bangladesh is kind of invisible in America. So it's like that part
     of me is invisible to other people.

It is important to note that such encounters as the above were situational
and occasional—they did not happen everywhere and all the time. They were
far less likely to occur in certain areas of the United States, such as around New
York City, where Bangladeshis have become a significant presence and thus
familiar to the local population. And notwithstanding the particular situation
described by Joi, they were far less likely to occur with friends and acquaintances who had personal knowledge of one's biography. But even when infre-
quent, these encounters served as important reminders of the "invisibility,"
as Joi puts it, of Bangladesh to Americans. Among the consequences of this
invisibility is the limited effectiveness of "Bangladeshi" as a counteridentity to
imposed labels. Scholars of the immigrant experience in the United States have
noted how the assertion of a national affiliation may be a strategy of resistance
to the homogenizing and often stigmatizing labels that are imposed on
migrants by members of the receiving society (Kibria 2002; Waters 1999). For
example, by choosing at times to assert a national origin affiliation over the
generic Asian label that has been assigned to them ("I'm Chinese, not Asian"),
second-generation Chinese and Korean Americans may gain a sense of agency
over the construction of their own identity. Bangladeshi Americans too may
assert their national origin when confronted with unwanted racial or ethnic
labels. But it tends not to be so effective a strategy given these conditions of
nonrecognition, when "from Bangladesh" is not accepted as a meaningful or
legitimate affiliation by others.

The experience of their national origins "invisibility" could thus highlight
to Bangladeshi Americans the comparatively greater significance of their
other affiliations—those that are generally more familiar to Americans. These
include the identity of "Muslim," which has gained prominence in post 9/11
America. Thus Tahmina, a nineteen-year-old woman who had grown up since
the age of seven in the Boston area, noted that her Muslim religious affiliation
was far more likely to provoke a response of recognition from others than
her Bangladeshi origins. Of note, too, is her observation that Bangladeshis
in the United States occupy a fluid racialized space, one in which they can
be "mistakenly" identified as a member of any number of racial and ethnic
minority groups:

> Americans don't see us as Bangladeshi. If they just see us on the street, maybe
> they think that we are Indian, or Mexican, Latin American, maybe Arab.
> It does depend on how one looks, and how one is dressed. If I say I'm from
> Bangladesh, the most common reaction is "Where's that?" Or: "Oh, that's

the place with all the starving people." They have no idea. But if they understand that I'm Muslim, either from my name or for whatever reason, then it's different. I'm not saying that they actually have real knowledge of Muslims either, but the idea of Muslim means something to them whereas Bangladesh means almost nothing to them.

As described earlier, the global national image of Bangladesh is such as to invoke not just nonrecognition in the United States but also an image of poverty, political instability, and corruption. Indeed, several second-generation Bangladeshi American informants admitted to me that they felt embarrassed about acknowledging that they were from Bangladesh because of this image. Both embarrassment and defiant frustration are apparent in the account of Jamshed, a twenty-four-year-old from Brooklyn, New York. Jamshed described reacting with self-mocking anger to the negative image of Bangladesh that was brought to his attention when he told people of his Bangladeshi origins:

When I tell people I'm from Bangladesh, they say, "Oh yeah, poor, starving people, floods and famines." It's a fact of course, what can you say? I say, "Yes, it's poor and starving and you know we've been ranked as the first or second most corrupt country in the world." [Laughing] Other countries are famous for their food or music; we're famous for being poor and corrupt.

For Bangladeshis in the United States, as in other parts of the world, the unfavorable image of Bangladesh was a source of considerable frustration. Not only was it hurtful to their sense of national pride but it was also distressing in its simplification, in its ability to reduce the rich and complex realities of a country they knew so well to a one-dimensional stereotype. There were also the dynamics of stigmatization around it, of "guilt by association" whereby the negative image of the country spills over into the presumed traits of those originating from it. Under these conditions, the Nobel Peace Prize of 2008 and other international recognition that has been given to Muhammad Yunus, founder of the Grameen Bank of Bangladesh, has been a particularly important source of pride for Bangladeshis abroad. Lamia Karim (2008) has observed how the Grameen Bank has become an important source of symbolic capital for middle-class Bangladeshis. Bemoaning how these conditions have worked to stifle critiques of the bank, she observes:

For the first time, we, the people of Bangladesh—Henry Kissinger's "bottomless basket"—have given a gift to the western development community. Now visitors, from former U.S. President Bill Clinton and Senator Hillary Clinton to Queen Sophia of Spain, come to Bangladesh to study a development phenomenon. It is a source of tremendous national pride for many Bangladeshis, which makes it all the more difficult to critique the Grameen Bank, or for that critique to be taken seriously. In fact, speaking out against the Grameen Bank makes one into a "traitor within." (2008: 24)

To summarize, Bangladeshi Americans often felt their national origins to be invisible and stigmatized within U.S. society. Social encounters marked by nonrecognition of their national origins seemed particularly memorable for younger Bangladeshi Americans, many of whom related a fairly fragile sense of meaningful connection to Bangladesh. Under these conditions, some felt the need to distance themselves from their Bangladeshi affiliation, perhaps coupling it with an assertion of "Muslim American" identity. But for others, certainly for first-generation migrants, these encounters with Americans who lacked knowledge of Bangladesh were unlikely to dislodge their firmly rooted identification with Bangladesh. It was a connection that drew meaning and strength from a rich store of memories as well as ongoing and active transnational webs of social ties and relations that stretched from Bangladesh to the United States.

TRANSNATIONAL WEBS OF FAMILY RELATIONS

Last summer, we went back [to Bangladesh] for two months. I am very excited about going back. Before I went I did shopping of $10,000, filling twelve suitcases. Everyone expects a gift. . . . We enjoyed ourselves very much. There was a lot of visiting and chatting (*adda*), shopping. I stayed with my sister in Dhaka and then my brother-in-law in Chittagong. We lived like royalty . . . no cooking, no cleaning, no laundry, no grocery shopping. I would like to go back, I dream about that day. Desh is desh.[4] As soon as my feet touch the ground there, I am crying. I feel like I am a changed person . . . I am back home. There are so many people, transportation is very bad, no one respects the law. The government is corrupt; the politicians do nothing but call strikes. In spite of all the problems, I miss desh. We are respected (*maan-shomman*) there. When I go there I forget about the hard life here, where you are nobody, just another dark-skinned person. What is most difficult about going is coming back here.

Nayla, whose account this is, was a forty-year-old Bangladeshi migrant from the New York area. She had been back to visit Bangladesh just three times over the course of her fifteen years in the United States. The relative infrequency of her trips back was far from unusual among the Bangladeshi Americans I interviewed. The high cost of plane tickets and the difficulties of obtaining vacation leave from jobs, as well as the legal problems for some migrants of reentering the United States after exit, were the most commonly cited reasons for not going back more often. Despite the infrequency, or perhaps because of it, the trips were often described as highly memorable occasions. For Nayla, the visits back home were filled with significance, generating a store of fortifying memories to which she could turn at moments of despondency about her life in the United States. She spoke of how no other country could pull her heartstrings in the same way as Bangladesh, whatever its many problems. From the moment of disembarking from the plane and touching the precious soil of Shonar Bangla (Golden Bengal), her senses flooded with intense feelings of belonging. Her beloved Bangladesh was, moreover, a place where she felt respected. During her time back home she regained a sense of middle-class honor and privilege that was so missing from her U.S. existence.

For Nayla, as for many other Bangladeshi Americans, family relations dominated their connections to Bangladesh. That is, it was relations with family members in Bangladesh that offered the most explicit, regular, and sustained anchor for maintaining connections with Bangladesh. It was family members to whom they sent remittances back home. It was family that they visited and stayed with during trips to Bangladesh. And it was with sisters, uncles, and other relatives that they stayed in frequent touch through phone calls and Internet communications. This family-centered transnationalism was, moreover, marked by its relative detachment from a local community. Reflecting the predominance in the United States of a migration stream of Bangladeshis from urban and middle-class backgrounds, many of my informants had grown up in the cities of Bangladesh and had moved across different homes and neighborhoods in the course of their lives there. Family members who were in Bangladesh tended to live in scattered areas of Dhaka or other cities. And so, even as Bangladeshi Americans were enmeshed in transnational webs of family relations marked by active flows of exchange, these connections tended not to be of such kind as to simultaneously embed them in a meaningful and well-defined territorial community such as the home village. In Bangladesh, the home village (*desher bari*) is used to refer to the patrilineal ancestral home and the larger rural community in which it is located. These places are understood to signify primordial roots, a site where ancestry and soil blend to signal an essential belonging.

Among my U.S. informants, Sajia was somewhat unusual in how self-conscious she was about the importance of having ties to one's home village. Sajia, who was in her forties, had been living in the United States for almost twenty years. She resided in a suburb in Connecticut with her husband and two teenage children. For many years now, she had worked as a bank teller while her husband held a clerical job at a local hospital. The couple regularly sent remittances to family members in Bangladesh. Sajia provided money for the care of her elderly mother who was living with her sister in Dhaka. And her husband sent money to his elder brother in order to assist him with the financial costs of schooling his three children.

In general, both Sajia and her husband seemed deeply enmeshed in a web of family relations and obligations that stretched from their lives in Connecticut to that of their family members in Dhaka. But Sajia was not satisfied. She yearned for something else, something that would give her a deeper sense of connection and belonging to the country of her birth. After thinking about it, she decided that establishing ties with her home village might be a way to address her discontent. And so just last year, when she had been visiting family in Dhaka, she had taken a two-day trip to her ancestral village. Sajia had actually never been there before that visit, although she had grown up hearing many stories about it. As a child, she had heard dramatic tales of how members of her family had been given shelter in the village in 1971, as they tried to escape the genocidal campaign of the Pakistani Army. She also remembered as a child how there had been times when relatives from the village had come to their home in Dhaka, at times carrying precious gifts of rice grown on the ancestral land (*desher dhan*). She also recalled how her father used to send money to the village on certain religious occasions such as Eid. But she and her siblings had not put much effort into maintaining connections with the village, especially since her father's death about eight years ago. This was true even though they still owned some property there. In fact, their only regular source of news about the village came through a first cousin who lived in a small town that was adjacent to the village and occasionally came to see them in Dhaka.

Before Sajia's time in Bangladesh last year, she had spoken of her desire to visit the village to her highly urbane and well-placed brothers and sisters in Dhaka. They had been a little taken aback. They had jokingly inquired if she was thinking of running for an MP (member of Parliament) seat from the home district and so wished to go to the village to campaign. And then they had discouraged her, citing the difficulties of reaching the village, which was not well connected to major transportation routes and required several river crossings by ferry boat to get there. Despite the opposition, Sajia had finally succeeded in making the trip, which had turned out to be a deeply fulfilling experience for her:

> S: I was not born there and I did not spend time there as a child. But still, there is something about it that cannot be put into words. I felt that it was my place, I belonged. You know how it is in this country [United States]: you have many things but you do not feel the intimacy. And in Dhaka

too, life has become very fast. Everyone is busy. Everywhere you look, the multistoried buildings are going up. Even though I had never been there, the people in the village know my family. They hold us, especially my paternal grandfather, in great respect because he built the school there. I had saved my *zakat* for the trip.[5] I used that money to provide a feast for everyone in the village. And I gave some money to the orphanage there that is run by the mosque. I asked everyone to say prayers for my children, my family. Just a few months ago, I faced a difficult family problem and I was able to send word to the Imam of the village mosque to say prayers for me.

NK: Are you planning to go back?

S: I would like to go back, but it is all in the hands of Allah. My elder brother is trying to sell our family land there and I cannot oppose him. He wants the money to start a new business. He also says, and it is true, that we do not have anyone trustworthy to look after our property there. As long as my father was alive, it was different because he had spent part of his childhood in the village and he knew people there. I don't know what will happen in the future.

NK: What about your children?

S: [laughing] Ahh, my children, they have no interest in my *desher bari*. Actually they have no interest in Bangladesh.

For Sajia, the ancestral village signified a place of community and true, authentic belonging. This was not only in comparison to the United States, where she felt marginalized and alone, but also in relation to the rapidly changing urban environment of Dhaka and the middle-class social circles to which she and her siblings belonged. As she describes, even after returning to the United States, the village and the ties she had established were a continued source of psychic comfort. The village was a place of honor, a location where she was given due recognition as a member of a family of high social repute. Indeed, through her various gifts to the village during the trip, Sajia had affirmed and consolidated this recognition. In short, as a result of her deliberate efforts, Sajia had made the home village a part of her life. Nonetheless, it was her relations with her immediate family members—her brothers and sisters in Dhaka—that continued to largely define and organize her active ties to Bangladesh. Because these family members were themselves hardly involved with the home village, these two sets of transnational anchors did not overlap and thus did not reinforce each other.

To summarize, among the consequences of the largely urban and middle-class background of Bangladeshi Americans is a pattern of familial transnationalism whereby ties to Bangladesh are organized around family relations without being nested in the supporting ties of a primordial territorially defined community. The case of Sajia is unusual in the degree of self-consciousness that she displayed about the absence of a specific community context for her ties to Bangladesh. Although few turned to the home village in the self-conscious manner that she had done, many Bangladeshi Americans did seek involvements with Bangladesh community associations as a way to strengthen, expand, and institutionalize their ties to Bangladesh. Especially among those who had suffered what they felt to be a loss of family social capital with migration, such involvements were seen to be a means by which to rebuild the contexts in which their family social capital held significance.

TRANSNATIONAL WEBS OF COMMUNITY ASSOCIATIONS

As Bangladeshi Americans have grown in numbers since the 1990s, a great variety of Bangladeshi community organizations have mushroomed across the country. Even though they are typically marked by multiple and evolving goals, these organizations can be broadly categorized by their primary stated mission. The organizations with the longest history in America are the cultural associations based in different parts of the United States (e.g., Bangladesh Association of Chicagoland) that aim to facilitate and encourage the practice of cultural traditions as well as foster a sense of community among Bangladeshis in the area. They often organize social and cultural events, such as annual picnics, Bangladesh Independence Day celebrations, and cultural shows featuring celebrity singers and performers from Bangladesh. They may also hold Bengali language classes for children on the weekends and conduct fundraisers for charity and disaster relief efforts in Bangladesh. While the emphasis is on social gatherings and cultural activities, some also work to establish ties with local U.S. political representatives and authorities in an effort to gain recognition and support for their projects.

Another important type of community initiative is the HTA (Hometown Association) which brings together those from a specific locale in Bangladesh with the goal of fostering social ties among them and collectively engaging in good works back in the home community. An important feature of community life among many migrant groups, the HTA has been especially prominent among British Bangladeshis, who tend to retain strong and ongoing ties with their ancestral village. Reflecting the greater representation of urban backgrounds in the U.S. migration stream, HTAs, though still important, are somewhat less prominent among Bangladeshi Americans. While not mutually exclusive, some Bangladeshi Americans have preferred instead to direct their energies to associations based not on regional origins in Bangladesh but on other types of shared histories and interests. These include, for example, alumni associations based on affiliation with schools and universities in Bangladesh as well as occupation-based groups such as the American Association of Bangladeshi Engineers and Architects. The activities of these associations typically include annual meetings, newsletters, internet chat groups, and fundraising for scholarships in Bangladesh.

Perhaps the most controversial of the Bangladeshi American community associations are those that are affiliated with the political parties in Bangladesh (e.g., Awami League of New England). At various times since the 1990s, political leaders in Bangladesh (especially when they are in power) have expressed concern about the activities of these overseas branches and chapters. These political groups, it is claimed, have tarnished the international image of the country with their often vicious and highly exposed squabbles. That is because these conflicts are often aired in public, and non-Bangladeshis are exposed to them and thereby form negative opinions of Bangladesh. Citing these concerns, the interim caretaker government of Bangladesh in 2008 put forward a law that not only made the official registration of political parties compulsory but also banned their branch organizations and chapters abroad. However, it was not clear that the ban has had much impact. This became apparent in September 2009, when hundreds of Awami League and BNP supporters in the United States staged a series of demonstrations and counterdemonstrations in front of the United Nations headquarters in New York on the occasion of Prime Minister Sheikh Hasina's visit there.

Associations based on political party have clearly been an important part of the visible divisions of Bangladesh community life abroad. But I do not think it would be fair to place all the blame on the shoulders of these groups and their rivalries. In reality, factionalism, as I was often told, was a more general and pervasive feature of Bangladeshi community life, both at home and abroad.

"WHERE THERE ARE BENGALIS, THERE ARE FACTIONS"

In the summer of 2008, my e-mail account was flooded with messages from several Bangladesh American newsgroups to which I subscribe about the annual FOBANA convention. FOBANA, or Federation of Bangladeshi Associations of North America, was formed in 1987 as an umbrella organization to bring together the hundreds of Bangladeshi associations that exist in the United States and Canada, fostering communication and cooperation among them (FOBANA n.d.). FOBANA's flagship event is an annual convention that is held in different North American cities on a rotating basis. At this gathering, representatives of the various Bangladeshi associations assemble together for a gala event with vendor stalls, business booths, featured speakers and discussions, cultural performances, fashion parades, and other activities. But in 2008, as had happened many times before, FOBANA appeared to have divided into warring factions. Several groups, each claiming to be the umbrella entity for Bangladeshi associations, held separate conventions of their own. On the Internet, there was much discussion of how this turn of events was both shameful and also entirely expected of Bangladeshis, who were naturally prone to factionalism (*dola-doli*).

The landscape of Bangladeshi American community life is rich, vibrant, and diverse, marked by a broad and varied spectrum of voluntary associations. And contrary to the image of dysfunctional factionalism that is evoked by the story of a divided FOBANA, these groups are able to engage successfully in a wide range of community projects. They bring Bangalis together, whether it is to commemorate Ekushe February, to organize a cultural show with the latest CloseUp stars from Bangladesh, or to raise funds to support flood victims in Bangladesh.[6] In general, then, Bangladeshi voluntary associations are clearly important and fulfilling forums of community engagement for many Bangladeshi Americans. Yet the dominant popular image of these associations is one of factionalism. It seems that it is the stories of conflicts that get recounted and discussed at length. Indeed, a splintered FOBANA was just one of the countless tales of Bangladeshi associations divided into warring sides that were in circulation when I was in the midst of fieldwork.

Because these association disputes are often freely and publicly aired, not only on the Internet but also in other community gatherings and other forums, they tend to be quite visible. Startling tales of fights and public humiliations are thus never in short supply, making for exciting gossip. In some cases, disputes are even taken to the courts, as the aggrieved parties file assault charges with the police and bring lawsuits for breach of contract or slander against each other. In one such case that was described to me, the opponents followed up their legal actions by each mailing lengthy letters describing what they felt to be the "real" story to all the association members. Although there were no doubt a variety of motivations driving these expensive and time-consuming efforts, the goal of preserving reputation—one's good name in the community—was often mentioned.

With the exception of cases that clearly revolved around political party affiliation, Bangladeshi Americans often spoke of the association disputes in highly personalistic terms, as the outcome of personal enmities between individuals—friendships and partnerships that had soured—perhaps due to the perceived dishonorable behavior of one or both parties. Such explanations were privileged over the more clearly sociological ones for which I searched, such as the varied interests of members due to differences in regional and class background. This favoring of personalistic explanations is apparent from my field notes below, which I recorded after a meeting with a group of community leaders in a city in the southern part of the United States:

> M. Ali said that he had been president of the ___ Association for four years. In fact he still considered himself the legitimate president although he had been apparently voted out of office in the last election which happened about a year ago. Jamshed, who had told me at an earlier meeting that he was "neutral" and tried to stay "out of the politics," chimed in to say that this was because there had been fraudulent votes cast in the last election. In fact M. Ali and his supporters were in the midst of consulting a lawyer about what possible legal steps to take against A. Mansur, who had engineered a win for himself in the election. A young man who had been secretary under M. Ali's presidency said that A. Mansur's supporters were thugs (*goondas*) and they had physically assaulted him the day of the election. They had ran-sacked his apartment and beaten him up before he reached the voting area. Horrified, I probed for explanations of the rivalry: Was it relevant that M. Ali was from Chittagong and A. Mansur from Noakhali? Were the two leaders different in other ways, such as in their levels of education or in the Bangladeshi political party they supported? All of these were dismissed. I was told that the two respective leaders and their supporters were quite mixed in terms of what part of Bangladesh they were from, whether they were sup-porters of BNP or Awami League, or what kinds of jobs they occupied. In fact M. Ali and A. Mansur had a long history of close friendship: when A. Mansur had first arrived in the U.S. in the 1980s, it was M. Ali who had helped him to settle into the area. Several people spoke of how the problems stemmed from the unscrupulous character and naked ambition of A. Mansur. Finally, M. Ali laughed and said, "You know it is in the Bangali character. Wherever you have a group of Bangalis, there will be fights and factions." Everyone agreed. As Jamshed walked me out, we chatted. He told me that there was a fair amount of back-and-forth movement across the M. Ali and A. Mansur camps, making it very difficult to understand what exactly divided them. It was also not clear that M. Ali and A. Mansur were particularly different in their visions of how the association should operate.

Studies suggest that migrant associations may be generally predisposed toward factionalism and division. In their analysis of migrant hometown asso-ciations among Salvadorans in California, Waldinger, Popkin, and Magana (2008) argue that it is the particular structural features of these groups that make them inclined to fracture. For one thing, migrant associations are voluntary and often informal in their organizational rules and hierarchy, making it easy for members to register their dissatisfaction through departure or challenge to existing leadership. In addition, leadership positions are highly coveted, offering as they do a means of gaining social respect, which migrants often feel to be lacking in their lives. The combination of these conditions favors volatility, making it often both possible and worthwhile to challenge existing leadership and to launch processes of organizational secession. As a result, migrant associations multiply, with one spawning another.

We see, then, that a high level and intensity of community factionalism may be a general aspect of migrant life, one that is not exclusive to any particular national origin group. In contrast, the popular discourse of Bangladeshi Americans was suggestive of national exceptionalism. Central to this discourse, which is prevalent among Bangladeshis everywhere, whether at home or abroad, was the idea that community factionalism is deeply, indeed primordially rooted in the national character of Bangalis. It is evident in varied situations and places, whether it is the turbulent national political scene of Bangladesh or the ongoing internal feuds of the local Bangladeshi association. We may recall that the M. Ali–G. Mansur schism as recounted in my field notes was viewed by those present to be a result of the flawed character of G. Mansur. This focus on personal qualities and enmities was nested, in a mutually reinforcing fashion, within a more general discourse of national character. That is, the disputes were seen to be the result of personal clashes to which Bangalis as a national group were naturally prone. In this ultimately self-denigrating perspective, there was an unconscious appropriation of racialized colonial constructs of Bengalis as inherently unfit to rule themselves. The global national image of Bangladesh as a poor and unsuccessful country only reinforced these notions.

Among Bangladeshi Americans, the discourse of an essential quality of factionalism affirmed the continuity of the field of Bangladeshi voluntary associations in the United States with the civic and political worlds of Bangladesh. That is, it was not only that they were Bangladeshi associations with activities that somehow focused on Bangladesh, it was also in their cultural character that they were part of Bangladesh. In fact, I would argue that this was precisely part of the appeal of these associations for many Bangladeshi Americans. They could provide a sense of continuity—of living in a social world that stretched seamlessly across the globe from the United States to Bangladesh. At the same time, it was this very continuity, in particular the quality of perceived factionalism, which gave a certain air of moral ambiguity to these organizations and thus to those who participated in them. The problem posed was of how to construct and to engage in forms of Bangladeshi community involvement that did not open one up to certain accusations. These included being self-serving, power hungry, and quarrelsome, as well as "backward" in orientation in the sense of being unschooled in the modern and rationalized rules and codes of civic life. Given these complexities, it is not surprising that even as many informants spoke of their involvement in Bangladeshi associations with both pride and pleasure, it was not uncommon for a certain ambivalence to accompany these accounts. Regardless of whether they actually did so, many spoke of wanting to stay away from the associations due to their unsavory character. Others spoke of their involvements with a tone of apology as well as apprehension and fear, given the constant possibility of accusations and loss of face.

And so the discourse of factionalism had many different consequences for Bangladeshi American community life. By strengthening an experience of continuity between the social and political worlds of Bangladesh and its diaspora communities, it contributed to a sense of ongoing presence in Bangladesh. But it also weakened the ability of Bangladeshi Americans to build an inclusive and effective sphere of civic engagement with Bangladesh. To be sure, as I have mentioned, the community associations of Bangladeshi Americans are in fact quite successful in achieving their basic goals. But they could arguably be even more effective if they were not encumbered by a discourse of factionalism.

Alternative Transnational Activist Organizations

You believe that every person has an equal right to be heard, and an equal right to dignity, compassion and opportunities.

You believe that safeguarding every individual's basic human rights will complement, and not hinder, the sustainable progress and economic development of Bangladesh.

You believe that there is so much more to Bangladesh—its culture, its language, its people—than the flood-ridden, poverty-stricken image portrayed in international news.

You read the news and feel the urge to speak out, to do something, to make a difference, however small.

You are, in spirit, already a member of the Drishtipat family.

Welcome to Drishtipat!

The early years of the twenty-first century have seen the emergence among Bangladeshis abroad of transnational activist organizations that identify themselves as agents of progressive social and political change in Bangladesh. There is, for example, BEN or Bangladesh Environmental Network, which aims to enhance awareness of environmental degradation in Bangladesh and to encourage policies that protect the environment. Drishtipat is a human rights organization with a broad range of projects, from poverty alleviation to protest against human rights violations in Bangladesh. With chapters in Australia, Britain, Canada, the United States, and Bangladesh, both BEN and Drishtipat are organized across multiple national nodes of the Bangladeshi diaspora. Their membership has tended to involve the highly educated segments of the diaspora, with leaders who have been educated and/or raised abroad. In general, as highlighted from the following segment of Drishtipat's (2007) Vision statement on its Web site, the emphasis is on fostering fundamental changes in Bangladesh: "Drishtipat comes to you with . . . a Vision to harness the cultural and nationalistic pride within the expatriate community, and to leverage the innovativeness, the technical skills and the professional expertise within this community, towards action-oriented projects that leave a real positive impact on the lives of the people of Bangladesh."

These transnational activist organizations tend to present themselves as alternative community spaces, different in character and sensibility from the more established array of Bangladeshi American associations discussed earlier. This is one important way in which they have been able to attract younger members of the diaspora, including those born or raised in the United States, who would not otherwise be involved in Bangladeshi associations. Whereas many Bangladeshi American community groups offer continuity with the social and political worlds of Bangladesh, these transnational activist ones identify themselves as a break from the past. This is not at all in terms of ties with Bangladesh per se but rather with the traditional culture of civic life as represented by HTAs or cultural associations. These alternative alliances self-consciously eschew regional and parochial ties, emphasizing instead national-level commitments and engagements with Bangladesh. They also strive for political neutrality, remaining nonaligned with the political parties of Bangladesh. Although there may be projects on which there is collaboration with the Bangladesh government, the primary emphasis is on activism in relation to the Bangladesh state. Thus whether it is the cause of greater rigor in the enforcement of national environmental laws or stopping human rights abuses against the minority peoples of the Chittagong Hill Tracts region, they often define their role to be one of watchdog in relation to the government.

To summarize, the formation of voluntary associations was an important strategy of community building for Bangladeshi Americans. They were at least one way in which this group could respond to the dilemmas of community and belonging that were posed by the U.S. environment. For example, participation in the activities of Bangladeshi cultural associations, where Bangladeshi culture and identity is cultivated and valorized, could serve as an important counterpoint to the experience of being invisible as a Bangladeshi. The social contexts generated by the associations were also important for their ability to make visible and significant the various forms of social capital that were rooted in the social and political landscape of Bangladesh. We have also seen how the voluntary associations have played a role in generating a transnational civic culture. The discourse of natural Bangladeshi predisposition to factionalism as a shared set of understandings about Bangladeshi civic life was an important point of reference in this culture. This was not only in terms of its ongoing reproduction but also in the deliberate efforts to move away from it, to build an alternative culture of civic engagement that was modern and rational in character. Indeed, the associations contributed to the development of a vital Bangladeshi American transnational context by strengthening the exchange of ideas and information as well as generating institutions and networks between the United States and Bangladesh.

Transnational Ties and American Dreams

The lives of migrants to the United States are shaped by the American Dream— the beliefs and symbols that affirm the notion of America as a land of opportunity and possibility for all who are willing to take advantage of what is available to them and work hard. In spite of the complex and often contradictory realities that surround these ideas, migrants tend to be among the most fervent believers of the American Dream. Indeed, it is a remarkably resilient nationalist ideology, one that continues to initiate newcomers into the American cultural fabric, inspiring them to "become American," at least in certain ways. I found this to be true of Bangladeshi Americans, who affirmed their belief in the American Dream even when faced with formidable obstacles to acceptance and success in the United States.

I also found that for Bangladeshi American, as is the case for many other migrant groups, a transnational sphere of ongoing connections between the sending and receiving countries played an important role in their efforts to respond to the challenges of life in the United States. For first-generation Bangladeshi Americans in particular, the transnational arena was a site of honor and belonging, one that gave them the emotional fortitude by which to cope with the experience of downward class mobility as well as the other adjustments that had been made necessary by migration. The transnational sphere supported their efforts to take advantage of whatever opportunities that America presented to them, and to maintain a sense of optimism about their future in America. In this sense, the transnational ties of migrants may be appropriately seen as part of the scaffold that underlies and props up the American Dream and its continued vitality and resilience.

But the Bangladeshi American case is useful to consider not only because it highlights the importance of transnational ties for migrants. It is also instructive in bringing our attention to the role played by specific interstate histories and dynamics in shaping the character and significance of the transnational sphere. Reflecting the large proportion of persons from urban, middle-class backgrounds in Bangladesh, the transnational ties of Bangladeshi Americans tend to be anchored in their geographically diffuse family networks rather than in spatially defined communities of village or neighborhood. Also of importance is the history of migration and relations between Bangladesh and the United States. As I have described, migration from Bangladesh to the United States is for the most part quite recent (dating back to the 1980s), and the Bangladeshi American population is relatively small in number. These circumstances, along with that of a global national image of Bangladesh that is weak if not invisible in the United States, shapes the scope of the transnational context in terms of its ability to be a powerful and effective vehicle of integration into mainstream American political and economic life for Bangladeshi Americans. Under these conditions, it is not surprising that Bangladeshi Americans are increasingly turning to their Muslim affiliation in order to understand their place in the United States and to build community and belonging within it.

CHAPTER 4

Becoming Muslim American

Scholars have long observed how in the United States, a country with high levels of religiosity, religion is generally accepted and, indeed, expected to play an important role in immigrant life. As Raymond Williams writes: "In the U.S., religion is the social category with clearest meaning and acceptance in the host society, so the emphasis on religious affiliation is one of the strategies that allows the immigrant to maintain self identity while simultaneously acquiring community acceptance" (1988: 29). In the United States, then, immigrants are expected to participate in religious institutions. This is so even when, as in the case of Muslim migrants, their religion is viewed with considerable suspicion. Indeed, the post-9/11 era has been widely observed to be a time of rising levels of religious identification and participation for Muslim Americans. Muslim Americans have become more politically conscious and engaged as they have mobilized to respond to the backlash against them. Many Islamic American leaders have called on Muslims to assert their rights as Americans and claim their American identity. Thus Imam Suhaib Webb, in his 2007 Eid sermon at the Islamic Society of Boston, excerpted below, asks Muslims to see their struggles as part of a history of "becoming American." It is through these struggles that Muslim Americans will ultimately come to assume their rightful place on the mantel of American diversity:

> Through all the struggles to build, and these struggles will continue, this Masjid [mosque], the attacks and vicious slanders laid upon this community, it is important to put it into perspective, the American perspective. After 9/11 our community faced an onslaught of attacks from every possible angle, from John McCain to Hollywood, we've met with some, what we could easily say, unfair and malicious opposition. . . . To stand up for justice in the face of this onslaught, to rise to new heights and declare your right to worship, your right to self-definition and your right to live in liberty, makes you part of the historic fabric that binds this country and her people. What I hope you

will understand is that you are an American community. This experience and this community's ability to overcome the odds, stand in the face of oppression, and use the system to overcome such obstacles is a defining moment which forces the book open, places the pen in your hands, and demands you to write! Write your narrative next to the Jews, the Irish, the Africans, and the Catholics! Write and blossom! Stake your claim!

If the post-9/11 era has been a time of greater engagement with what Imam Suhaib Webb describes as "the American perspective," it has also been a time of the growing significance of revivalist Islam among Muslim Americans. Jocelyne Cesari (2004) has described the growing diffusion of revivalist Islam across Muslim communities in Europe and the United States. She argues that the revivalist Salafi movement, with its literalist interpretations of Islam, has been successful in defining standards of religious orthodoxy among Muslims in these settings.[1] It has helped to produce and disseminate a set of taken-for-granted, general understandings of what it means to be a strictly observant Muslim, on matters ranging from veiling for women to prohibitions of certain types of music. Thus even as most Muslims do not actually follow or even necessarily fully subscribe to these notions, they nevertheless invoke them as guidelines of piety and orthodoxy.

In what follows I explore how the Bangladeshi American experience has been shaped by these social and political currents of Muslim American life. I begin by considering their impacts on community life and then move on to family relations, especially those between migrant parents and their U.S.-born and/or raised children.

THE POLITICS OF MUSLIM COMMUNITY
Bangladeshi Neighborhoods and Mosques in Hamtramck, Michigan

The city of Hamtramck, Michigan, a two-square-mile area bordering Detroit, is well known for its Polish roots. In the early 1900s, Polish migrants flocked to the area to work in the now-closed Dodge automobile plant. A hundred years later, Hamtramck has once again become a new immigrant city with settlers from Bosnia, Ukraine, Yemen, and many other countries, including Bangladesh.[2] It was in the late 1990s that the Bangladesh-origin population in Hamtramck grew rapidly. The growth was driven by a secondary migration into the area of Bangladeshi families whose first destination in the United States had been Astoria in New York (Kerhsaw 2001). The movement was largely Muslim but also included Hindu and Buddhist Bangladeshis. It was also, interestingly enough, predominantly from Sylhet, the region of Bangladesh that is also the primary point of origin for the British Bangladeshi community. Coming largely from rural backgrounds and with relatively low levels of education, the Hamtramck Bangladeshis had been attracted to the Detroit area for several reasons. There was affordable housing and the availability (at the time) of assembly-line jobs in small parts–manufacturing plants. There was also the presence in the Greater Detroit area of a large and well-established Muslim American community, estimated at 150,000 members, predominantly of Arab origin.

By the mid-2000s, Bangladeshis had become a notable part of the Hamtramck landscape. A visible Bangladeshi enclave had sprung up, with residential neighborhoods, businesses, and religious centers, including a Hindu temple and several mosques. The formation of the mosques had been facilitated by the R1 visa, a non-immigrant U.S. visa that allows ministers and other specified categories of religious workers to work in religious institutions in the United States for a period of up to five years and eventually to apply for permanent residence. The Bangladeshi American religious leaders I spoke to consistently emphasized the great difficulties in arranging for R1 visas for Bangladeshis, especially after 9/11. But even with these difficulties, in Michigan as in other parts of the country with significant Bangladeshi enclaves (such as Brooklyn and Queens, New York), by allowing for the import of imams from Bangladesh the R1 visa has played a role in the formation of Bangladeshi American mosques.

Along with the development of their own community institutions, Bangladeshis also made inroads into local politics, gaining seats on the Hamtramck City Council and other political bodies. In 2008, Hamtramck city officials approved a motion to place street signs saying "Bangladesh Avenue" on Conant Avenue, a bustling commercial district of Bangladeshi businesses. As symbols of the growing prominence of Bangladeshis in the area, the street signs were not, however, without controversy. A local media report noted resentment among some Hamtramck residents, one of whom is quoted as saying: "First they had the call to prayer, now they have street names, sooner or later I'll have nothing to say" (Sercombe and Hakim 2008).

In fact, 2008 was not the first time that Bangladeshis were in the Greater Detroit area spotlight. In 2004, the Hamtramck City Council unanimously approved the request of the Bangladeshi-led Al-Islah mosque on Caniff Street to amplify the *azan*—the traditional call to prayer that is given five times a day for Muslims. The azan was only to be heard for a block or two and not before six in the morning or after ten at night (Simon 2004). The decision, widely reported in the national media, sparked considerable controversy. Some Hamtramck residents expressed fear and suspicion about the language (Arabic) and meaning of what was being broadcast, and others spoke of how it infringed on their rights to privacy. In response, Detroit-area Muslim American leaders joined into the debate and lent their support to the mosque and the position of the City Council. They emphasized the importance of the azan to Muslim religious practice and also likened the azan to the ringing of church bells. In defense of their decision, City Council members pointed out that such broadcasts were actually not prohibited by existing laws and that official approval actually enhanced the ability of government officials to control the volume and hours of broadcasts from the mosque (Leland 2004).

Besides that of azan broadcasts, Bangladeshis have been at the center of a number of other public debates about Islamic practice in the Greater Detroit area. These include questions about the provision of halal food (to maintain Islamic dietary restrictions), space for voluntary prayers, and days off for Islamic holidays in public schools and work sites. The visibility of these community struggles over religious practices, struggles in which Bangladeshis have figured prominently, have contributed to the development of a Muslim political identity for Bangladeshis in the area.

It is important to note that the political projects of Detroit-area Bangladeshis have not just been about religion. Besides the placement of "Bangladesh Avenue" street signs in Hamtramck, Bangladeshi community leaders have also worked to introduce Bengali as a second language in the Detroit public schools and also to obtain permission for the building of a Shohid Minar monument— an important symbol of Bengali nationalism—in Detroit.[3]

These projects offer important and visible affirmations of Bangladeshi community and identity. But in terms of engagement with mainstream American institutions, they have also been less politicizing for Bangladeshis, exciting less controversy and interest from the general American public than those over Islamic practice in which the Bangladeshi community has also been prominently engaged. Besides the general currents of suspicion and hostility that surround Islam in the United States, struggles over Islamic practice are also associated with Muslim Americans as a whole—a larger population and of greater political significance than Bangladeshis. These forces work to draw attention to Bangladeshis as Muslims in the political arena.

Indeed, the Greater Detroit–area Bangladeshi experience is one that suggests the increasingly important role of Islam in the political identity of Bangladeshi Americans. There is little doubt that it does so in a manner that is exaggerated by the favorable circumstances of community formation for Bangladeshis in Hamtramck. The relatively small size of Hamtramck (a population of 26,000 and two square miles in area) has enabled Bangladeshis to gain a level of political prominence there that they may not achieve in larger cities. In fact, many Bangladeshis in other parts of the United States do not live in Bangladeshi neighborhoods. And even in comparison to such notable Bangladeshi enclaves as Queens, the Hamtramck community stands out in its clearly defined territorial boundaries as well as its high levels of internal social homogeneity. As mentioned earlier, the Hamtramck Bangladeshi community is heavily Sylheti in origins, a reflection of the regional social networks that drove the community's formation in the 1990s.

The community is fairly homogeneous in socioeconomic terms. Community formation has also been facilitated by the particular housing and business opportunities that have been available to new migrants to Hamtramck. That is, in the city's affordable neighborhoods of tightly packed homes that had been built in the early twentieth century to accommodate Polish factory workers, Bangladeshis have been able live in close proximity to each other. Bangladeshi entrepreneurs have also been able to take advantage of a declining commercial district to develop a distinct cluster of businesses in the city. Under these conditions, the community has been able to assert itself in the local political scene in a forceful manner.

Moving beyond the specifics, the Hamtramck case highlights the role of a more general set of conditions in encouraging the development of a Muslim identity among Bangladeshi Americans. In the course of their struggles to gain facilities and support for Islamic religious practice, whether it is the building of a mosque or the provision of halal food in school cafeterias, Bangladeshis have often gained visibility in the American political scene. To put it another way, it is not as Bangladeshis but rather as Muslims that Bangladeshis have been more likely to attract the attention of mainstream American political structures and institutions. While this is related to numbers—the relatively small size of the Bangladeshi-origin population in the United States—it also reflects the powerful significance, albeit at times of a stigmatizing nature, of being Muslim in the United States today. Furthermore, we have also seen how in their community-building efforts, Hamtramck Bangladeshis seemed to benefit from the presence of the larger and well-organized community of Muslim Americans in the Greater Detroit area. In the course of interviews, several Hamtramck Bangladeshi leaders mentioned the factor of inspiration and example. The successful engagements of Arab Muslim Americans with mainstream American politics had fostered a certain mimicry, with Bangladeshi Americans attempting to emulate these efforts. More generally, the Hamtramck case highlights the potentially important supportive role that the larger Muslim American community can play in Bangladeshi American political struggles for resources and legitimacy, especially when those struggles are about Islamic practice.

As we have seen, a strengthened Muslim political identity has been an important feature of Bangladeshi adaptation to the social and political environment of the United States. In what follows, I turn to another interrelated development. This was the emergence of bridging groups that positioned themselves as intermediaries between mainstream Islamic American organizations and Bangladeshi Americans.

Bridging Groups: Bangladeshi American Islamic Associations

During the course of my fieldwork, I encountered a number of associations dedicated to the support of Islamic values and practices among Bangladeshi Americans. These included the national-level association called NABIC— North American Bangladesh Islamic Community. NABIC was formed in 1990 as "an initiative of Bangladeshi Muslims in North America dedicated to promoting Islamic awareness and facilitating socioeconomic upliftment of the common people of Bangladeshi heritage in North America and those in Bangladesh" (NABIC 1990: 18). Its activities included a well-attended annual convention with seminars on such topics as education in Islamic schools, the concerns of Muslim youth in the United States, and the effectiveness of various development programs in Bangladesh. The convention's featured speakers typically included representatives of such major Islamic American associations as CAIR (Council on American Islamic Relations), ISNA (Islamic Society of North America), and IMANA (Islamic Medical Association of North America). Such collaborations helped to define NABIC's identity as a bridging group, one that worked to bring the resources and knowledge of these larger organizations to Bangladeshi Americans.

Activities dedicated to Bangladesh were also a major focus of NABIC, thus highlighting its identity as not only a bridging group but also a transnational one. The association has been a financial sponsor of several programs in Bangladesh. These include projects that provide eye care for the poor, safe drinking water for rural families, and shelter and education for orphaned girls. NABIC has also partnered with NUSRA (Network for Universal Services and Rural Advancement) to support an alternative type of micro-credit program that avoids interest-bearing loans that are viewed as contrary to Islam. Instead, the program uses a system of deferred payment to provide loans to needy families for investments in businesses, agriculture, and homeownership. In general, in its charitable activities in Bangladesh, NABIC has sought to simultaneously promote development as well as Islamic values and practices.

Besides NABIC, I also encountered several regional Bangladeshi Islamic associations. Among them was a dynamic group located in a mid-sized city that had been formed by a number of well-established Bangladeshi American professionals. The group's leaders were also active in local (multiethnic) mosques as well as in national-level Islamic American organizations. They had many activities: a newsletter, Eid celebrations, lecture programs on Islam, as well as weekend retreats for families at which there was prayer, religious discussions, and organized activities for the young. As highlighted by the fact that Bengali was the primary language of activity and communication among members, the association aimed to foster a sense of community among Bangladeshi Muslims in the area. In its efforts to support an Islamic way of life among members, the association also actively engaged in efforts to disseminate the ideas of revivalist Islam among members. Thus a notion of religious reeducation ran through their programs, in which members were urged to purify and reform their religious practices by stripping them of the extraneous popular influences that had been part of their experience of religion in Bangladesh. During an interview, a longtime leader of the group spoke to me about how migration to the United States was in fact an opportunity for Bangladeshi Muslims to educate themselves about the true Islamic path. Through their charitable projects in Bangladesh, the group leaders hoped to contribute to an expansion of these opportunities for religious reeducation to those in Bangladesh as well:

> In Bangladesh, most of us do not actually know much about our religion. Many of us learn more after coming here [to the United States]. Here we are encouraged to closely study the Qu'ran for ourselves and we have the opportunity to learn from the scholars who have been trained in the Arab countries. When Bangladeshis come here, it is usually a new system for them. We try to encourage them [Bangladeshis] to learn, to take advantage of the opportunities here to study the Qu'ran. In my home village in Kushtia, I also try to make a difference. A few of us pool our *zakat* and give to support an orphanage and madrassa there. I hope we can show the people there the true path of the Qu'ran.

In the course of further discussions, the group's leaders told me of how they had at times clashed with the local Bangladeshi cultural associations in the area. Disputes were often about such matters as the cultural association's sponsorship of a Bengali New Year's Festival, which went against the Islamic group's stance that such celebrations were not appropriate for Muslims. By taking on these disputes, the Islamic bridging groups contributed to the transnationalization of political conflicts over the role of religion in Bangladesh today. As I described in chapter 2, a core political fault line of Bangladesh has been that of the division between those who advocate for the central role of Islam in the state versus those who support the notion of secular nationalism that guided the country during its formation. The rise of Bangladeshi American Islamic groups that are willing to take on these battles abroad is thus part of the transnationalization of these fault lines. Under these conditions, it is not surprising that those at the forefront of these disputes could feel themselves to be in a battle whose stakes were very high—tied to the very foundations of Bangladeshi national identity. The battleground, moreover, was one that stretched from the streets of Dhaka and Chittagong to those of New York and other parts of the world.

The notion of a crisis of Bangladeshi national identity, a crisis spawned by the mounting forces of revivalist Islam, was prominent during a lunch meeting I had with a group of progressive Bangladeshi artists and writers in Queens. As suggested by my field notes below, those at the meeting identified the Bangladeshi Islamic groups in New York to have ties to the political party Jamaat-e-Islami in Bangladesh:

> I started off the lunch meeting by explaining that I wanted to learn more about how Bangladeshis saw themselves in the U.S. Before I could say anything else, several people began talking passionately about the growth of religious fundamentalism (*moulo-badi*) among Bangladeshis here. They felt that Bangladeshis in Bangladesh were far more progressive in their thinking than those here. A woman who had taught Bengali music to children in New York for about ten years talked of how there were a growing number of Bangladeshi families who preferred to send their children to the mosque for Islamic education on the weekends than to her for learning Bengali music. She complained bitterly about a local Bangladeshi Imam who had convinced families that the music she taught was filled with Hindu traditions and so their children should be kept away from it. A spate of comments followed about the political background of this Imam, who was apparently a member of Jamaat and had been actively involved in anti-liberation activities in 1971. Manik, who was a member of the progressive cultural group Udichi in Bangladesh, spoke emotionally about his heated conflicts with some people he had met at the Jamaica Muslim Center in New York who felt that Bangladeshis should not participate in Bengali New Year festivals because they were contrary to Islam. What was being destroyed, he declared, was the heart of what it meant to be Bangali.

To summarize, among the strategies used by Bangladeshi Americans to respond to the political and other challenges of the U.S. environment was to form alliances and relationships with larger, broad-based Muslim American groups. Those who formed bridging intermediary groups hoped to introduce a wider segment of Bangladeshi Americans to these forums, especially to the notions of Islam that they promoted. The bridging groups also offered an institutional platform from which to enter into the politics of Islam in Bangladesh. In general, their position was one of advocacy of a greater role for Islam, specifically a reformed Islam that was authentic and pure in its literalism, in comparison to the culturally informed Islam that prevailed in Bangladesh.

Concurrently, they tended to reject the ethos of secular nationalism for Bangladesh, citing its moral bankruptcy.

I turn next to a different dimension of the Bangladeshi American experience—family life and parenting strategies. Here too, as in the case of community life, the American context has been such as to bring religion into particular prominence.

PARENTING STRATEGIES AND ISLAM: "HERE IT'S DIFFICULT TO RAISE CHILDREN WELL"

Sara, the daughter of a high-ranking government income tax officer, had been born and raised in Dhaka. When I interviewed her in 2003 she was living with her husband and twelve-year-old son in Hillside, Queens. In Bangladesh, she had worked for several years as a model and an artist. In the United States, however, she had been unable to break into these fields and so had resigned herself to working in the advertising department of a local New York Bangladeshi newspaper. Sitting in the living room of their two-bedroom apartment, we had leafed through dazzling photographs of Sara in jeans, saris, and chic *salwar kameez* (long tunic and baggy pants) outfits, in striking poses that played up her long sleek hair and doe-like eyes. As we talked, Sara told me that at home, she had never given much thought to religion. She disliked those who were extreme about religious matters, and she expressed concern about how many Bangladeshis in her neighborhood were very conservative in their cultural outlooks. In her own case, movement to the United States had fostered a conscious attention to Muslim practice as she struggled to cope with a sense of "losing herself" and also to maintain cultural balance in her son's life. To a degree that she herself found somewhat surprising, the local Islamic Center had become a prominent part of her daily existence:

> S: After coming here, I have become much more conscious about religion. Here I feel, I will lose myself, so the consciousness goes up. I have become more serious about prayer and fasting. In Bangladesh we are not so worried about religion. There the environment is not so bad, there are fewer dangers. Here I constantly worry about my son. I try to teach him, I send him to the Islamic Center for religious classes. I go there sometimes to attend the women's circles. At home I would never think about attending these activities. I find that I have to constantly teach my son, which one is *halal* and which one is *haram*.[4] These are big changes for us; at home we were more relaxed about religion.
>
> NK: What do you worry about for your son?

S: We want him to have a good life. The problem with America is that there
is no balance. I see boys and girls who go astray, become ruined (*noshto*).
They don't obey their parents, they become involved in gangs. Our religion teaches us the right way, it gives us the strength to resist temptations.

A sense of dislocation, along with psychic and moral uncertainties about the
world and one's place in it, are often associated with the experience of international migration. As scholars have observed, these are conditions that can
foster religiosity, as migrants turn to religion to anchor themselves in the
receiving society (Smith 1978). For Sara, as for other migrant parents, the sense
of a moral vacuum in the United States and the subsequent need for a strong
religious anchor was deeply tied to the challenges that she felt about raising
children in the United States. In the course of my fieldwork, I was repeatedly
told that it was difficult to raise children well in America. As does Sara in the
above, many parents also spoke of an emphasis on religion as a key strategy
by which they sought to address these difficulties. This emphasis on Islam in
family life drew strength and significance from the political and institutional
developments of Islam in Bangladeshi American life, as I have described earlier.
That is, if Bangladeshi American parents wished to emphasize religion in the
upbringing of their children, their efforts have been increasingly buttressed
by such developments as the growth of Bangladeshi Islamic American
organizations.

Anxieties about raising children well are universal human concerns. However,
for Bangladeshi Americans, as for many other migrant groups, these concerns
can take on particular meaning and significance in relation to migration, especially to the dreams and goals that are part of it. The American Dream gave
Bangladeshi Americans a sense of hope, enabling them to cope with the hardships and challenges of life in the United States. Especially among those with
children, the dream was deeply tied to hopes for the next generation. That is,
for migrant parents, whatever the hardships of American life for themselves,
they were made bearable by the vision of a future made bright by the achievements of children. But this vision also provoked its own set of anxieties and
fears. If America itself was what made the dream possible, with its opportunities for children's education and socioeconomic advancement, it also brought
on the dangers of children's "Americanization."

Bangladeshi American parents spoke of two different faces, each with its
own set of dangers, of children's "Americanization" or integration into American
culture. Reflecting an intuitive understanding of what sociologists Portes and
Zhou (1993) have described as "segmented assimilation," there were fears of
children's assimilation into American youth cultures that disparage academic

achievement and so endanger the envisioned trajectory of upward class mobility in the family future.[5] And on a different note, there were fears that the child who assimilates into American society and indeed becomes successful, in the process will also become detached and distant from his or her family of origin. These were conditions that limited the rewards—psychic, social, and material— that the family of origin could derive from the child's achievements. In the eyes of migrant parents, both threatened the success of the migration project.

And so, as did Sara, many parents spoke of trying to achieve a "cultural balance" in raising their children in the United States. On the one hand, they valued the acquisition by children of skills and dispositions that would allow them to navigate mainstream American culture easily, to feel comfortable in it, at least enough to be successful. On the other hand, they strove to steer children clear of the negative currents of American culture and also to keep them grounded in "our culture"—a broad and loosely defined set of idealized traditions in which family solidarity and respect for the authority of family elders are core values. As one might expect, families took multiple and varied approaches to ensure the "cultural balance" of children, from restricting their extracurricular activities in order to keep them at home to taking them on trips to Bangladesh so that they could become acquainted with family there. Among them were self-conscious efforts to incorporate Islam into the routines of family life in the United States, through attention to Islamic practice in the home as well as participation in Islamic groups and associations.

Not too far away from Sara's place, in another neighborhood in New York, I met up with Seema, a woman with two young daughters who had come from Sylhet about six years ago. Like Sara, Seema also spoke of an emphasis on Islam as a parenting strategy. This commonality was there, although in many respects, Seema could not have been more different from Sara. Seema was the daughter of a small shop-owner in Sylhet. When she was in high school, her father had arranged her marriage to her migrant husband, a resident of New York who at the time of the marriage negotiations had been visiting his family in Sylhet. Seema described growing up in a devout family where regular prayer and study of the Qu'ran were encouraged and indeed required for children. Thus, unlike the situation of Sara, a parenting strategy that emphasized religion appeared continuous with her upbringing in Bangladesh rather than a change from it. However, like Sara, she too saw this strategy as taking shape in relation to the U.S. environment and its particular dangers. At the mosque near her home, she attended lectures, volunteered in the children's section, and also took her daughters to after-school Islamic education classes.

At the time of the interview, I also found her thinking about whether she should enroll her daughters in the full-time Islamic school that was attached to the mosque. Although she was attracted by the religious education assured by this option, she worried about whether it would place the girls at a competitive academic disadvantage when it came to college. She wanted to give her daughters the schooling opportunities that had been unavailable to her in her own life. Both an Islamic way of life and success in mainstream America were part of her vision for the future of her daughters:

> S: The environment here is not the same as in our country. At home, we as children learned our religion from our elders. Here it is different. As a guardian, I have to make a special effort to make sure that my daughters understand and follow our religion. I am thinking of enrolling them in the Islamic school that is with the mosque. I want to give them the opportunity for education in this country. I did not have the opportunity to study after high school, but the world is different now. I want the girls to go to university and to be able to get respectable jobs if that is what they want. But I also want them to learn our culture. The environment may be different here but I want them to live by *purdah*, to behave well with their parents.[6]

> NK: Do you think you will send them to the Islamic school?

> S: I would like to do that, if I am clear in my mind that the education there in the regular classes is good. Some people have told me that the students there are not able to do well later, at the university level. We worry about that.

If informed by the challenges of raising children well, Bangladeshi American parents also spoke of how an emphasis on Islam in parenting activities had shaped their own experiences of religion, as well. Olivier Roy (2004) has written of how Muslim migrants in Europe experience heightened religious reflexivity as their established notions of Muslim practice and identity come to be challenged. With migration to Europe, they find themselves to be a religious minority, often in contrast to their homeland circumstances. They also encounter Muslims of other national origins who bring their own diverse traditions of Islam with them to Europe. These conditions challenge what are often taken-for-granted expectations about religious practice, thus resulting in a more self-conscious stance toward religion.

The accounts of Bangladeshi Americans suggest that the activity of child rearing may be an especially potent context for generating such reflexivity. Many migrant parents spoke of having to think, perhaps for the first time in their lives, about the meaning of Islamic practice due to the demands of their children in the United States for explanation. We see this in the account below of Masum, an engineer living in a suburb outside of Boston and a father of three. Masum confessed to me a lack of personal interest and perhaps even ambivalence about religious involvements. Maybe because of these attitudes, he seemed especially conscious of the strategic character of his efforts to infuse Islam into the lives of his children:

> The education here is good, education is not a problem like it is at home. Children have opportunities, but it is difficult to raise them well. Here the children have more freedom and the laws are such that you have to constantly watch how you are dealing with the kids. At home we can be more tough and everyone can discipline. We see that there are a lot of children here who don't respect their parents and teachers and who don't seem to care about anything. Another difference is that here you have to persuade the children, you cannot force them to do anything. At home, you get a natural religious education from relatives. You grow up in a particular environment from which you naturally absorb the religion. Here it is not like that. Here you have to constantly answer the children's questions: Why can't we eat pork, why do we have to do *wudu?*[7] And then when my brother read the Qu'ran to my older son he challenged us and asked us to explain the meaning. Since it is in Arabic we are then forced to look up the translation. It has been an education for us all. It is a good thing, this American questioning of everything; we did not grow up like that. We have taken out books from the children's section of the mosque library and also looked up things on the Internet. Because I don't have much knowledge about these things, I take them to the mosque every week for classes and we also attend a summer camp where we pray together and talk about the Qu'ran. I do these things for my children, not for myself. I am personally very relaxed about religious matters; I do not pray regularly or fast and I am not inclined to go to the mosque except as a social occasion. But when you are raising children in this country you have to do it.

As we have seen, a self-conscious emphasis on Islam was an important strategy for Bangladeshi Americans in the raising of their children. Yet at the same time, many parents expressed considerable anxiety about the potential for religion to become a source of tension and rift in their relations with U.S.-born and/or raised children. This was for the most part not, as one might perhaps imagine, due to the rejection of Islam by the younger generation. Rather, in a political environment in which the threat of radical Islamists has loomed large, migrant parents were more inclined to worry about the possibility, however remote, of children turning to religious extremism. In discussing this matter, several informants spoke of the case of Tashnuba Hayder.

In March 2005, a sixteen-year-old second-generation Bangladeshi American girl by the name of Tashnuba Hayder was picked up by federal agents in a dawn raid on her home in Queens, where she lived with her Bangladeshi migrant parents. Just three weeks before, two FBI agents posing as youth counselors had visited Tashnuba at her home and gone through her schoolwork and other papers. The FBI's Joint Terrorism Task Force had identified Tashnuba as a potential suicide bomber, based in part on her interest in the sermons of Sheikh Omar Bakri, the militant Syrian Islamic cleric in London. After being taken away from her family, Tashnuba faced almost two months of interrogation at a center for delinquents in Pennsylvania. She was then released on the condition that she leave the United States because of her undocumented legal status in the country. She flew to Bangladesh with her mother and younger siblings, reluctantly returning to a country that she had left when she was five years old. Her father, a watch salesman, remained behind in New York with Tashnuba's fourteen-year-old brother, hoping to elude the immigration authorities long enough for his son to finish high school in the United States.

As portrayed in a series of *New York Times* reports by Nina Bernstein (2005a, 2005b), the story of Tashnuba was that of a child of Bangladeshi migrants who had embraced revivalist Islam in defiance of her parents. By the age of fourteen, Tashnuba had adopted a full Islamic veil and become an active member of several city mosques. Alarmed by her level of immersion in these activities, Tashnuba's parents had initially rejected her pleas for home schooling, which she sought as a strategy for removing herself from the secular environment of her high school. A frustrated Tashnuba had then impulsively tried to elope with Latif, a white American Muslim from Michigan whom she had met briefly at a local mosque. But she soon retreated from her plans and returned home to her frantic parents. It was just a few months later that Tashnuba achieved unwanted fame as one of the youngest terrorism suspects in the United States.

Bangladeshi Americans spoke of the case of Tashnuba Hayder as a cautionary tale on many levels. It captured the cruel and often mindless injustice toward Muslims that was part of the War on Terror, which thought nothing of bringing its full force to bear on the vulnerable family of a naïve young girl. But it was also a story of the diverse and somewhat unexpected dangers of the American social environment for children. Even as Tashnuba evoked a decidedly un-American image (in a popular sense), with her long Islamic veil and conservative ways, she also fulfilled the American teenager stereotype: angst-ridden, self-absorbed, and defiant of parental authority. It was a portrait that captured the dangers of "Americanization," even if it was an "Americanization" that seemed to be informed by Islam.

As is true of cautionary tales in general, the Tashnuba story is an exceptionally dramatic one. It is undoubtedly unusual, not only with respect to the FBI involvement but also the extent to which religion took over Tashnuba's life and the degree of rift with her parents that it created. Nonetheless, as suggested by its popularity as a story among Bangladeshi Americans, it was one that spoke to parents' fears, capturing certain aspects of their anxieties. Bangladeshi American parents spoke of how religion could be used by the younger generation to challenge the authority of their elders. Drawing on revivalist Islam and the notions of orthodoxy articulated by it, the younger generation was often critical of the religious knowledge of their parents, citing the polluting influences of Bengali culture on it. Similarly, Grewal notes in her study of Muslim American youth:

> Setting their parents' "cultures" in opposition to Islam, Muslim American children assume a moral higher ground and assert their own religious authority in the face of their parents' "cultural" authority. . . . The second generation's moral claims are persuasive because they draw on the same religious sources that their parents consider authoritative (Quranic verses, Prophetic example, sermons at their mosques, etc.). (2009: 325)

If parental anxieties about the role of Islam in their children's lives were embedded in its potential to become a source of challenge to their authority, they were also informed by concerns about the lack of importance given by children to their Bangladeshi identity. Parents spoke of the tendency of the younger generation to dismiss the significance of their national origins, to see it as of little importance in comparison to their religious affiliation and identity as Muslims.

"MUSLIM FIRST": SECOND-GENERATION BANGLADESHI AMERICAN IDENTITIES

Studies of young Muslim Americans have noted a trend toward "Muslim first" identification among them, whereby ethnic and national origin identities are given secondary importance to that of Muslim (Abdo 2006; Grewal 2009). Echoing this finding, I spoke to many second-generation Bangladeshi Americans for whom Muslim was a more important affiliation than Bangladeshi. But as we will see, a simple focus on this finding of "Muslim first" is one that tends to obscure the great variety of religious approach and experience that prevails among young Bangladeshi Americans. Defying the popular stereotype of the young Muslim who is extremist and dogmatic in his or her views of religion and the world, the narratives that I present below highlight the complex diversity of what it means to be Muslim American today.

Ferdousi: Finding Islam and Negotiating Family Pressures

I interviewed Ferdousi in the waiting area of a MAS (Muslim American Society) center where she was taking courses on Islam through the Islamic American University. These studies were in addition to her coursework toward a master's degree in education at a local state college. Dressed in *salwar kameez* with the *dupatta* (long scarf) wrapped loosely around her head, Ferdousi greeted me with a warm smile. She told me that she was glad to help with my research project. From her experience of working on her advisor's community health project last year, she knew how hard it could be to find people who were willing to be interviewed.

Ferdousi and her family had come to the United States when she was seven years old from a small town in Madharipur, a district in central Bangladesh. After a brief stay in New York, they moved to Boston, where her uncle had been living for many years. Ferdousi's father had worked as a security guard and also as a taxi driver for many years before a leg injury had forced him to retire. Ferdousi's mother worked as a cashier at a local supermarket, and her older brother held a part-time job at a pizza parlor.

Ferdousi, who was now twenty-three, had been married for three years. In the summer before the completion of her undergraduate degree she and her family had gone for a three-month visit to Madharipur, where her parents hoped to find her an appropriate groom. Although uncomfortable with the idea of "arranged marriage," Ferdousi had been persuaded to go along with these plans by her father's reassurance that she could choose whom she wanted to in Madharipur. For Ferdousi herself, the choice of whom to marry had been largely about finding someone who shared her commitment to Islam. Unlike her parents, she gave little importance to marrying a fellow Bangali or Madharipur native. After rejecting a string of suitors, she had eventually settled on the son of a family friend who had impressed her by his expressed commitment to her about living as a good Muslim.

When I asked Ferdousi about how religion had come to be so important to her, she told a story of personal crisis followed by the "discovery" of Islam as a complete way of life. For Ferdousi, the crisis had centered on a troubled adolescence in which she had suffered from deep bouts of depression. There had been conflicts with her parents stemming from her desire to fit in with "American" peers at school coupled with parental efforts to keep the influence of these peers at bay. She recalled feeling resentful of how she was not allowed to go out with friends and how she was discouraged from participating in after-school extracurricular activities. Things changed for her, however, as she began her first year at a local public university and began to learn more about Islam through a friend who took her to some Muslim Students Association (MSA) events on campus. In general, I found the MSA, with its active branches in colleges and universities across the United States, to be an important institution for many young Bangladeshi Americans. For Ferdousi, attendance at the MSA events triggered a life-altering transformation:

F: It's no longer about fitting in. What's important to me now is to live my life, my professional life, my family life, in a way that is true to Islam. I am learning Arabic now so that I can read the Qu'ran on my own. After I get my teaching certificate I hope to work in a public school, maybe one where there are Muslim children who I can help. They face so many problems; there are so many misconceptions about Islam out there. Eventually I may shift to teaching in an Islamic school.

NK: And your family life . . . ?

F: *Inshallah*, when we have children, I will raise them as good Muslims.

NK: Specifically how will that be different from how you were raised?

F: For my mother and father, it was all about raising children in the traditions of Madharipur, it was about . . . like Bangali culture. Religion was part of their way of life, but it was not a priority. For us, my husband and I have agreed, it's about Islam; we are not so concerned about Bangla culture. I mean, it's nice if they know the language and stuff, but it's not a big thing for us. You know, Islam is the same everywhere. There are no roots and branches. Islam is one God, one Prophet and one Book.

For Ferdousi, Islam had given meaning and purpose to a life that had seemed without bearings before. It had also given her a way to successfully negotiate the family pressures upon her—to concurrently comply with and resist them. She had agreed to marry a Madharipur native, to go along with her family's wishes. But she did so in a way that suited her own purposes, to fulfill her goal of marrying someone who shared her commitment to Islam, over and above the maintenance of Bengali cultural traditions. It was also clear from talking to Ferdousi that through her involvement in various Islamic groups and organizations, she had developed a large network of friends who were united in their shared commitment to Islam but diverse in other respects, such as racial and ethnic background and socioeconomic status. Her social world thus extended well beyond the confines of the Bangladeshi-centered world inhabited by her family in Boston. Religion had extended Ferdousi's social world, freeing her in some respects from the confines that had been imposed on her by her family.

A sense of agency was also evident in how Ferdousi approached the practice of Islam. Ferdousi spoke of Islam as a complete way of life, one that did not allow for compromise. Even as she affirmed her total commitment to Islam, she also spoke of the importance of individual agency. For example, at one point in the interview I asked Ferdousi if she always covered her head in public. Her reply emphasized the importance of spiritual authenticity—how maintaining correct practice was only meaningful when coupled with true inner conviction and desire to obey:

F: No, I don't always cover my head. I want to, but I'm not comfortable with it yet. Like I told you, I grew up trying to be very American, so it's a big jump for me. I am working toward it. But I only want to cover my head when I'm totally comfortable with it, when I can do so with an open heart. The most important thing is your belief, what's inside.

Akhtar: Islam and Antiracist Political Struggles

When I interviewed Akhtar in 2004 he was a pre-med student, a senior at an Ivy League university. Akhtar had grown up in the Chicago area. His father had come to the United States for graduate study in engineering in the 1980s and then stayed on as a faculty member at a large research university. Akhtar described himself as becoming interested in Islam after reading *The Autobiography of Malcolm X* as a teenager. The reading transformed his understanding of America, giving him a critical consciousness of its divisions and inequalities. He saw the power of Islam to be in its message of opposition and resistance to racism, imperialism, and other forms of injustice. If Akhtar's interest in Islam predated 9/11, it had also clearly been reinforced by the political and social developments that had followed. As he describes below, in the politically charged environment of post-9/11 America, political engagement was for him a central part of what it meant to be Muslim in America:

> Growing up, I knew I was Muslim but as a young person that did not mean much to me. When I was about fifteen, I read Malcolm X and that really got me thinking about Islam. Malcolm X did *Hajj* and he saw how there was so much brotherhood in Islam. It got me thinking about what America was really like.[8] I started to see the corruption, the corruption of the spirit, the endless buying of things, the superficial existence that most people lead. And I saw how the system divides people, pitting people against each other, white against black, black against brown. So I started getting more involved. I read more, and I took some classes at a Muslim center near my house. In college I have been trying to be a better Muslim. I belong to the MSA [Muslim Students Association] and I try to pray five times a day. Since 9/11, I have been politically active, encouraging Muslims to get out and vote, and informing them of their civil rights. In fact I've added political science to my courses here. I feel that it's the duty of all privileged Muslims in this country to speak up against the Bush policies, like the war in Iraq.

At one point in the interview, I asked Akhtar about how his family back in Chicago saw his religious involvements:

> I would say that my family has mixed feelings about the fact that I am so Muslim identified. They are always telling me that it's good to be religious but that religion has its place. At the same time they kind of like the fact that I'm not into American culture like alcohol, dating, that kind of thing. We do

have disagreements about what is actually part of Islam and what is not. My Mom and Dad are like the typical Bangalis. For them you know it's all about *Bangabandhu* and *Rabindra Sangeet*.[9] They do have a strong belief in Allah and they have good family values. But I would not say that they have studied Islam very closely. My mother, she's a great lady, but I think she is influenced by her sisters who are very involved with some *pirs* (popular saints) in Bangladesh. I disagree with the whole pir business, it is not part of Islam. So much of what passes for Islam in Bangladesh is superstition. And everything is so corrupt. The maulanas there charge money for reading the Qu'ran.[10] And they say things against women's rights that are contrary to Islam. But they use Islam to justify what they are saying. Islam is very progressive in women's rights. You cannot use Islam to justify a position that is against women's education or employment or women's freedom in terms of marriage decisions.

The veneration of pirs—popular saints who perform miracles in exchange for offerings—is an important aspect of folk practices of Islam in Bangladesh. For Akhtar, the pir tradition represented the backward hybridity of religious traditions in Bangladesh. He also emphasized how, in contrast to what often passed in the name of Islam in Bangladesh, true Islam was actually progressive in its approach to women's rights. As Akhtar described, his views had generated some friction between him and his parents, but not of an especially serious nature. I did not find this surprising. Akhtar's ties to his family were strong and active. And he seemed poised to enter a bright career in the field of medicine—a life that affirmed the American Dream.

Tanya: Bhangra, Fasting, and Marrying Muslim

I spoke to Tanya, a young Bangladeshi American woman in her early twenties, at a diner in Queens, in a neighborhood where she had been born and raised. She was visiting her parents that weekend, taking a break from her studies in marketing at a nearby state university. As she ordered a milkshake and fries, she repeatedly checked her cell phone, finally explaining to me that she was expecting friends to call her about going to a bhangra (South Asian dance) party that night.

Tanya was the daughter of an entrepreneur and community leader who had come to New York in the early 1980s and opened a profitable South Asian grocery store. He had gradually and fruitfully expanded into a variety of businesses, including the import of shrimp from Bangladesh for the U.S. market. Tanya spoke of growing up in a home where her parents had gone to considerable lengths to give their three outgoing and headstrong daughters a profound sense of both Bengali and Muslim identity. They had been sent to Bangla music and dance classes, and also to weekly tutorials in Islamic studies at a local mosque. She laughingly told me of how she and her sisters had not taken well to these efforts, to the extent that her indulgent parents had given up trying to force them to attend classes, concluding that it was a waste of time. There was, however, one religious practice that she steadfastly maintained:

> T: I can't say that I'm a good Muslim but I do believe in Allah and I do fast during Ramadan. I always try to fast the entire month if possible.
>
> NK: When did you start doing that?
>
> T: It was at the age of fifteen. At first I did it to please my mother, but now I do it for myself. It's difficult but it feels good, the discipline of it.
>
> NK: Do you fast in college?
>
> T: Oh yes. The MSA [Muslim Students Association] gives free *iftar* and it's usually pretty good.[11] It's the only time of year that I hang out at the MSA. It's a good time to meet other Muslims, you get a chance to know each other. I mean everyone, all the Muslim students regardless of how religious they are, they go there for iftar. So even if you're not a good Muslim like myself, it's OK.
>
> NK: You're not a good Muslim?
>
> T: No . . . I believe in Allah and I try to live by the basic principles of Islam, like honesty and compassion for people who are less fortunate. But I don't observe all the rules, like I don't cover my head and I don't pray five times a day. I know that these things are important in Islam, I've heard lectures and read things about them. But I can't say that I follow all of them.

If for Ferdousi (in the account discussed earlier), Islam was a complete way of life that could not be integrated into one's life in a selective or compartmentalized manner, Tanya's approach was quite different. With the exception of Ramadan and the avoidance of pork, she did not integrate other Islamic requirements into her daily life. This did not mean that she questioned the legitimacy or necessity of these requirements, which she seemed to accept as taken-for-granted features of observance. And with the exception of partaking of the free iftar at the MSA during Ramadan, she also did not frequent Muslim organizations and groups. In fact, much of her social life on campus revolved around the activities of the South Asian social clubs. She frequented South Asian dance parties and also described herself as a fan of Bollywood movies. In these settings she felt both a sense of belonging and marginality as a non-Indian. But when I asked her about marriage partner preferences, she was quite adamant that she wanted to marry a Muslim. Her words suggest a diffuse understanding of Muslim as a marker of cultural identity. She saw herself as an ethnic American, with Muslim traditions forming an ethnic culture that easily coexisted with mainstream American culture:

> T: I know it would make my Mom and Dad happy, but I really don't see marrying a Bengali to be a priority for me. Sometimes my Mom talks about it and my sister and I are like, "Oh God, no . . ." We're turned off by a lot of these Bengali guys who are so male chauvinist, especially the ones from Bangladesh. But I do want to marry a Muslim, that's much more a priority to me.
>
> NK: What about Indians or Pakistanis?
>
> T: If they're Muslim, yes. Well, the Pakistani is a problem for my parents, but not for me.
>
> NK: That leaves Indians. . . . But I still don't really understand. Why is it so important for you to marry Muslim?
>
> T: Well, I feel like we would have similar values and traditions like fasting during Ramadan. . . . Being Muslim is the one thing that my parents have passed down to me that's really important to me, in terms of passing down to future generations. Even though I've grown up in Queens where there are a lot of Bangalis, I'm very American. And I think to myself, what's distinctive about me that I really want to pass on. And it's being Muslim.

Despite their many differences, Ferdousi, Akhtar, and Tanya did all have one thing in common. Like many other second-generation Bangladeshi Americans, they felt that they were "Muslim first," that Muslim, rather than Bangladeshi, was a primary identification for them. But if the importance of being Muslim was a common theme, it was also clear that this was a wide umbrella, covering much diversity in terms of the lifestyle and approach to the practice of Islam that accompanied it. However, many described the "observant Muslim" in similar terms, regardless of the extent to which these ideas were reflected in the daily realities of their own lives. The observant Muslim was one who actively incorporated Islamic practice into every aspect of her or his life, following the examples set by the life of the Prophet and the dictates of the Qu'ran as closely as possible. There was a sense in which the acceptance of these ideals, even if only as aspirational points of reference, affirmed their sense of membership in a larger Muslim community.

BECOMING MUSLIM AMERICAN

For Bangladeshi Muslim Americans, religion is an increasingly important basis of political and social integration into the United States. This is especially so for second-generation Bangladeshi Americans, many of whom are active in pan-ethnic Muslim American community forums and identify themselves as "Muslim first." Ethnogenesis, a process whereby previously distinct ethnic groups gradually coalesce into a larger unified ethnic collectivity, has long been observed to be a possible feature of the migrant experience over time (Espiritu 1993; Herberg 1955). There is clearly a long way to go before amalgamation into a pan-national Muslim American collectivity becomes a significant reality for Bangladeshi Americans. Among the many conditions that potentially limit it is the tremendous diversity of the Muslim American population, in terms of culture, history, race, as well as other variables.

But whatever the scope of it might be, it seems likely that the development of ties with Muslim American institutions and groups will continue to be an important feature, indeed increasingly so, of Bangladeshi American life. Through these ties, the Muslim American arena with its varied currents may also come to play an important role in the transnational context of Bangladeshi American life, as it comes to be embedded in the cross-cutting institutions and flows of ideas that constitute it. The activities of Bangladeshi American Islamic bridging groups as I have described in this chapter are just one possible means by which such a role can take shape. Indeed, in terms of the character and type of influence that the Muslim American arena may exert, the range of possibilities is vast. In the realm of ideas, for example, they may include the influence of progressive reformist Islamic thinkers and activists such as the Islamic feminist Amina Wadud, who calls on Muslims to look at the "moral agency [that] is a mandate of the Qu'ran and cannot be restricted by any amount of historical precedent, social custom, or patriarchal aspiration" (2006: 204). It may also include the perspectives of revivalist Islam, with their emphasis on literalist interpretations of the Qu'ran and the need for emulation of the life of the Prophet and his Companions. In fact, it is the latter that has been the most visible religious thread in the transnational context of Bangladeshi American life. Among the particular strengths of Jamaat-e-Islami and other movements of revivalist Islam in Bangladesh is their ability to tap into a powerful web of global networks and resources for support. As a result, these movements have been especially well poised to enter into Bangladeshi diaspora communities and play a role of leadership within them. In the course of doing so, they have formed alliances with local Islamic organizations, thereby further consolidating their leadership as well as their ability to insert the ethos of revivalist Islam into the emerging transnational contexts of Bangladeshi American life.

CHAPTER 5

British Bangladeshis

CHANGING TRANSNATIONAL
SOCIAL WORLDS

In this chapter, I explore the lives of Bengalis/Bangladeshis in Britain, one of
the largest Muslim ethnic groups in Britain today.[1] As we will see, the British
Bangladeshi experience is powerfully shaped by a history of deep-seated
exclusion from mainstream British society along with limited opportunities
for socioeconomic advancement. In responding to these conditions, British
Bangladeshis have relied on a strategy of community transnationalism, one
that is focused on the maintenance of kinship networks and ongoing connections with the local community of origin in Bangladesh. In the late twentieth
and early twenty-first centuries, this strategy has come to face many challenges,
from increasingly stringent British immigration laws to the growing involvements of younger-generation British Bangladeshis in British Muslim community
forms.

THE EARLY DAYS: LASCARS AND POSTWAR SOJOURNERS

Sylhet is a region in the northeast of Bangladesh that borders the Indian states
of Meghalaya on the north, Tripura on the south, and Assam on the east.
During the era of British rule, Sylhet was a regional colonial outpost, especially
valued for the production of tea, an industry that continues to be important
in Sylhet today. Although colonial investments in the region were generally
minimal, in the early 1900s the Assam-Bengal Railway was extended into Sylhet
in order to bring it into the British Indian network of commercial and administrative centers. The British also administratively incorporated Sylhet into the
province of Assam (part of present-day India). However, during the time of
the partition of British India in 1947, Sylhet separated from Assam and joined
with East Pakistan, in accordance with the results of a popular referendum. With
this move, the political fate of Sylhet became decisively tied to that of the larger
region of what was then known as East Bengal.

The history of the Bangladeshi diaspora in Britain begins during the British colonial era. In the nineteenth century, young men from Sylhet found work as lascars or sailors on British ships that carried out goods from the region.[2] Some of them left their ships in London and other British seaports, where they took up work as peddlers, or as cooks and cleaners in restaurants and hotels. Among them were those who became permanent settlers in Britain, in some cases marrying local British women. Others returned home to Sylhet, armed with stories of life in *bilat*.[3] In either case, the experiences of these pioneering seamen laid the foundation of a culture of migration in the region with enduring social networks between Sylhet and Britain that would eventually, over time, facilitate further migration flows. No less important a part of the lascar legacy was the development in Sylhet of a migration vision—an understanding of international migration as both a possibility and opportunity. That is, as these men returned home to their villages in Sylhet carrying stories of their travels, they also ignited the imagination and curiosity of those around them about the wonders of life abroad.

It was, however, not until the Second World War that an active Sylhet-Britain migration circuit actually began to take shape. Faced with labor shortages after the war, the British government put forward the 1948 Nationality Act, which allowed the unrestricted entry into the country for the citizens of its former colonies. As South Asians began to flow into Britain under the provisions of this act, for Bengalis in what was then East Pakistan, the ability to take full advantage of this opening was constrained by the discriminatory policies of the Pakistani government, which sought to restrict the movement of Bengalis abroad by denying passports to them (Adams 1987). But even if many fewer in number than the Indian and West Pakistani migrants of this time, several thousand Bengalis entered Britain during the post–World War II period. There were two thousand Bangladeshis in Britain in 1951, a number that rose to six thousand in 1961 (see table 2.1). The majority of the migrants of this period were young men with relatively low levels of education, from the small towns and villages of Sylhet, in fact most often from the same areas, such as Beanibazar, Jagannathpur, and Maulvi Bazaar, that had dominated the lascar movements of the past (Choudhury 1993). In Britain, many found employment in heavy industry, in the factories of Birmingham and Oldham, while others took up jobs as pressers and tailors in the garment trades of London.

This postwar period of Bengali migration is often described as the sojourner era. This is a reference both to the widespread expectation of a temporary stay as well as the overwhelming dominance of men, without women and children, among the migrants. Akin to the classic labor migrant, the men aimed to work in Britain for awhile and then return home to enjoy the fruits of their labor.

A primary goal, then, of their time abroad was to maximize remittances and investments back home, in order to fulfill family obligations as well as to ensure their own comfort and well-being upon return. In their struggles to cope with and survive the often grinding realities of life in Britain, the migrants relied heavily on the support of fellow Bengalis, especially on kin and others from their home village and surrounding areas. We see this in Abdus Sami's account of his life in Britain in the 1950s, as recorded by the Oral History and Socio-Cultural Heritage Project of the Swadhinata Trust, U.K. As he describes, densely interwoven networks of kin provided him with the support he needed to find jobs and housing:

> There was an abundant number of mills and factories, so we had no shortage of jobs. I came here and lodged in twenty-four Great Windmill Street [Soho]. I had a relative of mine who had come here before me by . . . ship and he used to run a restaurant here. . . . He provided me a job. I had borrowed some money in Bangladesh . . . from my brother. . . . I was [under] pressure to [refund] the loan and also save some money. So I used to work hard. One of my nephews . . . used to work in a restaurant and the owner of that restaurant . . . offered me job with higher wages and free accommodation and food. It was a good offer for me and I could easily save some money in this process. I agreed with him and worked in his restaurant for five to seven years. Working in the restaurant, I was able to pay [off] all my debt. I then came to Aldgate . . . and rented a room from one of my friends. The rent was three and a half pounds. I took one partner and brought two single beds [to] the room and we two were living there. . . . Then someone advised me [to get a] tailoring job and tailoring had more money. I was busy with work and it was always crowded. People had sympathy for each other, which has dried [up] now. And all the people were single and no families were there. We had to work and eat. On the weekends our job was to enjoy cinema in the cinema halls like Naz Cinema. . . . We were always waiting for the letters from [our] country. We used to pass the weekend answering the letters also. We used to have a bath once a week and we used to go to bathe in groups of four or five. In the evening we never used to go to bathe, because the white people used to attack and beat us up. (Nirmul Committee 2006: 19)

Undergirding the tight-knit and clearly bounded Bengali community structures of the postwar years were conditions of sharp racial segregation from the dominant British society. As suggested by Abdus Sami's account, in an environment laced with intense and ongoing threats of racist violence from white British society, the Bengalis were encouraged to keep to themselves. The community's social isolation was further reinforced by its relatively weak ties with the other South Asian communities—of Indians and (West) Pakistanis also

entering Britain at this time. J. Rabbani, a restaurant owner in Manchester who
had lived in Britain for almost sixty years (since the age of seventeen), spoke to
me about the extremely wide gulf that had existed between Bengalis and other
South Asian–origin groups in the 1950s. While one might have expected a certain amity between Bengalis and (West) Pakistanis to have operated, given
their shared nationality as "Pakistani" at the time as well as the common adher-
ence to Islam, this was far from the case. In a foreshadowing of the dramatic
surfacing of divisions that was to occur in 1971, relations between the Bengalis
and (West) Pakistanis were especially strained:

> JR: In the factories at that time, there were Indians and Pakistanis working
> next to us [the Bengalis]. But the mixing was very limited, maybe there
> were some good relationships, friendships, but it did not go very far.
>
> NK: Was it a matter of religious difference?
>
> JR: No. Maybe that was there with the Indians, but not the Pakistanis. We
> were Muslim; we shared the religion but we did not feel any closeness.
> They saw us as their servants and at every opportunity they tried to cheat
> us. Also, we Sylhetis as you know, we Sylhetis are very attached to the
> Sylheti language. Many of those who came in those days did not even
> know how to speak *shuddho Bangla* [standard Bengali]. We did not know
> Urdu or Hindi; maybe a little bit here and there but it is not like today
> with the Indian films through which everyone picks up a bit of Hindi.
> We stayed close to each other and kept away from others. There was really
> no choice.

As suggested by J. Rabbani's remarks, besides racial segregation, the social
isolation of the British Bengali community in the postwar years was also
informed by the highly regional and localistic orientation of its members.
Conceptions of home and identity were deeply anchored in Sylhet and even
more specifically in the village of origin, where many had also often been born
and raised. Most had little exposure to the world beyond these local contexts
prior to their travels to Britain. Even as migration to Britain challenged this
localism, it also reinforced it, given the continued significance of kin and village
ties to the processes of migration and adaptation to life in Britain. Indeed, the
lives of the men were defined by a strategy of what I term *community transnationalism*. That is, the Bengalis organized their lives around ties with their local
community of origin, creating a world that stretched across the Atlantic, from
the British peninsula to the small towns and villages of Sylhet.

The transnational contexts that emerged in the postwar years were deeply
informed by patriarchal structures. That is, they were tied to the structures of
male privilege that organized kinship and village society in Sylhet and, more

generally, in Bengal. In her analysis of these structures, Katy Gardner (2006) notes the crucial role of wives and their labor to the postwar migration project. The expected division of conjugal labor was one in which wives were to remain at home in Sylhet and tend to the maintenance of the household and family, caring for children and elderly relatives. Under these circumstances, marriage had great strategic importance for the migrant men, providing a means for them to sustain the vitality of the kin group and their place of belonging and honor within it. Indeed, it was so important to have a wife at home that even in situations when the men married white British women, they often maintained Bengali wives in Sylhet as well. This was, at least in part, a way for them to ensure that there would be someone at home to take care of aging parents and meet other family obligations.[4]

Nonetheless, as is often the case with the unpaid work of caring for others, there was a certain invisibility to women's contributions to the migration project. Their significance was shrouded in ideologies of women's submission and deference to men and the kin group. To be sure, the migrant wives of the postwar era were not just passive victims of the migration project. Wives shared, at least to some extent, in the honor and respect accorded their migrant husbands. And in the absence of husbands, women could also gain a measure of latitude and authority over household affairs that they might not otherwise have had. However, the scope of these gains was circumscribed by a culture of male dominance that ultimately limited women's options and opportunities.

To summarize, the postwar sojourner era of Bengali migration to Britain was defined by a strong transnational community life that was dense, locally oriented, and structured around the dominance of men over women. The migrants were deeply embedded in transnational ties and networks based on kinship and village of origin. The 1970s, as I describe in what follows, brought an end to the sojourner era and the beginning of a period of family reunification for Bengalis in Britain. The community changed, from one composed of men who saw themselves as temporary labor migrants to one of families permanently settled in Britain. And following the events of 1971, the community came to identify itself with the nation of Bangladesh, even as it retained a strong regional Sylheti identification. But as we will see, even with these changes, the legacies of the sojourner era remain powerfully evident in the dynamics of community and family life among British Bangladeshis today.

THE ERA OF FAMILY REUNIFICATION: 1960S–1980S

The decades of the 1960s and 1970s were important periods of growth for the Bangladeshi-origin population in Britain. Their numbers rose from six thousand in 1961 to twenty-two thousand in 1971, and then to sixty-five thousand in 1981 (see table 2.1). The expansion coincided, somewhat ironically, with a period of tightening immigration laws in Britain. This suggests the possibility that there was preemptive migration whereby those in Britain began to sponsor family members in haste, in anticipation of the doors closing. Beginning with the Commonwealth Immigration Act of 1962, a series of increasingly stringent immigration laws were passed by the British government. The 1962 Act rescinded the unrestricted entry previously allowed Commonwealth citizens and also introduced a system of vouchers whereby those already in Britain could sponsor others to come in by obtaining guaranteed jobs for them. The Immigration Act of 1971 brought further restrictions, limiting sponsorship to family members and eventually only to those of the immediate family.

Along with these shifts in British immigration laws, several other developments of this time set the stage for a new phase of Bangladeshi community life in Britain.[5] Among these were the political events of 1971 and the birth of Bangladesh.

1971: The Birth of Bangladesh and British Bangladeshi Nationalism

In late 2004, on a chilly November evening in London, I visited a restaurant—one of the many Bangladeshi-owned and -operated Indian restaurants in the city. An acquaintance of my father had arranged a dinner meeting for me with several local Bangladeshi community leaders. A number of the leaders were active in the Awami League in Britain and, as I was to later find out, two even aspired to run for elections and become members of parliament (MPs) in the Bangladesh Parliament. As I sat down at a long table that had been set aside for the meeting, I was presented with a publication that had recently been produced by a community group to commemorate the birth of Bangladesh in 1971 and the important role played by Bengalis in Britain in support of Bangladesh.

In their introductions to me, several of the men offered brief biographies in which they spoke of their own personal contributions to the 1971 liberation efforts. An elderly man who appeared to be in his early seventies recounted the story of how he, along with others in Britain at the time, had raised money to send a barrister from Britain to support Bangabandhu Sheikh Mujibur Rahman, the leader of the liberation struggle, when he was sent to jail in 1968 by the Pakistani authorities in a sedition case known as the Agartala Conspiracy Case. As he finished, a young man at the table, who as I later confirmed had been born in the 1980s, turned to me and said in English in a crisp British accent: "We [Bengalis] here in Britain are very proud of our history, of our role in 1971."

The nationalist narrative of 1971 and the Bangladesh war of independence are often invoked by those who are in the Awami League, the political party that led the struggle. Beyond the divisions of political party, however, the events of 1971 culminating in the birth of Bangladesh are widely recognized by British Bangladeshis as a watershed in the development of their community life. In essence, the birth of Bangladesh nationalized the British Bengali community and transformed its relationship to the homeland state. During the postwar era of undivided Pakistan (1947–1971), the homeland state and its institutions were largely inaccessible and bereft of value as arenas of protection and affirmation for the Bengali migrants. As highlighted by the difficulties they faced in obtaining passports from the Pakistani government in order to travel to Britain (and other locations abroad), the homeland state was more often than not experienced as a site of oppression and constraint. The liberation struggles of 1971 drew on these grievances, and gave powerful meaning and expression to them through a framework of Bengali nationalism. With the emergence of Bangladesh, homeland politics became legitimate matters of investment and involvement for those in Britain. And the community came to identify itself with the nation of Bangladesh, moving away from the exclusively regional conceptions and loyalties of the past. This is by no means to imply that the notion of a Sylheti identity, deeply rooted in ties to the home village (*desher bari*), lost its significance. It was rather that "being Sylheti" came to be meaningfully nested within a national identity of "Bangladeshi." This shift set the stage for the emergence of a transnational context that was institutionally rich and robust, more so than might otherwise have been the case. As I will explore in more detail later, the contemporary community-building efforts of British Bangladeshis have included organizations and projects that draw on official intergovernmental ties between Bangladesh and Britain.

If the birth of Bangladesh effected a fundamental transformation in the relationship of the British Bangladeshis to the homeland state, it had implications for their relationship to the British political context, as well. As Sarah Glynn (2006) has described, the liberation war was a profoundly politicizing event that ultimately furthered the integration of Bengalis into British politics. As the Bengali community struggled to support the liberation effort, they formed grassroots organizations and forged relationships with political groups and parties in Britain, especially the Labour Party. These political ties came into play in the 1970s and 1980s as the community turned its attention to antiracist politics.

"Here to Stay, Here to Fight": Antiracist Politics

The 1970s and 1980s was a period of family reunification, a time when Bangladeshi migrant men were increasingly joined in Britain by their families. As this occurred, the previously "bachelor" community found itself struggling to find adequate jobs and housing for their families. The problems of racism, which were certainly there before, became particularly acute and visible at this time. There was the growth of the British National Front, a right-wing political movement with an ideology of racism that played on the fears and resentments of white working-class persons. For many Bangladeshis as well as those of other South Asian origins, racial attacks and harassment were endemic and an expected part of the daily experience of neighborhood, job, and school. Jamal Hasan, a community activist, describes his experiences of racial tensions at this time:

> When I came to this country in 1972, I realized that Asians, black people, and anybody who came from a colonial background were still perceived as subservient to whites. . . . As a result of that feeling; there was little or no interaction between white people and Asian people. Indians, Bangladeshis, and Pakistanis were all known to and described by many whites as "Pakis." Racists could get away with attacking "Pakis," who were seen as easy targets because there was no resistance from the Asians when they were attacked. . . . The younger generation was not prepared to stand idly by, turning the other cheek. . . . At that time, racist attacks by the National Front were a daily occurrence in East London. The police would hardly take any action or do anything to stop such racial attacks. (Nirmul Committee 2006: 100)

Racial tensions reached a breaking point with the murder of Altab Ali in 1978. Altab Ali was a young Bangladeshi garment worker who was stabbed and killed in the East End in London as he was making his way to a bus stop after work, on a day when local borough elections were taking place. His murder served to galvanize the British Bangladeshi community into political action. A protest march took place in which thousands of Bangladeshis participated. They were joined by a vast array of supporters and political allies, all braving their way through the heavy rains of that day. In the march from Whitechapel to the House of Commons and back, the slogan chanted was "Here to stay, here to fight." The message then was clear—the sojourner era had ended and these former subjects of the British colonial empire were committed to carving out their rightful place in British society. Moreover, they would not sit back in silence but actively resist the harassment and incursions of racists.

Among the organizing forces behind the protests of 1978 were several Bangladeshi youth groups (i.e., Bangladesh Youth League, Bangladesh Youth Front, Federation of Bangladesh Youth Organisations) that had sprung up in the 1970s. John Eade (1989) has written of the mushrooming of grassroots organizations among British Bangladeshis that occurred at this time. They were nurtured through such British government initiatives as the 1975 Spitalfields Project that aimed to improve the conditions of impoverished neighborhoods. In the years following the Altab Ali murder, the community groups continued to form, especially around the issue of access to public housing. These activities were increasingly supported by a generation of young British Bangladeshi activists whose political consciousness as well as leadership and organizing skills had been honed in the youth groups of the 1970s.

Many of the activists were young men who had been born in Bangladesh and come to Britain in the 1970s, perhaps as children, or as teens and young adults. Eschewing what they felt to be the community's prior stance of passivity in the face of unjust treatment, they instead sought conscious and assertive engagement with mainstream British politics. In comparison to the earlier generation of leadership, they were indeed better equipped for such engagement, armed as they were with English-language skills as well as the knowledge of local political structures that they had gained through youth group involvements. But if different from the earlier generations in these respects, they were also similar in one important way—in their embeddedness in the transnational worlds of Bangladeshi British life. In keeping with the politics of the time, they advocated solidarity with other minority groups and the adoption by Bangladeshis of an Asian or Black political identity. But even as their politics took them outside the Bangladeshi community, their social and familial lives were largely defined by it.

Many of the younger generation of activists continued to live and work in the Bangladeshi neighborhoods where they had grown up or spent their young adult years. Of note, too, is that many of them had grown up in Sylhet or at least spent a great deal of time there as children during extended trips and stays. Thus the transnational ties that had so tightly organized the lives of their elders— of kinship and home village—had meaning and importance for them as well. The significance of these ties was further reinforced by the widespread practice of transnational arranged marriage. The second-generation British Bangladeshis tended to marry in Sylhet, to young men and women who had been chosen for them by their families from within their kinship and village networks. These marriages solidified transnational ties and ensured their continuity over time.

Many of the second-generation activists eventually found jobs in local government offices, schools, and social service organizations (Eade and Garbin 2006). Some joined the Labour Party and came to assume posts in local government. From these positions, as we will see, they have continued to play an important role in British Bangladeshi community life.

Strategies of Community Transnationalism

By the opening of the twenty-first century, the era of intensive family reunification, especially evident in the 1970s and 1980s, had ended for British

Bangladeshis. The community changed, from one composed largely of first-generation migrants to a predominance of second- and third-generation British Bangladeshis. This shift was one of many that augured a new environment, with new challenges and possibilities. Even as established strategies of community transnationalism have faced a growing set of obstacles, the transnational social worlds of kinship and home village have continued to hold great meaning and significance. Among the conditions that have sustained their value is the widespread persistence of socioeconomic disadvantage among British Bangladeshis. Thus, as we shall see, the strategy of building transnational worlds of kinship and village has come under challenge. At the same time, it has also been sustained and strengthened by certain conditions.

Persistent Disadvantage

In May 2010, Rushanara Ali became the first British Bangladeshi to be elected to the House of Commons. The thirty-five-year-old Oxford University graduate was born in Biswanath, Sylhet. She came to Britain at the age of seven and grew up in Tower Hamlets, East London. Running for the constituency of Bethnal Green and Bow on a Labour Party ticket, she made a successful bid for the seat that had previously been held by the controversial Respect Party leader George Galloway.

As highlighted by the example of Rushanara Ali and her life story, the first decade of the twenty-first century has seen growing numbers of British Bangladeshis who are overcoming the barriers to achievement and power in British society that had so firmly circumscribed the lives of the generation before them. But it is also clear that disadvantage and exclusion continue to be pervasive features of the British Bangladeshi experience. The rap song "Rebel Warrior," the lyrics of which are excerpted below, conveys a sense of the widespread and deeply rooted sense of anger and frustration felt by many young British Bangladeshis. "Rebel Warrior" was produced by the Asian Dub Foundation, a community rap organization with musicians of Bangladeshi as well as Indian and Pakistani origin. The song was inspired by the poem "Ami Bidrohi" that was written in the 1920s by the beloved Bengali poet Kazi Nazrul Islam. Drawing on the powerful, searing verses that Kobi Nazrul had penned at the time of India's struggles against British colonialism, "Rebel Warrior" issues a call of protest and resistance to racism and other social injustices:

Ami Bidrohi! I the rebel warrior
I have risen alone with my head held high
I will only rest
When the cries of the oppressed
No longer reach the sky

When the sound of the sword of the oppressor
No longer rings in battle
Hear my war cry!
I'm here to teach you a lesson
I'm here to torture your soul
I'm the itch in your side that's got out of control
Gonna prey on your conscience
You'll be praying for forgiveness
Seen all the evidence
No longer need a witness
So take my word man
Here's my sentence
One hundred thousand years of repentance . . .
I'll be sowing the seeds of community
Accommodating every colour, every need
So listen to my message and heed my warning
I'm telling you now
How a new age is dawning
Ami bidrohi![6]

In 2007, there were an estimated 353,900 persons of Bangladeshi origin in
Britain (Office for National Statistics 2009). Almost half lived in London, especially in the East London boroughs, of which Tower Hamlets had the highest
concentration. Table 5.1 offers information on the socioeconomic status of
British Bangladeshis. For purposes of comparison, I also include information
on British Pakistanis and Indians. We see that for British Bangladeshis, rates of
economic inactivity and unemployment are relatively high. In general, the
margin of intergroup difference suggested by these measures is far wider
between Bangladeshis and Indians than between Bangladeshis and Pakistanis.
Among British Bangladeshis, 9.8 percent were reported to be in professional
jobs, compared to 17.8 percent for British Indians. The data also show the proportion of those in the labor market who have educational qualifications to be
lower for Bangladeshis than for Indians or Pakistanis. There are, however,
some signs that the educational profile of young British Bangladeshis may be
improving. Among secondary school pupils in 2002, 50 percent of British
Bangladeshi girls and 40 percent of British Bangladeshi boys received five or
more grades of A–C, thus receiving a Level 2 qualification under the U.K.
National Qualifications Framework. Although these rates were lower than that
reported for whites and a number of other ethnic groups, they exceeded that of
black Africans, black Caribbeans, as well as Pakistanis (Office for National
Statistics 2006).

TABLE 5.1

SOCIOECONOMIC INDICATORS OF SOUTH ASIAN–ORIGIN
POPULATIONS IN BRITAIN

Socioeconomic indicators	Bangladeshi	Indian	Pakistani
Unemployment rates of men of working age (%)	18	7	14
Self-employment rates* (%)	10	13	23
Professional employment rates* (%)	9.8	17.8	9.3
With educational qualifications** (%)	56	82	66
Men of working age who are not available for work or seeking work (%)	30	20	28
Women of working age who are not available for working or seeking work (%)	77	33	68

* as a percentage of all economically active.

** those with GCSE (O-level) attainment or higher.

Source: Office for National Statistics. 2006. "Ethnicity and Identity: Employment Patterns." Newport, UK: Annual Population Survey, January 2004 to December 2004. http://www.statistics.gov.uk/CCI/nugget.asp?ID=463.

Studies also show second- and third-generation British Bangladeshis to be heavily concentrated in the unskilled service sectors; intergenerational occupational mobility has been limited (Dale, Shaheen, Kalra, and Fieldhouse 2002; Salway 2008; Twomey 2001). In 2002–2003, 60 percent of British Bangladeshi men were employed in the distribution, hotel, and restaurant industries. Indeed, the restaurant industry has been an especially important source of employment for British Bangladeshis. In the 1960s, there was a decline in British manufacturing industries resulting in the widespread closure of the factories where British Bangladeshis had worked. Many turned to the food service business and worked to expand the appeal and accessibility of curry restaurants for the general British population. Today an estimated eight out of ten of the 8,500 Indian food restaurants in Britain are Bangladeshi-owned and -operated. Audrey Gillian (2002) notes the remarkable expansion of the sector since the postwar years: "In 1946 there were twenty restaurants or small cafes owned by Bengalis; in 1960 there were three hundred; and by 1980, more than three thousand. Now, according to the Curry Club of Great Britain, there are eight thousand five hundred Indian restaurants, of which seven thousand two hundred are Bengali."

The curry restaurant business has undoubtedly been an important and valuable source of livelihood for many British Bangladeshis. But with the exception, perhaps, of those who are the business owners, the jobs that they offer are limited in their pay and lacking opportunities for advancement. In her study of the labor market experiences of young British Bangladeshi men, Sarah Salway (2008) describes the men as viewing Bangladeshi restaurant work negatively, as low status and more suitable for "hashpots"—a derogatory term for new arrivals from Bangladesh—than those who are British-born and raised like themselves. She also describes a variety of conditions operating to constrain the young men's labor market opportunities and options. These included pressures to drop out of school and earn money to support an often struggling family. There was also the problem of discrimination in the labor market—of employers who refused to hire or to promote them because they were Bangladeshi and/or Muslim. Under these circumstances, the young men often found themselves in low-skilled and low-paid jobs in retail sales and fast food outlets, usually located in close proximity to Bangladeshi neighborhoods. In these jobs, as well, Bangladeshi community networks played an important role in terms of referrals and finding employment.

In certain ways, then, not much has changed; with respect to employment, the lives of many young British Bangladeshis today are not significantly different from the sojourners of the postwar years. As in the past, many continue to be deeply embedded in a local Bangladeshi community, one that is segregated from mainstream British society, territorially defined, and organized around dense and interwoven social networks based on kinship and home village in Sylhet. The high levels (77 percent) of economic inactivity (i.e., non-participation in the formal labor force) reported by British Bangladeshi women also suggests that the family migration project continues to be informed by the patriarchal structures of rural Sylheti society. Of course, these days, unlike in the postwar years, the Bengali wives of migrants are likely to actually be present in Britain, as are their children. Among other things, this has generated access for both sons and daughters to the British educational system, thus potentially providing girls with the resources to challenge the culture of restrictions for girls that continues to pervade British Bangladeshi life.

The concentration of minorities in disadvantaged urban neighborhoods tends to produce self-perpetuating cycles of poverty and discrimination. Under these conditions, minority groups become deprived of access to important social resources (such as high-quality schools) that could facilitate their socioeconomic mobility. The dynamics of neighborhood concentration and disadvantage have been a notable feature of the British Bangladeshi experience. Among the many consequences of these conditions is the supportive context that they have created for a transnational community life. That is, in an environment where access to resources outside the community has been limited, the cultivation of the transnational sphere has been seen as a strategically valuable focus of effort.

Transnational Politics

Today a tourist who is new to London may well decide to make her way over to the East End of the city. After exiting the Tube station there, she might follow the signs that point to Brick Lane, a street that has gained a certain notoriety from Monica Ali's best-selling novel of the same name, which was also made into a movie. She may decide to try out one of the many Bangladeshi restaurants she sees there for lunch. Sitting at one of the tables with a window onto the street, she might notice that the street signs are not just in English but also in Bengali. And the lamp posts are in green and red—the colors of the Bangladeshi flag. In fact, everywhere she looks she finds visual cues of the Bangladeshi and, even more specifically, the Sylheti presence in the area. Storefronts advertise flights from London to Sylhet, some on Bangladesh Biman (the national airline of Bangladesh) and others on Air Sylhet, a private airline company formed by British Bangladeshis. There is a sign for Sonali Bank—the major state-owned commercial bank of Bangladesh. There is a food store advertising frozen fish from Sylhet's Shurma River. The visitor watches two elderly men with long, grey beards enter the store; they are dressed in long white tunics, baggy pants, and white head caps. She sees a group of teenage girls walking down the street in animated conversation. One is dressed in a black *burkha* and the others are in jeans and long shirts, along with bright sequined *hijabs* on their heads. Looking through her London guidebook, she reads about how this neighborhood is in "Banglatown."

In 2001 British Bangladeshi leaders, including many of the second-generation activists, led a successful bid via the Tower Hamlets council to gain the official designation of Banglatown for Brick Lane and its surrounding neighborhoods. With the help of street signs and an advertising campaign, the hope was to give the area a distinct cultural identity that would be attractive to tourists and thus beneficial for Bangladeshi businesses located there. In fact, the area has a number of visible Bangladeshi landmarks, such as Altab Ali Park, the Kobi Nazrul Cultural Centre, and the Shohid Minar Monument. Along with the official designation of Banglatown, these landmarks are matters of considerable pride for many British Bangladeshis, symbols of their hard-won presence and political voice in Britain.

But, if British Bangladeshis have used local political structures to assert their place in Britain, they have also drawn on them to strengthen and to institutionalize transnational community structures. In 1996, for example, British Bangladeshi leaders successfully negotiated a Twinning Accord between Sylhet Municipality and Tower Hamlets in East London. By formalizing the relationship between the two communities, the accord aimed to: "increase co-operation and understanding between the two municipalities; encourage mutual trade and investment; promote both Tower Hamlets and Sylhet as magnets for economic growth." Under this accord, Tower Hamlets has sponsored the Sylhet Partnership Project. Funded by the European Commission, the project works with Sylhet City Corporation to improve public services in the city of Sylhet.

If engagement with local British political structures has supported these transnational initiatives, the cooperation of the Bangladeshi state has been important, as well. Reflecting growing worldwide interest since the 1990s in the role of diasporas in fostering development, the Bangladesh state has taken measure to encourage ties with expatriates in Britain. The early 1990s also saw the restoration of democracy in Bangladesh, following a long period of military rule. This change has been important for British Bangladeshis, enabling them to play a greater political role in Bangladesh, especially in Sylhet. They have done so through support and funding of candidates for elections at both the national and local levels. Moreover, invoking dual citizenship (British and Bangladeshi), there are British Bangladeshis who have run for office themselves. In their campaigns to garner votes, they move between social and political networks that stretch across the national borders of Britain and Bangladesh. Indeed, those who run for political office in Bangladesh may begin their political career in city councils and other local political structures in Britain. These British political activities may garner them the necessary contacts and funding to make a successful political bid in a local election in the home village region.

Back to Sylhet: Of Transnational Honor, Respite, and Safety Nets

Besides politics, the transnational strategies of British Bangladeshis have taken a number of other different forms. Among these are remittances to Bangladesh. While family reunification in Britain may have reduced the most immediate pressures on British Bangladeshis to send money back, many continue to have some financial obligations in Bangladesh. In general, these obligations relate to the welfare of the kin group and the upkeep of the institutions of the home village. Thus my informants spoke of remitting money for such purposes as the care of elderly and sick relatives or for the schooling and wedding expenses of the children of needy kin. Money was also sent for the building and mainte- nance of village institutions, such as mosques, madrasas, orphanages, health clinics, and so forth.

Besides their contributions to kin group and village, some British Bangladeshis also invested in the purchase of land and the building of houses for themselves in the home village region. Indeed, the sight of the many modern multistoried luxury homes that have been built by Londoni families is perhaps the most visually striking sign of the British Bangladeshi presence in rural Sylhet.[7] In 2009, on a trip to my own home village of Jalalshap in Nabiganj, Sylhet, after many years of absence, I remember gazing with disbelief at the mansions that had been built there amid the peaceful and seemingly unchanged landscape of paddy fields, ponds, and wandering goats and chickens. Referring to what was a rooftop pool, a village resident informed me in a tone of awe that one of the houses had a pond (*pukur*) on the top. Despite such ostentatious amenities, many of the houses seemed to be uninhabited. I was told that in some cases elderly relatives lived in them, and in other cases they were left vacant but under the supervision of caretakers who were paid to guard and clean the houses, preparing them for the times when their Londoni employers would come back to visit and stay there.

Studies have noted the importance of the community of origin as a site of status and honor for migrants. Especially in developing societies, the expenditures of returning migrants have great value, effectively allowing them to use consumption to elevate their social status (Smith 2006; Thai 2008). These transnational dynamics of honor were part of what underlay the continued financial investments of British Bangladeshis in the home village. But there were other motivations, as well. Reflecting deep-seated anxieties about British society and their place as Bangladeshis and Muslims within it, investments in the home village were also seen as a safety net. If, for whatever reason, life in Britain became untenable, these investments would facilitate their ability to come back and live in relative comfort there. Some also related plans to follow other British Bangladeshis who had retired to their home village. There they could draw on the housing and other investments they had made and also, perhaps, draw on the savings and old-age pensions they had accumulated during their years in Britain.

Besides providing a safety net as well as a possible site of retirement, the home village was widely described as a place of respite by British Bangladeshis. In comparison to what I found among Bangladeshi Americans, homeland trips were in general both far more frequent and prolonged in length among British Bangladeshis.[8] Many British Bangladeshis felt these trips to be their only meaningful breaks from the daily and often difficult routines of their lives in Britain. Among the consequences of these frequent back-and-forth movements is the growth in Sylhet of a business sector that caters to the tastes and needs of returning Londonis. In the city of Sylhet and in the larger district towns of the region (i.e., Beanibazar, Maulvibazar), there are health clubs, hotels, restaurants, and shopping malls with stores that sell such items as diapers and canned baked beans for those coming from Britain.

Although I expected the theme of respite to be part of the narrative of trips back to Sylhet among first-generation British Bangladeshis, I was surprised to find it to be prominent in the accounts of the second and third generation as well. It is important to emphasize that even with the luxury homes that have been built there by Londonis, much of rural Sylhet remains quite undeveloped and isolated, lacking such modern amenities as stable electricity, running water, Internet access, and so forth. Nonetheless, as suggested to me by sixteen-year-old Shompa, there were other aspects of life there that could compensate for the absence of these amenities. In London, Shompa shared a cramped room with three younger sisters in her family's two-bedroom flat in East London. Her parents strictly monitored and restricted her activities in London, allowing her only to walk to school and back without them. In Sylhet, they were far more relaxed about her movements, and so she felt a certain freedom. She enjoyed being away from the hustle and bustle of London, which she otherwise never had a chance to escape:

> We spent three months there and I loved it. London is always so busy and crowded. We went to Sylhet for my cousin's marriage. There are a lot of people there who are my age and we can just muck around. . . . It's comfortable. I would go around with my cousins, we would go and talk with people in the village, ride rickshaws and village boats, even swim in the pond. And I could just go out and walk around without anyone telling me what to do. My Mum and Dad let us go. Here my Mum and Dad are very strict . . . "Don't go here, don't go there." Last year there was an overnight field trip from school to Scotland and they wouldn't let me go, "What will people say, what will people say?" They worry about what Bengalis would say about a girl going on an overnight trip.

If for Shompa the trip to Bangladesh was welcomed as a respite from what she described as the restrictions of her life in London, for other young British Bangladeshis the circumstances of such trips could be quite different. A strategy of sending unruly children back to the home country as a disciplinary method has been noted by studies of migrant families of other backgrounds (Smith 2006; Waters 1999). That is, when it is feared that children are heading down the wrong path, perhaps through involvement in drugs and gangs, migrant parents may decide to send them back to stay with relatives in the community of origin for an extended visit. In that setting, it is hoped, removed from the negative influences to which they had succumbed in the receiving society, they might reform themselves. This strategy of sending at-risk youth back home was also practiced by British Bangladeshis. I was told by informants that there were now several drug rehabilitation centers in Sylhet which admitted young British Bangladeshis who had been sent there by their families to treat them for drug and substance abuse. But it was also the case that sending teenage children "back" to Sylhet for a long visit could be related to another prominent British Bangladeshi family strategy—transnational arranged marriage.

Transnational Arranged Marriage

It is late morning and I am sitting at a Bangladeshi restaurant in London. I have come to talk to the waiters, trying to catch them before the restaurant opened for lunch and they became too busy to speak to me. Fuad, neatly dressed in a white shirt and black pants, carefully dried a set of wine glasses as we talked. He had been in Britain for about four years. He had come over from Sunamganj, Sylhet, after his family had arranged his marriage to a third-generation British Bangladeshi woman; they were distant cousins. Now a father of two young children, he lived with his wife and her relatives in a flat not far from the restaurant. When I asked him how he liked it in London he shrugged his shoulders and smiled in silence. He asked me if I was going to write in my story about the poor service given to Sylhetis on Bangladesh Biman (the national airlines of Bangladesh); he had recently experienced such problems in the course of a trip back home. Soon a thin young man in jeans strolled into the restaurant, a cigarette dangling from one side of his mouth. His name was Sammy and he was about to start his shift in the restaurant kitchen. Our conversation switched from Bengali to English as Sammy, a second-generation British Bangladeshi, was more comfortable in English. It turned out that Sammy too had recently been married, about three years ago, to a second cousin in Sylhet. Flashing a grin that revealed several missing front teeth, Sammy was happy to tell me the story of how this had come to happen. He had been "mucking around," doing little else but getting into trouble. To emphasize this point he pulled up his shirt sleeve and showed me an impressive collection of tattoos. I noticed a small Bangladesh flag next to a water lily (shapla), the national flower of Bangladesh. He told me that this was a symbol of a Bangladeshi gang in East London to which he had belonged few years ago. Fearful for his future, his father had packed him off to Sylhet, to their village in Maulvibazar. After a few months, he was introduced to the teenage daughter of his father's cousin, with the intention that they would marry. Fortunately, it was love at first sight for him and he quickly agreed. They eventually came back to Britain together, and his wife gave birth to a baby girl. They planned to go for a long visit to Sylhet soon, to visit the family there. Sammy spoke passionately about his attachment to the home village: "Man, I love it. It's my home, my place, it's here" [thumping his chest].

The practice of families arranging the marriages of their British-born children to young men and women from Bangladesh has been an important strategy of transnational reproduction for British Bangladeshis. In the face of restrictive British immigration laws, these marriages have offered a means for the community to replenish its ranks, as young men and women have entered Britain from Bangladesh through marriage to British citizens. As in the case of Fuad and Sammy, many of these marriages occur among kin or within village-based social networks. They thus serve to strengthen these ties and also to ensure that the British-born generations remain part of them.

The importance of transnational arranged marriage for the continuity of British Bangladeshi life was highlighted by the tremendous anxiety I encountered, especially among older British Bangladeshis, about the growing challenges to this practice. There were widespread fears that it would not continue, thereby jeopardizing an established way of life. Mr. and Mrs. Khan, a couple in their fifties, talked to me at some length about these matters. Mr. and Mrs. Khan were raising four children—three daughters and one son—in London. Mr. Khan was a successful entrepreneur and the family lived in a comfortable home in a suburb of London, in a neighborhood that was largely white. As we talked, they told me that their eldest daughter, aged twenty, had recently married a boy she had met at university. Seeing the grim expressions on their faces, I started to imagine that she had married someone not of Bangladeshi origin. So I was surprised when they told me that her husband was third-generation British Bangladeshi. They rushed to assure me that their son-in-law was "a good boy" (*bhalo chele*) and that the young couple was doing well. But they were nonetheless disappointed, as they had expected their daughter to marry in Sylhet. This was what Mrs. Khan, a British-born Bangladeshi, had herself done many years ago in the 1970s. At the age of sixteen, her parents had arranged her marriage to Mr. Khan, who had been a college student in Sylhet at that time:

MR. K: It is a big problem now in our community that a lot of our girls especially do not want to marry boys from back home.

MRS. K: They feel that they will have a hard time adjusting, because the boys raised back there have a different mentality. The girls here would prefer someone who was raised in England. Of course in my day we didn't question these things. We married, we adjusted, we made our happiness.

MR. K: My daughters are all good students. Inshallah, they will do well here. But when it comes to marriage we feel very protective of our daughters. There are many advantages to getting them married to someone from back home. In that way we know much more about the background of the boy. We know their family, in fact we know them for generations and generations. We know where they live, how they live. And the most important thing is that if there is a problem in the marriage, it is easy for both sides of the family to talk and to try and solve the problem.

NK: I don't understand how it's different if it's a marriage to a Bangladeshi who is already here in Britain, someone who grew up here?

MRS. K: Yes [hesitantly]. It is possible for it to be a good match if the two families [in Britain] are from the same village area back home. In that case it would maybe be OK. But if you don't have that in common, then you don't have the same family support.

MR. K: Marriage is so important. You have to know as much as possible about the family.

For Mr. and Mrs. Khan, shared village origins were a critical ingredient in a successful marriage. From their point of view, the presence of these ties provided a level of trust and family support for the marriage that could not otherwise be there. While emphasizing the significance of shared village origins, they also expressed a clear preference for their children to marry someone who was in Sylhet. For those in Britain, a marriage that is not transnational may be disadvantageous in its inability to harness the value of British citizenship in marriage negotiations. In other words, in the marriage market in Bangladesh, marriage to a British citizen is likely to be valued for the access it provides to legal entry into Britain. Among those already in Britain, this asset is not likely to carry the same weight.

While transnational arranged marriage continues to be an important part of British Bangladeshi life, it is also facing challenges. As suggested by the example of Mr. and Mrs. Khan's daughter, there are signs of resistance to this practice among the ranks of the British-born for whom a sense of compatibility may override any other considerations. Besides these cultural changes, the legitimacy of transnational arranged marriage has been weakened in certain respects by the emergence since the 1990s of "forced marriage" as a public issue. "Forced marriage" is defined as coercion into marriage; when a person is married against his or her will. The Department of Children, Schools and Families in Britain has estimated that five thousand to eight thousand cases of forced marriage to occur in the country each year, with most involving victims of South Asian origin (Jones 2009). These cases typically involve a young person who is taken from Britain to the home country by their family on a visit, perhaps forcibly or perhaps on the pretext of seeing a sick elder grandparent or celebrating the marriage of a relative. Once there, when they are socially isolated, they find themselves coerced into entering into a marriage that had been planned for them. In one such case that received media attention, a British Bangladeshi teenager named Nasrin Begum was taken to Sylhet to marry the son of her mother's uncle. After Nasrin managed to telephone the British consular office in Sylhet, embassy officials came to the village with the police and rescued her (Barrowclough 2008).

In Britain as in other European countries, the forced marriage issue has been informed by human rights discourse as well as concerns about immigration. Specifically, it has come into prominence as a social problem within a political environment of anxiety about the failure of some minorities, especially Muslims, to adopt core European values of individual rights. Thus the British government has been increasingly interventionist in its stance toward forced marriage. It has set up a Forced Marriages Unit (administered through the Foreign and Home Offices) to provide assistance to victims. In 2008, a law was passed to raise the minimum age for approval of marriage visas from eighteen to twenty-one, with the specific goal of deterring forced marriages in which the victims are often in their teens. Before that, in 2007, there was the passage of the Forced Marriages Act under which judges in Britain are able to issue protection orders for British citizens and residents either to prevent forced marriage or to rescue victims married under these circumstances. Under the act, anyone convicted of forcing a person into marriage can be jailed for up to two years. One of the first cases to be heard under the act was that of Humayra Abedin, a Bangladeshi resident in London. Humayra indicated that she had been taken to Bangladesh and held captive there by her parents who planned to coerce her into a marriage. Using the Forced Marriage Act, the British High Court successfully issued an injunction to Abedin's family in Bangladesh to allow her to return to Britain (Guzder 2008).

Indeed, the forced marriage issue has strengthened the visible presence of the British state in Bangladesh, especially in Sylhet. The British High Commission in Bangladesh maintains a consular office in Sylhet that provides a variety of services to British citizens in the area, ranging from issuing passports to providing information about local health care facilities. Among the most visible and well-publicized of its services is that of intervention in forced marriage cases. Between 2007 and 2008, the Consular Office reported assisting fifty-six forced marriage cases in Bangladesh, most in Sylhet (Barrowclough 2008). In order to assist its citizens, the British High Commission has also placed large placards on the road from the Sylhet airport to the city (British

High Commission, Dhaka 2009). These signs provide information on how to contact the Consular Office and the help that British passport holders can get in a variety of matters, from lost passports to forced marriage. These activities highlight the institutionalization of British citizenship in Sylhet and the concurrent development of a transnational legal sphere.

When I talked to British Bangladeshis about their thoughts on forced marriage, all were quick to indicate their disapproval of it. Forced marriage, I was repeatedly told, was contrary to the dictates of Islam, which required the consent of both the man and the woman to the marriage. Echoing the findings of Samad and Eade (2002), some informants, especially those of the older generation, also denied the existence of forced marriage in the community. According to them, what was present rather was a practice of arranged marriage. In speaking of this practice, these informants articulated notions of family relations that sharply diverge from those that have guided forced marriage activism. In arranged marriage, consent to marry is understood to be rooted not in the preference of individuals but rather in their respect for elders and their sense of family duty and obligation to the kin group. In this framework, the presence of these values among the young is assumed, especially given that their absence brings dishonor to the kin group. There is thus a certain presumption of the consent to marry, signaled by the passive acquiescence of those involved. In fact overt enthusiasm for marriage, especially from the girl, is viewed as unseemly. As a result, a certain degree of resistance to marriage is expected from girls. Under these conditions, the question of when arranged marriage ends and forced marriage begins may not be easy to answer.

Besides reflecting a lack of understanding of arranged marriage practices, British Bangladeshis also spoke of the forced marriage issue as an expression of mainstream Britain's antipathy toward them and their presence in Britain. The announcement in June 2010 by the British government that all those coming from outside the European Union in order to marry or join their British spouse would have to pass an English-language test has only solidified these perceptions.

To summarize, starting in postwar sojourner days, strategies of community transnationalism have been an important part of the Bangladeshi migration project in Britain. These strategies have evolved in important ways over time. For example, the emergence of Bangladesh as a nation-state in 1971 along with the growing involvements of British Bangladeshis in local British politics have contributed to the institutional enrichment of the transnational sphere. At the same time, as demands for immigration restrictions in Britain have grown more heated, the practice of transnational arranged marriage has been made more difficult, thereby threatening a central means by which the continued vibrancy of transnational ties has been ensured in the past. In what follows, I turn to another emerging feature of British Bangladeshi life—changing religious perspectives and involvements in the community, especially among the younger generation.

British Muslim Politics, Youth, and Revivalist Islam

In response to the postwar flow of immigration from its former colonies and the dilemmas of managing diversity posed by it, Britain established a policy of multiculturalism in the 1960s. Under this rubric, "the state encouraged cultural groups to create their own organizational structures, to safeguard their customs and religious practices as they saw fit, and to introduce an awareness of and celebration for Britain's cultural pluralism into the state education system" (Fetzer and Soper 2005: 30). During the 1960s to 1980s, multiculturalism supported the formation of community organizations based on national origins for British Bangladeshis. Local administrative authorities encouraged the development of Bangladeshi youth groups and social welfare organizations. But in the 1990s, there was an important shift. Multicultural policies began to support the Muslim affiliation of British Bangladeshis. Eade and Garbin (2002) describe the change in state funding that occurred at this time, away from Bangladeshi-based groups. The focus instead was on mosques and Islamic community organizations, which were invigorated by public funds as they began to successfully enter into partnerships with local authorities for the delivery of social services to British Muslims.

The strengthening of Muslim identity that resulted from these developments was also informed by the growth of British Muslim politics. The 1989 protests by British Muslims against the publication of Salman Rushdie's *Satanic Verses* are often cited as a watershed event. Reflecting global trends at this time, Islam became an increasingly prominent basis of political identity and community among British Muslims. Among the conditions that fueled these developments was the widespread anger of Muslims against the U.S.-led and British-supported "War on Terror" and its military engagements. The invasion of Iraq by the United States and its allies in 2003 led to the growth in Britain of a large antiwar movement in which Muslim participation was prominent. The politicization of British Muslims was also a response to the rising flames of anti-Muslim sentiment and the related concerns throughout Europe about the alleged failure of Muslims to integrate into mainstream society. In a statement on December 11, 2006, the year after the London bombings, Tony Blair, prime minister of Britain from 1997 to 2007, gave voice to these anxieties as he spoke of the obligation of all groups, including Muslims, to adopt Britain's core values:

> These murders [July 2005 bombings] were carried out by British-born sui-
> cide bombers who had lived and been brought up in this country, who had
> received all its many advantages and yet who ultimately took their own lives
> and the lives of the wholly innocent, in the name of an ideology alien to
> everything this country stands for. Their emphasis was not on shared values
> but separate ones, values based on a warped distortion of the faith of
> Islam. . . . Multicultural Britain was never supposed to be a celebration of
> division; but of diversity. The right to be in a multicultural society was
> always, always implicitly balanced by a duty to integrate, to be part of Britain,
> to be British and Asian, British and black, British and white.

In 2006 Tony Blair also made controversial comments against the donning by British Muslim women of the *niqab* or full-face veil, calling it a "mark of separation" (Cowell 2006). These and other such remarks by prominent British politicians have provoked considerable frustration among British Muslims, galvanizing them to unite politically in order to protect themselves from the hostile intrusions of non-Muslims.

"Jamaat Is in London": Transnational Networks of Revivalist Islam

Within Bangladesh, Sylhet is well known as a historic center of Islam in Bangladesh, a fact of considerable pride for many Sylhetis. In 1303, the Sufi saint Hazrat Shah Jalal came to Sylhet from Mecca via Delhi and Dhaka. He and the 360 disciples (*awliya*) who traveled with him settled in the region, converting much of the local population from Hinduism and Buddhism to Islam. What resulted was an enduring regional culture that is deeply defined by Islam, specifically an Islam that is embedded in popular Sufi traditions, includ- ing that of reverence for Muslim saints. Today the mausoleum of Shah Jalal, located in the city of Sylhet, attracts visitors from all over Bangladesh and beyond. The rural landscape of Sylhet is also dotted by the shrines (*mazaar*) of his 360 disciples who are revered as pirs or saints. Many of these popular sites of prayer and homage have benefited over the years from the patronage of Sylhetis abroad and their financial contributions toward the upkeep and refur- bishment of the shrines.

As in Sylhet, in Britain as well, Islam has been integral to Bangladeshi identity and community life. As the migrants of the postwar years began to bring their families to Britain, they also built mosques and madrasas, led by

Imams who had come over from Sylhet. In general, the goal was to cultivate religion and to teach children about Islam in much in the same manner as had been done back home. As with other aspects of British Bangladeshi life at this time, the emphasis was on continuity rather than change. But in the 1980s, the landscape of British Bangladeshi Islam began to change, with revivalist Islam becoming an increasingly important strand. Among the forces giving rise to this change was the growth of British Muslim politics and the widespread politicization of British Muslims. Concurrently, there were shifts in Bangladesh as well, including the political rehabilitation and institutionalization of Jamaat-e-Islami.

When I spoke to British Bangladeshi community leaders in London about the rising influence of revivalist Islam, a number of them referred to the looming presence of the East London Mosque as symptomatic of it. The East London Mosque was built in 1985 with money from a variety of sources, including donations from British Muslims and from the governments of Saudi Arabia and Kuwait, as well as funding from the British government. The mosque proffers a revivalist Islam that is grounded in Deobandi traditions.[9] Along with its affiliate, the London Muslim Centre, the mosque is also an extensive service complex, with a school, gym, nursery, library, radio station, and youth center. The mosque has ties to the Islamic Forum Europe and its influential youth wing, the Young Muslim Organisation (Garbin 2005). In fact, it has been especially active in working with Muslim youth, partnering with local government authorities in neighborhood campaigns against drugs and gangs. In its extensive size and scope, the East London Mosque offers a sharp contrast to the London Jamme Masjid, also known as the Brick Lane Mosque or the Bangladeshi community mosque, which offers an approach to Islam that is grounded in the traditions of Sylhet. The Brick Lane Mosque maintains ties with the Bangladesh Welfare Association of London as well as U.K.-based Awami League groups (Garbin 2005).[10]

For many British Bangladeshis, especially those of the older generations, the East London Mosque and its growing influence have been troublesome on many levels. It is important to note that British Bangladeshis are by no means a homogeneous population with respect to their Bangladeshi political affiliations and loyalties. There are supporters not only of the Awami League but also the Bangladesh Nationalist Party (BNP), the Jatiya Party, Jamaat-e-Islami, and other political groups. However, the Awami League appears to have maintained a dominant albeit contested presence among them. As I described earlier in this chapter, the war of 1971 nationalized the British Bangladeshi community, giving it a sense of being a nationality-based diaspora—a community of Bangladeshis abroad. The 1971 war of independence and the important role of support for the country that was played by those in Britain have become enduring and defining elements of the collective memories and consciousness of the community. Thus, especially among older generation British Bangladeshis, there is a widespread sense of loyalty to the Awami League as the party that brought the country to independence. This tends to be coupled with revulsion toward Jamaat for the violent anti-liberation role that it played in the conflict.

For those British Bangladeshis who hold these viewpoints, the growth of the East London Mosque has been deeply troubling because it has also represented a transnational expansion of Jamaat-e-Islami. A number of mosques and Islamic organizations in Britain, including the East London Mosque, are believed to have close ties with Jamaat-e-Islami of Bangladesh. The one with the longest history is the Jamiatul Ummah, Bigland Street Mosque. This mosque is the home of the organization Da'watul Islam, which was formed in London by members of Jamaat-e-Islami Bangladeshi who took shelter in London after 1971; a number of them are accused of 1971 war crimes. Since that time, the Jamaat Bangladesh networks in Britain have proliferated, running through not only the East London Mosque but also such organizations as the Islamic Forum Europe, Muslim Aid U.K., the Muslim Council of Britain, and the East London Mosque. These connections have been made visible by such occasions as the public appearance of the Jamaat leader Delwar Hossain Sayedee at the East London Mosque to raise funds for his party (Hussain 2006). Thus the growth of the East London Mosque has also been seen by some to represent the expansion of Jamaat, in Bangladesh and beyond. In effect, Jamaat has successfully used the expanded political and institutional space for Muslim organizations in Britain that emerged in the 1990s in order to consolidate its transnational presence. It has used this space to develop a large international network, strengthening ties with Jamaat-e-Islami of Pakistan and other allied groups. In short, Britain has been an important node in the networks that exist between Jamaat-e-Islami and its allied movements to others across South Asia and beyond.

But the expansion of Jamaat has also produced countermovements in the British Bangladeshi community. Among these is the Nirmul Committee, whose central platform is the demand for trials of those who committed war crimes in 1971, including members of Jamaat. More generally, the Nirmul Committee affirms the ideology of secular nationalism that guided the country's founding in 1971. The organization has an active branch in London that has protested the appearance at the East London Mosque of the Jamaat leader Delwar Hossain Sayedee and demanded a revocation of his British visa. In 2000, the committee's leaders also formed the Swadhinata Trust, which is "a London based non-partisan secular Bengali group that works to promote

Bengali history and heritage amongst young people" (Swadhinata Trust 2010). The organization's activities have included workshops, seminars, and cultural performances, as well as a British Bengali oral history project. All of these aim to generate knowledge and pride, especially among younger British Bangladeshis, about their history and identity as Bengalis in Britain. However, as leaders of the organization informed me, the group has felt constrained in its activities by limited funding. In comparison to such religious organizations as the East London Mosque, they have had access to a narrower range of funding sources.

"I Am 100 Percent Muslim": Islam and the Intergenerational Divide

If for some British Bangladeshis, the growth of such institutions as the East London Mosque provokes anxiety on political grounds, for many others it is most troubling for its contributions to the growing intergenerational divide in the community. I often heard older-generation British Bangladeshis speak of how the youth of the community who had come of age in the 1990s and beyond were different from those of an earlier time. The British Bangladeshi youth of today were more inclined to reject a way of life that centered on transnational networks of kinship and home village, along with their attendant obligations. They questioned a way of life in which the needs of the kin group and the wishes of elders were the primary compass for one's life. These rejections, the elders felt, stemmed from the young's growing detachment from Bangladesh and Sylhet coupled with the growing lure of many British Muslim organizations with their incendiary messages.

Karim, a father of three boys, told me that he had forbidden his two younger sons to join the Young Muslim Organization after seeing how it had impacted his elder son, now aged eighteen. Karim lived with his family in Tower Hamlets, East London. He had worked for years at a restaurant before entering into a business that imported betel nut and leaves to sell in the British market. He seemed to have been caught off guard by the rebellion of his son, which he felt had been encouraged by the Young Muslim Organization, a group affiliated with the Islamic Forum Europe and the East London Mosque:

When my eldest son Javed was about fifteen, he joined the Young Muslim Organization (YMO) with some friends. I thought it was a good thing for him to mix with other Muslims and learn about Islam. In the neighborhoods around here, the environment is not so good for young men. There are opportunities for them to get into trouble. But then after he joined, we saw him change, his attitudes and behavior towards us changed. He went on camping trips with the YMO for days and days. Every night he was out of the house, attending their activities. He did not want to listen to us. What he would say to us is: "I only obey the Qu'ran, nothing else." And he argued all the time, he talked of things he had learned at the YMO meetings. He said he was 100 percent Muslim. Our country [Bangladesh] was nothing to him. We come from a long line of religious people and scholars; my older brother is the Imam of a large mosque in Sylhet. I would say to Javed, What is this that you're learning at the YMO? Are you learning to disrespect your parents? I tell you, they poisoned his mind.

Much has been written of the angst and anger that has pushed some British Muslim youth to become involved in movements of revivalist Islam (Glynn 2002; Jacobsen 1997; Masood 2005). There is the frustration born of persistent socioeconomic disadvantage, including widespread unemployment. There is the anger felt from being negatively stereotyped by mainstream British society. There is also the alienation felt from being unable to relate to the cultural orientation and priorities of parents, given limited exposure to the homeland. Under these conditions, revivalist Islam can articulate a sense of difference from mainstream society that is both sharply distinct and affirmative in its sense of superior morality. It also provides a sense of membership in a global community that transcends citizenship and nationality. And by offering as it does a well-defined set of rules by which to live one's life, it may appeal to those who feel a sense of moral and cultural void in their lives.

To further explore these themes I turn next to the accounts of three British Bangladeshis for whom involvements in British Muslim organizations and groups were an important part of their lives.

Tanvir: A Professional British Muslim

Tanvir, in his mid-twenties, had been born in Birmingham and spent his early years there before his family moved to East London. Throughout our interview, Tanvir described himself as unusual—an outlier in his family and the community into which he was born. In contrast to those around him, he had done very well at school. He had gone to a well-regarded university outside of London and he now held a management post at an international bank. His parents and siblings were still living in East London. He had, however, chosen to live in another part of the city, sharing a flat with friends from his university days.

As we sat at a café just outside Banglatown, sipping cappuccinos, Tanvir told me that he came to East London on the weekend to spend as much time as possible with his family. When he was there he liked to counsel his younger brother and cousins about their schoolwork and career plans. He also assisted

his mother and other elderly relatives with such matters as how best to deal
with the housing authorities and paying bills. At one point, I asked him if he
participated in any Bangladeshi associations. I was a little taken aback by the
vehemence of his negative response:

> T: Oh no, no . . . bloody waste of time. They quarrel a lot. I also think that
> the Bengalis here need to look at education, why the results are not better
> for us and why Bengalis are not moving ahead like the Indians or the
> Caribbeans.
>
> NK: Do you think Bengalis should integrate into British society?
>
> T: Hmm . . . yes and no. Yes, as far as education and jobs. But we are
> Muslims, that's the key to it. I always see myself as Muslim first and
> Muslim last. I am 100 percent Muslim. There is no compromise to it. I've
> always tried to make sure that I know enough about British or Western
> culture—the literature, the art, the classical music. No one can say that
> I'm ignorant, not good enough. But I have not forgotten my roots. When
> I compare myself to my white colleagues at work, I definitely see a differ-
> ence. I feel that as a Muslim I have a sense of discipline and purpose about
> myself which is quite lacking in the average white person. I don't drink
> and smoke, I don't womanize, and I work hard. I know what is important—
> my commitment to being a good Muslim.

Tanvir saw himself as a Muslim professional. He was an active member of
an organization that aimed to offer a forum for educated British Muslims,
a place for them to engage in open intellectual discourse, discussions about
Islam, community activism, and social networking. Even as he continued to
maintain ties with his family and the community in which he had grown up, he
felt himself to be distant from them by virtue of his education and career
achievements. In fact, with respect to these relationships he perceived his role
to be that of a bridge to mainstream British society, or perhaps a role model for
those aspiring to enter into it. He placed little importance on his Bangladeshi
origins. He had been to Sylhet and his home village many times as a child,
although not in recent years. He found the idea of going for another visit
"interesting" but not a priority at all. In fact, his relatives had been urging him
to go to Sylhet to find a bride. He did not see this as an attractive option for
himself. He wanted a partner who was a committed Muslim as well as a professional who was at ease in mainstream British society in much the same manner
as himself. I asked him to elaborate on what exactly it meant to be a committed
Muslim. He spoke of the importance of aspiration and effort; he felt himself to
be committed by virtue of the fact that he was working toward living as closely

as possible to what was written in the Qu'ran. He was aware that he did not fulfill this goal, but he was driven by a desire to do so in the future, saying, "Being a good Muslim means living by the Qu'ran, as close to the words as possible. I would like to pray at the mosque five times a day and Inshallah, someday I will be able to do that. Right now I'm working at a typical European bank. But I'm trying to move to a bank or at least a branch that follows Islamic principles of banking. Someday I hope to open such a bank myself."

Asif: Tablighi Jamaat and Following the Call to Travel and Preach

I interviewed Asif at the home of his uncle in London. When I arrived at the appointed time I was told that Asif had gone for prayer at the nearby mosque and would return shortly. As I waited in the living room, Asif's wife brought me tea. She was wearing a long black burkha that covered her hair but not her face. She told me that she and Asif were expecting their first child. They had married a year ago in Maulvibazar, Sylhet, where she had grown up. Asif, however, who was in his late twenties, had been born and raised in Manchester. When I asked how the two had come to be married, she spoke of how her father was active in a mosque in Maulvibazaar. When Asif had traveled there and gone to the mosque, the elders of the mosque had conferred and decided that she and Asif should marry.

Asif soon came in, apologizing for being late. He was a tall, fair-skinned, bearded man who was wearing a white cap and a long, black robe with a leather jacket over it. Unlike his wife, he spoke to me mainly in English, clearly feeling more comfortable in it than Bengali or the Sylheti dialect. He asked me many questions about my project, indicating that he had read some sociology and found it interesting. When I asked him what he was doing these days, he said that he had just returned from a trip to Sylhet. He had gone there on a trip that had been organized by the Tablighi Jamaat mosque to which he belonged. Tablighi Jamaat is an international Islamic movement that was founded in the early twentieth century in India. Among the notable features of the movement is the requirement for members to regularly go on missionary trips during which they work to revive the faith of Muslims, encouraging them to emulate the life of the Prophet. The movement maintains a stance of detachment from politics and worldly affairs. However, Tablighi Jamaat has also come under growing suspicion in Britain and other Western countries for its possible links to militant Islamist groups.

Asif indicated that he had been drawn to the Tablighi Jamaat movement as a teenager growing up in Britain. His elder brother, who had raised him, had also frequented a Tablighi Jammat mosque. But as Asif's involvements grew, so did a rift between the two. Asif was urged by his brother to find a job so that he could contribute money to the household. After a period of intense conflict, Asif found a job as a caretaker of the mosque that they both frequented. He soon dropped out of school and moved into the mosque. Since that time, Asif had traveled to many different parts of the world on missionary trips. Besides Bangladesh, he had been to Pakistan and many parts of Europe. He told me that he was about to go to Sylhet again; he planned to travel with others to several remote areas in order to revive the faith of people there. When I asked him about whether he had thought about getting a job in Britain, especially with a baby on the way, his answer was vague:

A: Allah has always shown me the way. When I was on the brink of ruin, Allah showed me the way.

NK: But you will need money for the baby. . . .

A: [Laughing]. Sister, you have lived too long in America, where they worship money. We will manage. Look, if necessary I can get a job for some time. But I will follow the call to travel, to invite Muslim brothers to the path of Allah. This is written for us.

At one point I asked Asif about how Tablighi Jamaat was viewed in Britain. In the soft and melodious tones that he had used throughout the interview, he spoke of the war against Muslims that was being waged by the United States and Britain. Mosques in Britain were under constant surveillance. Traveling had become more difficult; several leaders of the mosque had not been able to get a U.S. visa. But he bore no resentment for these difficulties. He affirmed the nonpolitical stance of those who were part of the movement, "Sister, I invite you to come to a women's meeting. In the end, the truth will prevail. They [pointing outside] think that all of this is important, their guns, their bombs, their money. But in the end they will face the anger of Allah. It is written. We have no interest in politics. The politics of Britain, the politics of Bangladesh; we have no interest in them."

Zarina: Finding Her Voice as a Muslim Woman

I met Zarina at a local social services office where she had been working for about a year. The organization offered after-school academic tutoring to children. Besides working there, Zarina was also attending a local university for a degree in education. Her goal was to eventually work as a primary school teacher at an Islamic school. Zarina was in her early twenties, and she had been born and raised in Britain. She was wearing a black sequined headscarf that covered her hair and entire upper body, along with jeans and black high-heeled boots. As we settled down to talk in an office that was empty, I asked her if she wanted to be interviewed in English, Bengali, or Sylheti dialect. She laughed and told me, "Definitely, English." She had some knowledge of Sylheti dialect but none of standard Bengali.

As we chatted, Zarina told me that she was going to Sylhet the next week. When I asked her if she was going for any specific reason, she smiled shyly and told me that she was getting married. A year ago, her family had arranged for her to marry Samir, the son of a distant uncle who was a wealthy businessman in Sylhet. Samir and his family had actually visited Britain last year and Zarina had spent some time (supervised by elders) with her future husband. After he left, they had exchanged e-mails and talked over the phone; Zarina gradually became sure that he was her "Mr. Right."

Zarina was an active member and leader of the women's section of a Muslim youth organization. Her brother (one year older) had joined the men's section of the organization first and then persuaded her to try out the women's section. She began attending the weekly meetings and other activities. There she blossomed; she found a sense of purpose and independence that she had not had before:

> Z: We [the organization] are very active. We do a lot of community work, fund-raising, and we have seminars and speakers on many topics: environmental issues, Muslim issues. We also study the Qu'ran together and also with the help of teachers. It's helped me a lot. I came to believe in myself and think independently. My Mum and Dad are not as restrictive towards their children as a lot of the Bengali families around here. But still, they have a different mentality. Like they don't think that women should work. I want to have a career and they've come to accept that. It was only by learning about Islam, the true Islam that I had the courage to stand up to them.
>
> NK: How about your future husband, what does he think?
>
> Z: Oh, he supports my career and what I want to do. He was telling me that things have changed in Bangladesh; there are a lot of women there who work. And my brother also showed Samir around, took him to the mosque and had long conversations with him. He's fine. He understands that in Bangladesh they use Islam to justify why women shouldn't work or go out or speak their mind. That is contrary to Islam.

Zarina described herself to be "very close" to her parents, who seemed to accept her involvements in the Muslim women's organization to which she belonged. These involvements had given her access to an Islamic discourse that legitimated an expansion of women's roles and activities in the public sphere, beyond what was expected in the traditional culture of Sylhet. In contrast to the stereotype of coercion that often surrounds arranged marriage, Zarina seemed quite happy to accept the match that had been negotiated for her by her parents. Of course, it helped that Samir's family was wealthy and relatively cosmopolitan; they lived in Sylhet city and they traveled abroad frequently. And so Zarina did not feel a large cultural gap with Samir.

The Intergenerational Divide on Both Sides of the Atlantic

In many respects, the accounts of younger generation British Bangladeshis and their engagements with religion echo those of their American counterparts as I have described in the previous chapter. Informed by global political and cultural trends as well as family and community pressures, in both settings the younger generation emphasized the primacy of their Muslim identity. They also rejected Bengali Islam as practiced by their families in favor of what some have called "the new Islam" (Glynn 2002)—an Islam that claims authenticity and true commitment to the words of the Qu'ran. And finally, in both settings, the ethos of revivalist Islam was an organizing feature, albeit a fluid and contested one, of the younger generation's religious perspectives.

But underlying these broad commonalities were also some notable differences. More than in the United States, in Britain the younger generation's turn to Islam has been accompanied by an anger born of persistent socioeconomic disadvantage and exclusion from mainstream society. In general, these are conditions that are more likely to provoke the embrace of separatist and extremist viewpoints. Concurrently, these same conditions of segregation also mean that even with their involvements in British Muslim forums, younger-generation British Bangladeshis tend to remain ensconced within the tight-knit Bangladeshi social worlds of their parents. Thus in comparison to Bangladeshi Americans, they are less likely to actively disengage from their Bangladeshi affiliation. In the British context, as well, the gravitation of the younger generation toward the new Islam has generated a community discourse of intergenerational conflict and crisis that has given public visibility to these developments and also disseminated a sense of their potentially grave implications for British Bangladeshi life. These developments have, moreover, become a focus of community politics, actively opposed by groups that are aligned with the secular nationalist traditions of 1971. In their ability to attract attention and gain sympathy, such opposition benefits from the British Bangladeshi community's collective sense of history and pride in 1971 and their own role as a community at that time. In the United States, where the Bangladeshi community has grown only since the 1980s, secular nationalist groups have not been able to similarly draw on a popular reserve of collective memories and sentiment to generate public concern over religious trends among the young.

Transnationalism in Motion

In the post–World War II period, strategies of community transnationalism, with their emphasis on transnational kin and home village networks, came to organize British Bangladeshi life. Even as community transnationalism has remained important, since that time the British Bangladeshi transnational sphere has also expanded. With the independence of Bangladesh in 1971 and the growing engagements of British Bangladeshis in local British politics came new transnational opportunities. Especially as dual citizens, British Bangladeshis have had the ability to appeal to both the Bangladeshi and British states in their efforts to expand the transnational sphere.

These expansionary efforts are, perhaps, especially significant given the growing frailty of community transnationalism. Younger-generation British Bangladeshis are increasingly doubtful about the social and moral logic of kin and home village that guided the lives of their parents. More generally, there are the challenges to community transnationalism that stem from the unfolding forces of modernity. The small towns and villages of Sylhet are not immune from the forces of urbanization, the global media, and other modernizing developments. We can expect these changes, along with others, to shape the course of British Bangladeshi transnationalism in the years to come.

CHAPTER 6

Muslim Encounters in the Global Economy

LABOR MIGRATION TO THE GULF STATES AND MALAYSIA

The very idea of international migration is suggestive of change, of altered social and political circumstances that produce novel opportunities as well as challenges for those who are part of such movements. In the case of Muslim migrants, the experience of becoming a religious minority is widely understood to be the critical shift implied by international migration. Reflecting a predominance of research on Muslim movements to Western societies, there has been much attention to issues of Muslim migrant integration into societies that are largely non-Muslim. But what of the many Muslim international migrations of today that involve the movement of Muslims to Muslim majority societies? What are the dynamics of identity under these conditions, when it is not Muslim affiliation that sets the migrant apart in the destination society?

In this chapter, I consider these questions as I explore the experiences of Bangladeshis who migrate to the Muslim majority societies of the GCC states and Malaysia. Unlike those who have been the focus of previous chapters, these Bangladeshis do not become a religious minority when they go abroad. Furthermore, for the vast majority of Bangladeshis who go to work in the GCC states and Malaysia, the experience of international migration is definitively defined by its temporal, political, and social limits. Recruited as contract labor, they are expected to enter into the receiving society for a brief and specified period of time and work without the presence of their families with them. After fulfilling their contract, they are expected to leave, creating no disturbance and leaving behind no footprints—no apparent trace of the fact that they were once there. As in the case of Turkish guest workers in Germany or of Mexican braceros in the United States, the history of international migration is filled with examples of how these receiving society expectations may not always be fulfilled. Temporary workers can drift into permanent settlement, often to the consternation of their reluctant host states. But in the circumstances explored here, of Bangladeshi workers in the Arab Gulf states and in Malaysia, the potential for such drifts have been extremely limited, sharply curbed by a tightly woven web of restrictive policies. As we will see, the labor of these Bangladeshis is embedded in a regime of difference—of institutionalized distinction and disadvantage from the citizens of the destination country.

THE POLITICS OF LABOR MIGRATION FROM BANGLADESH

In 2009, the creeping tentacles of a major global economic recession began to make their way into international migration streams out of Bangladesh. Newspapers in Bangladesh carried distressing reports of labor migrants returning home, having lost their jobs abroad. For many of these returnees, their time abroad had been prematurely cut short, robbing them of the chance to recoup the costs that they had incurred in order to migrate, and so plunging them into economic destitution (see Palma 2009a; 2009b). The sad plight of these returning workers gained dramatic coverage in March 2009 when the Malaysian government announced that it was canceling the work visas that it had issued for more than fifty-five thousand Bangladeshis. The migrants reported paying about 2,500 dollars each to recruiters to obtain three-year employment contracts in Malaysia (Daily Star 2009b).

Although at the time of the announcement by the Malaysian government most of the would-be migrants were still in Bangladesh, waiting to go, several hundred had already flown to Malaysia. There they found themselves in the unfortunate position of being stranded at the airport and unable to enter the country. In an attempt to avert a possible domestic political crisis, the foreign minister of the newly elected Awami League government of Bangladesh rushed to Kuala Lumpur to try and persuade the Malaysian government to reverse its policies. As reported in the press, the ensuing discussions revealed a variety of factors that sparked the Malaysian decision to not honor the visas, including concerns about the tendency for Bangladeshi workers to drift into undocumented status and become a source of social problems for the country.[1]

In fact, 2009 was not the first time that the Malaysian government had voiced anxieties about Bangladeshi workers and decided to close the doors to them. In 1994, Malaysia agreed to recruit Bangladeshi workers, but then imposed a ban on their entry in 1997. The doors reopened ten years later, in 2007, before closing again in 2009. Furthermore, this "now it's open, now it's not" pattern has been apparent not only in the case of Malaysia but other important destinations, as well. Kuwait, for example, imposed a ban on Bangladeshi labor migrants in 1999, lifted it in 2000, and reimposed it in 2006.

Thus even as the global economic recession of 2008 has added an external source of volatility to Bangladeshi international labor movements, disruptions due to regulatory factors have been chronic rather than exceptional.

For the Bangladesh state, the management of this volatility as well as other issues surrounding the international labor migration of its citizens have been increasingly important political matters. This reflects the growing significance of remittances—the money sent back by Bangladeshis abroad—for the national economy. As shown in figure 4, remittances into Bangladesh grew steadily in the opening years of the twenty-first century, peaking in 2007 before declining in response to the 2008 global recession. In the 2007–2008 financial year, official remittances into Bangladesh totaled seven billion nine hundred thousand dollars, making it the largest source of foreign exchange followed by the export garments manufacturing sector (Paul 2008). In response to these trends, international labor migration or "manpower export" has become an increasingly important focus for the country. In 1990, the Bangladesh government established the Wage Earners Welfare Fund. The fund, which requires contributions from each migrant worker, was set up to help migrant workers and their families in emergency situations such as illness, death, or legal problems in the receiving countries. And in 2002, the Ministry of Expatriates Welfare and Overseas Employment was created with the goal of facilitating labor migration, exploring new labor markets and ensuring the welfare of Bangladeshi migrant workers. Since the 1980s, successive governments in Bangladesh have also tried to secure and expand outflows of labor migrants through diplomatic negotiations with labor-receiving countries.

Bangladeshis and the Migrant Worker
Regimes of the GCC States and Malaysia

Since the 1970s, the primary labor migrant destinations for Bangladeshis have involved the Arab Gulf states—members of the GCC or Gulf Cooperation Council (see figure 4). The GCC, also known as Cooperation Council for the Arab States of the Gulf (CCASG), is a trade bloc that was formed in 1981 among the six oil-producing states of Bahrain, Kuwait, Oman, Qatar, Saudi Arabia, and the United Arab Emirates. Since the oil boom of the 1970s and the economic developments generated by it, the GCC states have relied on an international labor force. From oil production, construction, and domestic service to finance and trade, workers from other Arab countries as well from South Asia and Southeast Asia have been recruited to fill a variety of jobs. According to the official figures of the Bureau of Manpower, Employment and Training (BMET) of the Government of Bangladesh, over the 1976–2008 period, about five million Bangladeshis had gone to work in the GCC states; Saudi Arabia and

United Arab Emirates were the top country destinations. The majority have
been men, with a predominance of semi-skilled and unskilled (66 percent)
workers.

In the 1990s, growing national concerns in the GCC states about economic
dependence on foreign workers resulted in such programs as "Saudization" or
"Kuwaitization" that aimed to move citizens into jobs previously occupied
by migrants. Nonetheless, as the first decade of the twenty-first century closes,
foreign workers, including Bangladeshis, remain an important presence in the
GCC states. Indeed, in the United Arab Emirates (UAE) and in Kuwait, nonci-
tizens were estimated in 2004 to outnumber nationals, constituting 81 percent
and 64 percent of the total populations, respectively. In Saudi Arabia, the
largest of the GCC states, the foreign population was approximately six
million, or 27 percent, of the total population. In all of the GCC countries,
nonnationals are a majority of the labor force (Kapiszewski 2006).[2]

Although the GCC states remain the dominant destination, international
labor migration from Bangladesh has also expanded since the 1990s to include
a wider range of countries, including Japan, Lebanon, Malaysia, Mauritius,
Singapore, and South Korea. Of these destinations, Malaysia has been the most
important, officially receiving 686,334 Bangladeshi workers from 1976 to 2007
(BMET 2007). For Malaysia, the import of foreign labor surged in the 1980s
because of labor shortages produced by the success of the country's export-
driven industrialization policies. Workers from neighboring Indonesia as well
as many other Asian countries—Bangladesh, Burma, India, Nepal, Pakistan,
Philippines, and Thailand—were sought for the plantation sector as well as the
booming construction and manufacturing industries. By the end of 2007,
Malaysia had an estimated two million two hundred thousand foreign workers,
constituting almost a quarter of the country's labor force. In 2008, rising rates
of unemployment among Malaysians intensified concerns about the presence
of foreign workers, especially the large numbers of those without legal documentation. The government responded by stepping up efforts to detain and
deport unauthorized foreign workers, and also asking employers to fire foreign
workers before laying off Malaysian workers (Migration News 2008). Whether
these measures can successfully restrict foreign workers remains an open question, given the extent to which the Malaysian economy has relied on migrant
labor in the past, especially for jobs that have not been attractive for citizens.

Not unlike other migrant receiving countries around the world, the GCC
states and Malaysia have approached and treated international migrant workers differently based on their skill levels and class resources. Professional and
high-skilled workers as well as wealthy entrepreneurs have been subject to less
restriction and enjoyed far more hospitable treatment than less privileged

migrants. Among other things, they have been more likely to have had the option of bringing family members with them during their time abroad. The class-differentiated character of migration policies is likely to become even more pronounced in the future, as countries strive to position themselves favorably in the global economy of information and communications technology by actively recruiting "the best and the brightest" (Bunnell 2002). But whatever their social class background, foreign workers in the GCC states and Malaysia share limited opportunities for permanent settlement and the acquisition of citizenship in the receiving country. For the most part, naturalization in these countries has been limited to the foreign wives of national men, and citizenship has not been automatically granted to those born in the territory.[3]

Guided by this framework of restricted citizenship, the migrant worker regimes of the GCC states and Malaysia have sought to achieve several goals. For low-wage migrants, the aim has been to access a labor force that is flexible in supply, nonthreatening to citizens, and of course willing to perform low-status jobs for highly competitive wages. Under ideal conditions, such a workforce provides labor without making demands on state resources or legitimacy. It also offers flexibility in that worker supply and characteristics can be adjusted in response to whatever economic and political exigencies may arise. Bans on workers from one country or region can quickly be followed by opening the doors to others who can readily fill the jobs; the expansion of the global economy has ensured that low-wage workers are never in short supply. In the GCC states, for example, a policy of bringing workers from neighboring Arab countries such as Egypt and Yemen was abandoned in the 1980s in favor of labor from Asia. Underlying the shift were political concerns, such as fears that these Arab workers would demand political inclusion in the receiving states on the basis of shared Arab heritage (Kapiszewski 2001; 2006). In Malaysia, an implicit policy of "national switching"—of periodically shifting worker recruitment from one country to another—has been informed by anxieties about the impact of foreign workers on the balance of power between the three major ethnic groups (Malay, Chinese, Indian) in the country (Dannecker 2005).

In what follows I turn to the institutional heart of the low-wage migrant worker regime in these receiving states—the sponsorship system. As we will see, although the sponsorship system has been the key mechanism by which the receiving states have sought to restrict and police low-wage migrant workers, the system has nevertheless generated its own set of problems. As a result, toward the end of the first decade of the twenty-first century, there were important signs that the sponsorship system in its prior form was on its way out as many of these receiving states began to initiate reforms.

The Rise and Demise of the Sponsorship System

Since the 1970s, the official system of recruitment for low-wage foreign workers in the GCC states and Malaysia has involved a system of employer-based sponsorship. To provide a general overview: the process begins with potential sponsors stepping forward with guaranteed jobs for the foreign workers, either in their own business or in that of others to whom they are providing the service of procuring foreign labor. After workers from the sending state are identified, contracts are signed between the sponsor and worker in which the terms of employment are laid out, such as the type of job, pay, hours, provisions for leave, and other conditions. Travel and work visas are issued only after all the relevant documents are inspected and approved by government officials in both the sending and receiving countries.

For the receiving states, the sponsorship system, at least in its idealized form, has been seen as a means of accessing a labor force that is flexible and readily adjustable to market shifts. And especially when accompanied by laws that impose strict limits on the duration of the work contract available to migrants, the system also ensures a rotating labor pool. This is useful for restricting the opportunities for migrants to become socially embedded and to seek permanent settlement in the country to which they have come to work. Most important, perhaps, the migrant dependency on the sponsor that is at the heart of the system can also potentially serve as a means of surveillance and policing of migrants on behalf of the state. Under the terms of the sponsorship, it is the sponsor's role to oversee the legalities of the migrant's stay in the country and to bring any visa infringements to the attention of the authorities.

But as is often the case with state efforts to regulate migration flows, the sponsorship system has not always worked as intended. As suggested by the case of Bangladeshi labor migrants to the GCC states and Malaysia, its unintended consequences have included the growth of a transnational industry composed of an array of intermediary services in the foreign worker recruitment and placement process. These services include, for example, the entrepreneurial "scouting" agents in Bangladesh who locate would-be migrants in rural parts of the country and negotiate on their behalf with recruiting agents located in cities. There are the recruiting agencies in Bangladesh that locate jobs abroad and arrange the necessary paperwork for migrants. And there are the sponsoring companies in the receiving states that work with local employers as well as recruiting agencies in Bangladesh to identify job vacancies for Bangladeshi workers.

As one might expect, this transnational foreign worker industry has mushroomed as labor migration flows out of Bangladesh have grown. The intermediary service nodes have multiplied, resulting in higher transaction costs that are often passed down to migrants. According to a 2009 national survey by the IOM (International Organisation for Migration) in Bangladesh, intermediaries generated almost 60 percent of the costs of going abroad for Bangladeshi labor migrants; these costs were the highest in South Asia (*Daily Star* 2010). Furthermore, in an ugly dynamic that has received much media coverage in Bangladesh, some intermediary service providers have not refrained from engaging in dishonest practices in order to jack up their profits. That is, in operations that involve the transnational collusion of multiple businesses as well as corrupt government officials, false documents are produced and agreements reached over jobs that actually do not exist or are in fact quite different from what was represented in the contract.

In 2009, several GCC countries announced reforms of the sponsorship system. Bahrain declared that it would replace employer-based sponsorship with a system in which the government would take over the responsibility of providing international migrant workers with work permits that would be issued for renewable periods of two years (*Daily Star* 2009c; 2009d). In addition, both Saudi Arabia and Kuwait announced that they would allow workers to switch jobs, thus ending the complete dependency of workers on sponsors—circumstances that had given rise to frequent abuse and exploitation of workers. While the actual consequences of these developments are yet to become fully clear, they undoubtedly do signal important shifts in the foreign worker regime of the GCC states. In what follows I further explore some of the driving forces behind the reforms.

The Problem of Illegals and the Racialization of Bangladeshi Workers

Among the developments that have driven the call for reform of the sponsorship system is the presence of substantial numbers of undocumented foreign workers in the GCC states and in Malaysia. As analysts of the GCC *kafala* (sponsorship system) have noted, the tendency for migrant workers to drift into the underground economy reflects the costs of the recruitment and migration process, costs that have been inflated by the ever-expanding transnational migrant worker industry (Shaham 2008). Employers may prefer to hire an undocumented migrant worker over a documented one, given the high costs of freshly recruiting and training workers from abroad. For the migrant workers, too, given how much it has cost them to get there, they may feel it worthwhile to overstay their visas and to work abroad for a longer period of time rather than return home.

Furthermore, in tragic fallout of the corrupt practices of the transnational foreign worker industry, the worker may find himself to be "illegal" upon arrival because of the fraudulent documents that he (often unknowingly) had purchased. Under these conditions he is basically trapped, unable to pay the government fines that are often imposed on illegals at the time of departure, not to mention the loans incurred for the costs of migration. Thus in describing the growth of an undocumented foreign labor population in the GCC states in the 1990s, Shaham notes, "Unsupervised, many agencies thrived in selling sponsorship documents that had either been obtained illegally from shell companies or were not backed by the employment offer presented to the workers. Upon arrival in the Gulf, these workers found themselves underemployed, underpaid or in debt, and resorted to the illegal job market" (2008: 5).

For the receiving states, demands for reform of the sponsorship system have stemmed in part from the acknowledged role that the system has played in generating an undocumented migrant worker population. Across migrant receiving societies around the world, it is not unusual, especially during periods of economic and political crisis, for migrants to be blamed for social problems. Because they give such anger an air of legitimacy, "illegals" or those who have violated visa laws may be a convenient target of public ire. Yet migrants of varied legal status—both "legals" and "illegals"—are affected by these currents of animus, which often take on a racial character.

In the GCC states and Malaysia, low-wage workers from Bangladesh have often been seen as naturally different from and inferior to nationals of the receiving society as well as other, "better" migrant groups, at least in certain times. In these racial constructions, Bangladeshis have been associated with a natural inclination toward criminality. Indeed, many of the receiving state bans on the recruitment of Bangladeshis have occurred in response to specific incidents of crime in which a Bangladeshi migrant was the perpetrator. Kuwait's 1999 ban (lifted in 2000) on Bangladeshi migrants, for example, occurred after a horrific incident in which a Bangladeshi worker murdered his elderly Kuwaiti employer, stole his money, and left the country. And as reported in the *Gulf Daily News* of Bahrain, a proposal to ban Bangladeshi workers was put forward in the Parliament of Bahrain in 2008, after the death of a Bahrain national who was killed in an attack after an argument with a Bangladeshi mechanic (Pradeep 2008). Commenting on the proposal, a member of the Bahrain Parliament noted that Bangladeshis stood out in their unsavory character not only from Bahrainis but from other Asians as well: "It has been observed that people from the Bangladesh community are involved in many ugly crimes and murders. We don't want to live with people of such criminal nature. We have been receiving many complaints and requests from Bahrainis to get rid of Bangladeshis from their neighborhood. Why should we live our lives like mice in our own country because of foreigners? Bangladeshis seem to have a culture different even from other Asian expatriates, which we find hard to adjust to" (Pradeep 2008).

Besides these concerns about the criminal proclivities of Bangladeshis, the often hostile reception to Bangladeshi workers has also been embedded in more general fears about the cultural impacts of international migrants in these highly migrant-dependent societies. As Kapiszewski (2001) observes, in the GCC states, rapid social change in combination with the high proportion of foreign workers has generated considerable anxiety about a loss of cultural identity. There have been public debates about the declining influence of local culture in the home, especially in the raising of children, because of the wide-spread use in the GCC states of nannies and other domestics from Asia. In Malaysia, fears about Bangladeshis and their inclination toward criminality have been accompanied by anxieties about the alleged tendency of Bangladeshi men to enter into unions with Malaysian women as a way of remaining in the country. Despite the presence of laws that prohibit foreign workers from marrying citizens, Bangladeshi migrant men have been accused of trying to court Malaysian women in order to stay in the country. In the late 1990s, the Malaysian media gave voice to these fears by reporting on clashes between Malaysian and Bangladeshi men that were supposedly over women but later discovered to be over money (Abdul-Aziz 2001). And in 2001, the matter was discussed in the Malaysian Parliament as a social problem. It was alleged that the women in these unions often became single mothers, left behind to fend for themselves as the Bangladeshi men returned home, perhaps to the other wife that they had left there. As Dannecker (2005) has noted, a notion of Malaysian women as vic-timized and in need of protection ran through these parliamentary discussions.

International Pressures for Reform

In 2008, Kuwait was rocked by a general strike held by thousands of Asian migrant cleaning workers, many from Bangladesh. The protests had begun with a dispute over the nonpayment of salaries to the workers of a particular com-pany, and then rapidly spread through the entire cleaning industry. With a back-drop of soaring inflation rates, the workers had asked for better pay and working conditions. As the protests turned violent, there were clashes with the police fol-lowed by the arrests and deportation of hundreds of workers. Besides increasing security patrol in "expatriate bachelor" (i.e., male labor migrant) areas, Kuwait's Interior Ministry issued statements warning of strict and firm action against any further agitation. The Kuwaiti government also announced that it would not renew the residency visas of Bangladeshis in menial jobs because of the threat they posed to state security as well as the negative international publicity they had brought to Kuwait (Barrett 2008; *Daily Star* 2008; *Kuwait Times* 2008).

As highlighted by the 2008 Kuwait strike, for the GCC states and Malaysia, the task of managing migrant workers has become increasingly onerous.

The 2009 GCC initiatives toward reform of the sponsorship system have emerged in relation to these problems, which have created a greater willingness on the part of the receiving state to acknowledge that the existing practices need to change. Among the forces that have operated to generate support for reform is a growing transnational migrant worker rights sector. Composed of fluid networks of NGOs that span the sending and receiving societies, the sector is also informed and supported by a larger international human rights regime (Alekry 2005; Piper 2004; Piper 2005). Affirming the concerns of migrant worker rights groups, for example, the well-established international watchdog organization Human Rights Watch has in recent years issued a number of highly critical reports (2006; 2009) on the treatment of foreign workers in the UAE.

Since the 1990s, a cluster of organizations has developed in Bangladesh that is devoted to protecting the rights of the country's international migrant workers. These include WARBE, the Welfare Association of Repatriated Bangladeshi Employees, which was formed in 1997 with the goal of promoting the rights and welfare of Bangladeshi international migrant workers. The Refugee and Migratory Movements Research Unit (RMMRU) at Dhaka University has been a leader in research and advocacy work on behalf of migrant workers. There is also a broad coalition of human rights organizations in Bangladesh that have taken a public stand on these issues, including such groups as Ain-o-Shalish-Kendra, BSFEHR (Bangladesh Society for the Enforcement of Human Rights), and Manusher Jonno Foundation. In their advocacy on behalf of migrant workers, these groups are also increasingly enmeshed in transnational linkages and networks that connect them, in both direct and indirect ways, with organizations in the migrant receiving states.

In the receiving countries, the work of advocacy for foreign workers has involved the associations formed by the migrants themselves as well as local human rights organizations. Even as these groups have been constrained in their activities by state restrictions that are present to varying degrees across the GCC states and Malaysia, they have nonetheless been an important part of the transnational Bangladeshi labor migrant rights sector. In Bahrain, for example, those who have called for reform of the sponsorship system include the Bahrain Human Rights Society, which has drawn attention to how the system "contradicts international conventions in human rights" (*Daily Star* 2009c). In Malaysia, an organization called Tenaganita has played an important role in exposing poor working conditions for migrant Bangladeshis and also in providing legal services to those in Malaysian detention for visa violations.

Besides its activities in the receiving states, the transnational Bangladeshi labor migrant rights sector has also taken on the Bangladesh state in its activism. The sector has actively lobbied the Bangladesh government, calling for better protection and opportunities for Bangladeshi migrant workers. Its victories include the introduction by the Bangladesh government in 2006 of the Overseas Employment Policy, a policy brief that was produced in consultation with a variety of groups, including different government ministries and NGOs devoted to human rights and migrant welfare. In this comprehensive statement, Bangladesh affirms the goal of expanding overseas employment as a strategy of economic development for the country. Also mentioned are such goals as ensuring that remittances travel through official channels and that remittances are used by the communities that receive them in productive ways. The rights of both men and women to choose to go abroad are affirmed, thus signaling a shift away from the ambivalence of the past in state policy toward the migration of women.

Another focus of activism has been the passage of the 1990 UN Convention on the Protection of the Rights of All Migrant Workers and Members of Their Families: "a set of binding international standards to address the treatment, welfare and human rights of both documented and undocumented migrants as well as the obligations and responsibilities on the part of the sending and receiving States." As of 2009, Bangladesh had signed but not ratified the convention. In arguing for its ratification by Bangladesh, Tasneem Siddiqui (2007) notes that its passage has been blocked by fears that it might discourage labor receiving countries from recruiting Bangladeshis for work in their countries. Quite apart from whether or not these anxieties are justified, their presence among Bangladeshi government officials highlights the felt weakness of those who represent Bangladesh in their dealings with other, more powerful players in the global economy. The importance of migrant remittances for the Bangladesh economy has resulted in the government's general reluctance to intervene politically on behalf of its migrant citizens. In a newspaper column, Farid Bakht (2006) bemoans this passive stance and makes an impassioned plea for the government to take better care of these "unsung heroes of the economy":

> Turn off the tap of migrant remittances and you shut down the government, economy and normal politics. . . . Because we are poor and we have failed economic policies, we are unable to provide jobs to the one million people who come onto the job market every year. With 250,000 flying out every year as temporary migrants, we are avoiding a social explosion and at the same time receiving irreplaceable foreign exchange. . . . The majority of these migrants are poor, badly educated, and unaware of their rights or their future. They need their government . . . to ensure that their rights are being protected.

MODERNITY, ISLAM, AND THE GOOD SOCIETY

For many international labor migrants from Bangladesh, the experience of traveling abroad and living and working in another country is a novel one. Professionals and highly skilled workers from Bangladesh (and elsewhere) tend to be seasoned travelers, adept at dealing with procedures for showing passports and boarding airplanes, and familiar with the sights and sounds of skyscrapers, high-speed trains, and the other trappings of global cities. But this tends not to be the case for low-wage international labor migrants. Indeed, a number of the labor migrants we interviewed had never been to Dhaka, the capital city of the country, before making their way for the first time to the city's international airport in order to board a plane that would take them to work abroad. In places such as Dubai, they could find themselves standing next to such immense structures as the Burj Khalifa, which in 2010 was the tallest building in the world.

For many labor migrants to the GCC states and Malaysia, then, going abroad to work was an excursion into modernity. Concurrently, reflecting the central place of Islam in these destination societies, it was also a journey into Islam. In their writings on Kerala's Muslim elites, Osella and Osella (2009) have noted the importance of the Gulf States and of Malaysia as referential points in the production of Muslim modernities around the world. As we will see, the narratives of Bangladeshi labor migrants to these societies were often marked by an assessment of the character and role of Islam they had observed there in comparison to what they understood to prevail in Bangladesh. It is of note, too, that on an official level, the rhetoric of Muslim brotherhood has not infrequently been used to put forward and legitimate the recruitment of Bangladeshi workers to these destination societies. Thus Petra Dannecker (2005) has described how Bangladeshi workers headed to Malaysia may be clothed at the airport by the recruiting company in t-shirts that say "Malaysia and Bangladesh, Muslim brotherhood."

However, if the GCC states and Malaysia all offered models of modernity, specifically of Muslim modernity, to the Bangladesh migrants who went to labor in them, they did not necessarily do so in the same ways. Reflecting their shared histories and ongoing ties as a region, the political and social environments of the GCC states do have important elements in common. All are monarchies in which the ruling families exercise considerable authority and power, even with the establishment of separate, and in some cases elected, legislative bodies. Across the region, Islam is the state religion and the legal system is usually based on a combination of civil and *Shar'ia* (Islamic) law codes, with the latter dominating family and personal matters. These conditions affirm the centrality of Islam in these heavily state-controlled societies. But an over-emphasis on the commonal-ities of the GCC states also obscures their great diversity. Perhaps no other single issue better captures the varied political and social landscapes of these countries than the treatment of women. Reflecting a commitment to the ultra-conservative Wahhabi doctrine, Saudi Arabia has taken the most restrictive approach to women's rights and participation in civic and political life. Besides not having the right to vote, women are also not able to drive a car or board a plane without the permission of a male guardian. While in much of the GCC region, women's dress is not subject to legal dictates, in Saudi Arabia the laws require women to cover their bodies. In contrast to Saudi Arabia, in Bahrain, Kuwait, Oman, and Qatar, women have gained the right to vote, and a number of women have assumed ministerial posts (Taboh 2009). Bahrain and Kuwait have also led the region in terms of women's labor force participation. In 2000, women constituted 31 percent of the labor force in Kuwait and 21 percent in Bahrain. In Oman, Qatar, Saudi Arabia, and the United Arab Emirates, these rates have been much lower, ranging from 15 to 17 percent (Willoughby 2008).

In Malaysia, the integration of Islam into the political and social fabric of the country is quite different from the Gulf states, where it is embedded in the history and politics of ethnic pluralism in the country. The country's citizenry is diverse, including ethnic Malays or *bumiputera* (65 percent) as well as Chinese (26 percent) and Indians (8 percent). The New Economic Policy (NEP), instituted in 1971 after ethnic riots rocked the country, established a sys-tem of "ethnically differentiated citizenship" (Hefner 2001). Chinese, Indians, and other non-Malays who met certain residency requirements were given citizenship in exchange for Malay dominance in politics and culture. Affirmative action policies for Malays in the areas of education and employment were put forward, along with state programs to develop an economy centered on export manufacturing. Malay was declared the official language of the country. And Islam—the primary religion of the Malays—became the religion of the state, even as freedom of religion was assured to all Malaysians. Thus the legal system is one in which all Malaysian citizens are subject to national (statu-tory) laws while only Malays and Muslims are subject to *Adat* (customary laws) and *Shar'ia* (Islamic laws), respectively. Even as the official centrality of Malay culture as established by the NEP has continued, the early twenty-first century has also seen the development of an official discourse of multicul-turalism. This shift has been informed by the government's efforts to establish Malaysia as a global high-tech hub. To this end, there has been great interest in wooing highly skilled international labor and encouraging the active economic participation of Malaysia's extensive Chinese and Indian diaspora (Bunnell 2002).

The role of Islam in Malaysia has also been shaped by the state's response to the Islamic resurgence that developed in the 1970s among the newly emerging Malay middle class. By the 1980s, the state had launched its own Islamization campaign as part of a strategy to co-opt and undercut the political challenges posed by this resurgence. In a vigorous campaign to build state-sponsored Islamic institutions, mosques were constructed and refurbished, an Islamic University was created, and a nationwide system of Islamic banking and finance was established by the state (Peletz 2005). As a result of these efforts, by the 1990s the Islamic resurgence in Malaysia had, as described by Aihwa Ong, become "low-key, integrated into the fabric of a rapidly modernizing society in which the domination of Malays is now well-assured" (1995: 184).

In what follows I explore the narratives of Bangladeshi labor migrants about their lives while abroad, with particular attention to developments of identity. These narratives, as we will see, were rich in variation, reflecting the diversity of destinations involved as well as in other circumstances. But across these differences, the experience of migration was widely understood to be an eye-opening experience. As I explore in what follows, it could foster self-conscious reflection on the nature of national and religious identities, specifically on what it meant to be Bangladeshi and to be Muslim in the world today.

NATION MATTERS: NATIONALITY, CITIZENSHIP, AND THE LIMITS OF MUSLIM SOLIDARITY

The labor migrants I interviewed included Afroza, a vivacious young woman in her late twenties. As a child, Afroza had attended a school in her home village in Comilla for about six years. She had started working in a garment factory in Dhaka in her late teens, shortly after her husband had taken up with another woman. Her brothers, already employed in the factory, had helped her to find a job there. About three years after she began working in the factory in Dhaka, a "foreigner" who was a friend of the factory owner had come and recruited her and five others (two men and three women) to work in a garment factory in Oman. According to Afroza, the foreigner had chosen them on the recommendation of his friend the factory owner, who had pointed them out as the best workers in the factory. When we talked to Afroza, she was at home on vacation after working in Oman for just over four years:

> In the garment factory in Oman where I worked, there were workers from India, Pakistan, Oman, Philippines, Indonesia, Sri Lanka, and China. There were about fifty Bangalis, including about twenty-two women. The workers from Oman were all women and as citizens of that country they were paid more than us. On the factory floor there were four rows of men workers,

then four rows of women workers, and so on. The first owner was Indian, then he sold the factory to a man from Oman who put Pakistanis in charge of the factory.

I lived with other women workers in a building next to the factory. I shared a room with six Bangali women and also later with a Chinese woman who became my closest friend in Oman. This building had a big hall with a television. I knew a little Hindi from Bangladesh and I soon learned more. Most of the time Indian movies were shown and in this way we all learned to speak Hindi. Actually almost everyone in Oman speaks Hindu or Urdu.

I was friendly with everyone but there were occasional quarrels too. Once in our building there was a quarrel with the Pakistani women over a bathroom. The Pakistani women had more influence because the boss was Pakistani. Twenty to twenty-five women shared a bathroom and there used to be a long line both morning and evening. We used to wait in the line but the Pakistanis kept buckets and mugs to reserve their places while they rested and chatted. They were very nasty. Then we Bangalis started protesting and this resulted in a big quarrel. Later the supervisor intervened and solved the problem by providing them with a separate bathroom. Sometimes the Pakistani supervisor was rude to the men. If they made mistakes or spent a little more time for lunch or tea he used to shout at them. Once a Bangali man was punished for coming late from the bathroom. The next day he was not allowed to go to the bathroom for seven hours. We protested this treatment but the employer threatened to send us back to our country. We kept quiet after this. Sometimes he abused us by calling us names. For one year I had worked for an Indian supervisor who was a Sikh; I never heard of this religion before. The Sikh supervisor was very good to us. But the two Pakistani supervisors never behaved well with us in spite of being Muslims. Apart from this, there were Chinese Buddhist and Sri Lankan Hindu women who behaved well with us. Once I told the Pakistani supervisor that the Hindus, Sikhs, and Buddhists were much better people than the Muslims like him. He didn't punish me but he said that if I ever spoke like that then he would convert me into a Hindu.

Afroza's account of the factory and dormitory where she lived in Oman depicts a lively and complex social world. The separation of men and women was a basic feature of this world. That is, while both men and women worked in the factory, there were separate housing facilities for them as well as a factory floor that was arranged by separate rows of men and women workers. As suggested by Afroza's remarks about trying to keep her distance from the men, these gender-segregated arrangements were also enforced for her by the presence of transnational networks in the factory. Thus Afroza restricted her interactions with the men, in fear of the gossip that could travel back to her home village through the networks of Bangladeshi workers in the factory and so damage her reputation.

Even with these social constraints, Afroza's account makes clear that the time in Oman had expanded her outlook on the world in important ways. For her, as for many other labor migrants, the experience of living and working abroad had placed her in a multiethnic environment that held opportunities for interacting not only with Bangladeshis but also with people from a range of national and religious backgrounds. In this environment, there had been times when "Bangladeshi" as a basis of community and unity had been prominent. These included incidents of dispute between Bangladeshi and Pakistani workers in which the currents of animus ran deep, informed as they were by the history of Bangladesh. Afroza plays on the memories of this history, perhaps unknowingly, as she chides the Pakistani supervisor for his misbehavior as unbecoming to a Muslim. Such conflicts did not, however, mean that Afroza simply kept to other Bangladeshis. In fact, Afroza describes her "best friend" in Oman as a Chinese Buddhist woman with whom she had developed a relationship far closer than those with her fellow Bangladeshi women workers. And in a theme that was echoed often by those of my informants who had lived and worked in the GCC states, she also described the formation around Bollywood films and culture of a shared basis of community and sociability among workers of diverse backgrounds. Migration then had extended her social world beyond the village networks that had organized it in the past, evoking the emergence of what Habibul Haque Khondker has described as "cosmopolitanism from below" (2010: 19).

The challenges of navigating a social world composed of persons of many different national backgrounds were the foreground of a sharpened nationalist consciousness among the Bangladeshi labor migrants. They described how they had come to understand that nationality and citizenship mattered, in ways that they had not fully appreciated or perhaps even been aware of before their sojourns abroad. In this regard, perhaps the most powerful experience was that of pay discrimination by nationality. My informants spoke of being paid less than others, not because of their work skills or experience but because they were foreigners and Bangladeshi nationals. Abedin, who had worked in factories in Malaysia for almost sixteen years, remarked on how the Malaysian citizens with whom he had worked had received better pay and benefits than his own. Among other things, these experiences had caused him to reflect on the significance of citizenship. Echoing the comments of many others, he mused on the question of how things would be if the situation was reversed—if Bangladesh was an importer rather than an exporter of labor. Even under these conditions though, he was not so sure that Bangladeshi citizenship would confer the same privileges in Bangladesh that Malaysian citizenship did in Malaysia:

> A: They gave special benefits to those who were Malaysians, citizens of that country. Their pay was higher, for the same work. For example, when I started I was paid fourteen *ringit* [Malaysian currency], whereas they started at thirty ringit. In the last few years I received fifteen ringit, whereas those with the same experience were getting fifty ringit. They were paid more for overtime and they took more vacation. This was the system; there was nothing to say about it. It is after all their country and we are just there to work. What is there to say about it?
>
> NK: You did not feel bad about it?
>
> A: Of course I felt bad but what is the point of being upset? Sometimes I imagined what would happen if Bangladesh was prosperous like Malaysia and we brought in people from abroad to work for us.
>
> NK: Do you think we would pay them less?
>
> A: I cannot say for sure, but I don't think so. Our country is not like that country [Malaysia]. We don't value our own people in the same way.

As suggested by Abedin's remarks, the privileges given to citizens of receiving countries in terms of pay and other work benefits were often seen by the Bangladeshis to have some degree of legitimacy. In contrast, observed pay differentials by nationality among foreign workers were seen to have no legitimacy, thus generating much resentment and anger. Those who had worked in the GCC states often described a differential pay scale that had operated among Asian workers in the labor market. Bangladeshis held a distinct position in this hierarchy—at the bottom. That is, in comparison to workers from India, Pakistan, the Philippines, and Sri Lanka, Bangladeshis were paid less, even if their skills were commensurate or perhaps even superior to others. Abul, who had worked in a metals shop in Kuwait for over three years, was among those who had been subject to such pay discrimination. He noted with some anger that it was the poverty of Bangladesh that made its people vulnerable to exploitation:

> A: At that factory there were people from many countries. Egyptians, Indians, Filipinos, Pakistanis. We Bangalis kept to ourselves. We naturally had some contact with the others since we had to work with them, but it was minimal. The Egyptians got the most pay and were treated the best, then it was the Indians and Filipinos. Bangalis were paid the least, even for the same work.

NK: Did you ask for more pay?

A: Yes, we asked the supervisor. He laughed and said, "If it's not good then you can go back to your miserable country." What is the use of complaining? This is our destiny. Our only fault is that we are poor. The rule in the world is that the rich will torture the poor. This is our luck. If we Bangalis had been rich today, then they would have to come to our country to work.

Unlike many if not most other aspects of living and working abroad, that of pay discrimination by nationality was one that could extend across the otherwise very diverse experiences of Bangladeshi professionals and low-wage workers. Amin was a civil engineer who had worked in Saudi Arabia for almost twenty years. At the time of the interview, he and his wife were in the process of retiring to Canada, where both of their children had settled after attending university there. As we see in the account below, Amin felt that he had experienced pay discrimination as a Bangladeshi, although he also seemed somewhat vague about the details and a little reluctant to discuss them:

A: The company was Saudi-owned, but it was very cosmopolitan. My relations with colleagues were excellent. I had close friendships with the people I worked with, who were from everywhere ... Egypt, India, France, Britain.

NK: What about pay, were there differences?

A: The pay issue was a delicate matter ... it was not so openly discussed, I don't know much about it. But I know that in my own case and that of the other Bangladeshi professionals, there was discrimination in pay. I believe that the Arabs made more, and so did the Europeans and Indians. You know there is a bias in the region against Bangladeshis because we are a poor country. And then there is the fact that many of our people who go there are uneducated rural folk. But I have always been treated with great courtesy by the locals. Because they [the locals] are lagging in education themselves, they have great respect for educated persons, even if they are from Bangladesh. There were a few times when I was checked at the airport in Riyadh. The checkers are mainly Arabs. I was always carrying Bangladeshi or American magazines. If there were photos in there that they did not like they would never tear those themselves but tell me to take them home and tear them up at home. They were very polite.

As Amin describes, in a workplace environment that was generally quite convivial, there had been a code of silence among the professional employees about salary matters. Yet Amin seemed quite sure that he and other

Bangladeshis had been paid less than the professionals from other countries. As did Abul the factory worker, Amin attributed this pay disparity to the poverty of Bangladesh and its weak stature in the global hierarchy of nations. But even as he spoke of discriminatory dynamics that affected all Bangladeshis, he also affirmed the privileges of his class location. With the exception of the "delicate" pay issue, he was well protected, by virtue of his professional status, from the indignities heaped on his less privileged Bangladeshi brethren.

Indeed, if professionals such as Amin spoke of how well they had been received abroad, low-wage Bangladeshi workers were far more likely to report hostile treatment. As discussed earlier, the scapegoating of migrants has been an important political current in the GCC states and Malaysia. Reflecting these conditions, many Bangladeshi migrants described experiences of verbal and even physical harassment, not only in the workplace but on streets and buses as well as in stores and other public spaces. Those who had gone to the GCC states spoke of being called *miskin* (beggar) or persons from a miskin country. To be sure, miskin, with its connotations of naturalized poverty and inferiority, is not an exclusive reference to Bangladeshis but one that is widely used in the GCC states against marginalized populations. Nonetheless, for many of my informants, it was a symbol of the exceptional stigma from which Bangladeshis suffered, even in comparison to other South Asian origin workers. Mamun, who had worked in a variety of jobs in Bahrain for almost six years, was painfully aware of the dehumanizing connotations of the miskin label:

> M: All over the region, we Bangalis are known as miskin. They see us as less than human, below them in every way. The behavior of the locals is very bad.
>
> NK: How exactly is it bad?
>
> M: They call us names, they don't hesitate to kick and hit and throw stones. They don't care if we're Muslims. I feel that they treat Christians better than us. One of the customs in the Arab countries is that they greet and give salaams to everyone, young and old. It is not like in our country where the young must first greet the old. But sometimes I felt angry. The meaning of salaam is to wish peace. At one minute they give us salaam and the next minute they kick us. What kind of salaam is that?

In describing "life while abroad," a number of informants organized their narratives around comparative and generalized assessments of the cultural character of the various national and ethnic groups that they had observed while abroad, in relation to each other, as well as in relation to Bangladeshis. For example, Fahim, a high school graduate, had worked in Malaysia for almost seven years. During this time, he had met and observed foreign workers of different nationalities as well as Malaysian citizens of different ethnicities. In noting the Chinese prominence in the Malaysian business sector, he described the Chinese as "hard-working" and prosperous as a result of their diligence. He felt that Bangladeshis, in contrast, did not have this work ethic, a fact that was reflected in the poverty of Bangladesh:

> There were Malay workers in the factory and also workers from different countries, from Nepal, Vietnam, and India. The company gave us housing. They called it "containers," which were large rooms with four sides made of wood. Each container had bunk beds and a small refrigerator and TV. I lived in a container with five other Bangalis. There were Nepalese in the next container and I was friendly with them. We talked in Hindi and a bit of English and we watched Indian movies together. Everyone got along. People from Nepal are very simple and honest. The Indians are clever but not sincere in what they do.
>
> The factory was owned by a Chinese man. All the factories there are owned by Chinese. The Chinese are behind everything in Malaysia. They are so hard-working, I have never seen anything like it. The owner worked from morning till night. It is not like our country where the big boss sits and drinks tea in his office for a few hours and then goes home. It's because the Chinese are so hardworking that they are so prosperous. If we Bangalis were like that we would also be prosperous, our country would be different.

As suggested by Fahim's account, developments of national consciousness while abroad involved the emergence of a globalized and critical lens on the meaning and significance of Bangladeshi nationality. Like Fahim, many other labor migrants referred to the issue of work habits in their reflections on why Bangladesh was not as prosperous as the country in which they had labored. Thus Jhintu, who had been in Kuwait for almost three years, spoke of how his time abroad had exposed him to the rhythms and discipline of the modern capitalist workplace. He had learned the value of time—that time is money and that time spent in idle chatter rather than labor is time that is wasted, "Certainly I have changed a great deal because of my time in the Arab countries. I look at things differently now. I pay attention to time, I know the value of time. And I have come to understand the value of work. In Bangladesh, we don't value these things in the same way that they do abroad. Maybe that is why we do not progress. We spend too much time in idle chatter (*adda*)."

If the absence in Bangladesh of a modern work culture was among the specific issues around which these informants expressed a critical nationalist consciousness, another was the absence of national solidarity among its citizens. Echoing the discourse of Bengali factionalism as discussed in chapter 2, the

Bangladeshi labor migrants spoke of how Bengalis were inclined to stab each other in the back rather than help each other out. For example, Bokul, who had worked in a jewelry store in Dubai, described tense relations with workers of other (non-Bangladeshi) national backgrounds. But rather than coming together in solidarity, Bangladeshis were more inclined to exploit each other. Thus echoing the comments of so many other informants, Bokul spoke of how the poor stature of Bangladesh in the global order was attributable in part to the failure of Bangladeshis to look out for each other. As described earlier, the transnational foreign worker industry is rife with corrupt practices, the brunt of which is often borne by the worker. If Bangladeshi nationals are not the only players in this web of corruption and exploitation, they are certainly part of it:

> B: I met people from all over the world in Dubai and I have naturally learned things as a result of that experience. I had never really met people from abroad before that time.
>
> NK: What have you learned?
>
> B: With Pakistanis, especially the Punjabis, even though we share the same religion we have nothing in common. They look down on us and I despise them. With Indians, I found that they can be very different depending on their region. The Gujaratis, for instance, are very different from the others. But all the Indians, wherever they are from, they look down on us. What I have learned is that Bangladeshis are viewed badly everywhere, because we are a poor country. We are not respected anywhere; this is to some degree our own fault. When I was abroad I also saw Bangladeshis exploiting other Bangladeshis. How can we as a country make any progress when we are like that?

A sense of disillusionment about the realities of Muslim solidarity in the world often accompanied these discussions about the problems of Bangladesh and its weak stature in the global hierarchy of nations. This was sharply evident in the account of Salman, whom we interviewed when he was at his village home in Manikganj. Salman was on a three-month leave from his job as an ambulance driver in Kuwait, where he had been working for five years. His wife and two children lived with his elderly parents in Manikganj; the household was dependent on the remittances that he sent back to them. It was only after a long and frustrating string of degrading and poorly paid jobs in Kuwait that Salman, who was a high school graduate, had obtained work as an ambulance driver there. While he was content with his current circumstances in Kuwait, the long years of struggle had left him embittered about the country where he was working. At several points in the interview he spoke of an assumption that he had held dearly before going abroad. This was that Muslim employers in a

Muslim society would treat Muslim workers well, regardless of their national origins:

> I am satisfied now with the job that I have as an ambulance driver in Kuwait. By the grace of Allah, I was able to obtain a driver's license and get a decent job. As a Bangladeshi, I get less pay than the other drivers there [from Egypt and India], but I don't complain. Everybody behaves well with me at this job. I thank Allah that I can work now in Kuwait with some respect. I went to a Muslim country with a lot of hope but I received no privilege, just harsh treatment. At all of my jobs [shop assistant, office boy, ambulance driver] I have been paid less than non-Muslims. At my first job, the Egyptian shop owner said prayers with me, and we observed fasting and *iftar* together during Ramadan. But in other ways his behavior was rude and rough. He paid only 18 *dinars* [Kuwaiti currency] and I was spending 8–9 dinars on food. Through a friend I then found a job as an office boy. When I joined I found that I received 28 dinars whereas the other office boys working there who were from Pakistan got 35 dinars. With a lot of courage I once told the employer, "We all do the same work, then why is my salary low"? He replied in Arabic, "You belong to a country of *fakirs* (beggars), you're getting more than you would in your country . . . go and work . . . or else you can leave." I felt like crying but what could I do? As an office boy I was constantly abused by the Kuwaiti men at the office. Once, after completing my chores I started saying my prayers. The manager just took hold of my shirt collar and punched me and asked me to make tea again. Their only concern was tea and alcohol. Going to America would have been better. In a Christian country I would never have expected them to give me time for reading the Qu'ran and saying my prayers.

RETURNED MIGRANTS AS AGENTS OF RELIGIOUS CHANGE

Studies of low-wage Bangladeshi international labor migrants have noted the diversity of economic outcomes among them (Kibria 2004; Murshid et al. 2002; Rahman 2000; Siddiqui and Abrar 2001). While some migrants struggle and perhaps even fail to pay back debts and cover the basic living expenses of their families, others are able to use their overseas earnings not only to maintain families but also to finance such investments as land purchase, home construction, and business ownership. For the Bangladeshi labor migrants we interviewed, as well, the migration episode has produced a wide range of economic outcomes. There were stories of success in which overseas work had turned out to be a financially effective and perhaps even personally fulfilling strategy. But there were also those who described the migration episode to have brought minimal economic and other rewards for them. The most heartbreaking stories came from those whose economic circumstances had actually declined as a result of migration. There were migrants who had found themselves abroad without a valid work permit, often after being cheated by migration agents. This eventually led to their arrest and deportation, often before they had had the opportunity to recover even the costs of going abroad.

As one might expect, the extent to which the migration episode had been a financially profitable venture shaped the lives of migrants after their return home in many ways. Among other things, variations of economic outcome were reflected in the likelihood that the migrant would take on the self-conscious role of religious reformer upon their return. As we will see, there were some returned migrants who saw themselves as agents of religious change, working to bring Islamic practice in their home community into line with what they had observed while abroad. Others, however, were far less likely to take on this role, even consciously desisting from it, in part due to skepticism about the value of such emulation.

Returning with Religious Reform

Joshim had worked for twelve years in Saudi Arabia as a truck driver. After returning to Bangladesh he took up a well-paying job in Dhaka as an office driver for a multinational company. He told me that he planned to work for just a few more years before retiring to his village in Barisal, where his wife and children were living with his mother. There he had bought a fish pond and farm land with savings from his time in Saudi Arabia and he hoped to live comfortably from these investments in his old age. As we see in the account below, Joshim was confident that he had gained from his time in Saudi Arabia, not just economically but also in the religious knowledge that he had acquired there:

> By living in a Muslim country [Saudi Arabia] I have learned a great deal about the correct practice of Islam. As soon as the *azan* [call to prayer] is heard, the shops close and all Muslims are required to pray. The punishment is that the person is made to read fifty to sixty *rakat* [a unit of Islamic prayer] of extra prayer. Sometimes he may be locked up in a bathroom or a red mark put on his work permit. So even if one does not want to say his prayers, one is forced to do so and it becomes a habit. In our religion it is said that you should encourage people to do good. It is because their laws are strict that they do not have crime. In our country we have laws that are not followed and nobody fears the police.
>
> The way they say their prayers is also a little different. For example, there is no head cap required there for prayer. And here in our country we say "amen" softly after *Sura Fateha* but there they say it loudly.[4] In our country

the *monajat* [invocation] is given more importance. I've talked to the imam of our mosque in the village and I have told him to start these practices.

Since returning to Bangladesh I try my best to live in accordance with Islamic rules as I have learned in the land of Allah. My eldest son used to be in an English medium school in the village but the standards there are not good. So I have put him in a *madrassa*. I hope he becomes a *hafiz* [scholar of Islam who has memorized the Qu'ran] as it is of great value if one's son reads the Qu'ran at the grave of his parents. I have also asked my wife to tell the women workers of our house to maintain purdah [separation of men and women]. We do not let the women go near the men workers in the farms and the pond. They have separate places to eat and the men are not allowed to come inside the house. I try to do all the transactions with the men and my wife with the women.

The story of Joshim affirms the growth of religiosity that has so often been described in studies of South Asian Muslim men labor migrants and their lives after return to the homeland (Ballard 1989; Gardner 1995; Kurien 2002; Simpson 2004). These analyses bring attention to the religious sphere as a focus of status and identity negotiations for migrant men in their home communities. That is, religious practices and involvements offer a site within which to deploy the economic and symbolic capital of migration for the achievement of status and mobility. Gardner and Osella have noted the importance of consumption, of the simultaneous displays of religiosity and prosperity that can mark these strategies: "as migrants and their families reinvent themselves as high-status members of their community, how they worship and how they spend their earnings—activities which are often closely linked—tend to take centre stage" (2004: xxxiii). Such displays may also serve to establish the acquired religious knowledge and thus the religious authority of the returned migrant. The value of this knowledge derives from its claims of both authenticity and modernity. That is, the returned migrant may claim to have acquired knowledge of an Islam that is universalistic and steadfast in its commitment to the core principles of Islam. This is in contrast to the folk Islam of the community, steeped as it is in local tradition and superstition.

In the case of Joshim, the potency of migration capital was evident in the strong authority that he exercised in his family and home village. If the under-girding to this authority consisted of the economic resources that he had accumulated through his work in Saudi Arabia, it was also formed around the "authentic" religious knowledge that he felt he had gained there. Indeed, in his role as community leader and family patriarch, he drew on the strength and legitimacy of an identity that he had self-consciously adopted. This was of an agent of religious change—someone who was carrying back from the "land of Allah" to Bangladesh what he felt to be the true and authentic practice of Islam.

In general, the self-conscious role of Islamic reformist was far more apparent among those for whom migration had been an economically profitable venture as well as among those who had been to the GCC states rather than to Malaysia. Migrant claims of religious authority are clearly supported and indeed enforced by the scaffold of economic resources and the status and power generated by them. And as in the case of Joshim, these claims can also be bolstered by the popular image and understanding of the particular country of destination, especially the character of Islam there and its integration into institutions and culture. Reflecting the country's identity as the birthplace of Islam and also its reputation as a strict Islamic state, migration to Saudi Arabia seemed especially fertile as a history against which to invoke authoritative knowledge of Islam. However, just as not all Saudi *pherot* (i.e., migrant returnees from Saudi Arabia) made claims of greater religious knowledge, such claims were also not confined to those migrants who had been to Saudi Arabia. In fact, a story similar to that of Joshim in terms of acquired religious knowledge with migration was offered by Ilyas, who had worked in the construction industry in Malaysia. He had returned home to Chittagong after five years and eventually, using the contacts and networks he had acquired in Malaysia, had begun to work as a recruiter of labor migrants to Malaysia. He told us that he was employed as a subcontractor for an international recruiting company with offices in Bangladesh, Malaysia, and other countries around the world:

I: We have a lot to learn from other countries about Islam. In Malaysia, the government funds the mosques and even pays the salary of the imam. In that way they ensure the upkeep of the mosques. This does not happen in our country which does not follow the rule of Allah. In Malaysia the young children start learning the Qu'ran from a young age. There they also do not patronize the *mazaars* [shrines of saints] as we do here. I have learned that these practices are forbidden in the Qu'ran.

NK: Did you go to the mazaars before?

I: Yes, when I was ignorant of these rules. Now I have forbidden my wife and children to visit them. I have tried to influence my brothers and other relatives to follow the true path, but that is more difficult. They do not listen to me. I have also told them that in marriage, the *mehr* [dower] money should be given as soon as possible by the husband to the wife. After returning from Malaysia I gave the mehr that I owed to my wife. She was astonished and at first she did not want to take it. I told her, this is what I must give you as written in the Holy Qu'ran. She took the money and bought a sewing machine with which she makes clothes for the children.

Toward the end of the interview, Ilyas informed us that he was a member of the Islamist political party and movement, Jamaat-e-Islami, in Bangladesh. Along with his work as a migrant recruiter, these interests informed the rather uncomplicated picture he offered to us of Malaysia as a Muslim country; its ethnic and religious diversity were not matters that he chose to dwell upon. In speaking of the true practice of Islam as he had learned in Malaysia, Ilyas also referred to issues and perspectives that have figured in the public platform of Jamaat-e-Islami as well as other movements of revivalist Islam in Bangladesh. This includes the popular and deeply entrenched practices in Bangladesh of pilgrimage and prayer at the mazaars or shrines of popular saints (pirs). That is, if Ilyas's knowledge of how mazaar patronage was wrong came from his time in Malaysia, as he told us, it had also perhaps been reinforced by the position that Jamaat has taken against it as well. However, as also suggested by Ilyas's comments about being unable to prevent members of his family from continuing to visit the shrines, such opposition has had questionable success in dampening popular enthusiasm for the shrines.

The influence of Jamaat ideology was evident also in the other issue raised by Ilyas, that of mehr or mohrana. This is a condition of marriage in Islam in which the bridegroom is expected to make a payment to the bride at marriage. In Bangladesh, however, the actual practice of mehr has not been that of immediate and direct payments to the bride, but rather a contractual agreement at the time of marriage that the husband will pay a specified amount of money to the wife in the event of divorce. In exchange for this agreement, the bride agrees to forgo receipt of the mehr payment at the time of the marriage. Indeed, rather than receiving mehr, what has been prevalent in Bangladesh since the mid twentieth century, as in much of South Asia, is the practice of dowry (joutuk or dabi), whereby the bride and her family are required to pay money and/or goods to the bridegroom at the time of the marriage. In her book Reshaping the Holy, Elora Shehabuddin (2008) writes of how the practice of dowry has been denounced in Bangladesh not only by women's rights groups but also by Jamaat-e-Islami. Jamaat leaders, however, have also seized on the issue as an opportunity to criticize what they see as women's lack of conformity to purdah or veiling. According to them, it is women themselves who are responsible for their own terrible predicament. That is, the rise of dowry comes from the devaluation of women by men, a devaluation that is the result of women's growing physical immodesty, making women "cheaper" in the eyes of men than they supposedly were in the past. Migrants such as Ilyas then are able to draw on the expanding movements of revivalist Islam in Bangladesh to garner support for the role that they have taken on, of religious reformer who has been duly educated in the correct practices of Islam by his time abroad.

These movements offer powerful institutional and ideological frameworks that support those migrants who are inclined to take on this role.

Secret Histories and Critical Reflections

When we interviewed Matin, he had been back in his village in Manikganj for eight months, after spending five years in Dubai. As a child, Matin had attended the village madrassa for about seven years before starting to work on the family land. When the family's financial situation deteriorated, leaving them with overwhelming debts and little cultivable land, Matin sought work abroad. He borrowed eighty-five thousand *taka* (unit of Bangladesh currency) from a local moneylender to pay fees to a recruiting agent. But when he landed in Dubai, he discovered that he had been cheated. He was placed in a job that paid less than and was also different from what he thought he would be doing there. Even though he switched jobs several times, he was unable to improve his circumstances. After about five years of drifting around from one disastrous situation to another, he was picked up and jailed as an unauthorized worker and eventually deported to Bangladesh. He told us that far from improving, the family's financial situation had deteriorated as a result of the migration episode, leaving them with even more debts than before.

These experiences, as we see below, had left him quite bitter and disillusioned about the Arab states, which he had held in high regard before going abroad. He expressed anger about the realities of Islamic practice as he had witnessed there and the empty rhetoric of Muslim brotherhood. For him, the pampered treatment of pet dogs by local residents, a sharp contrast to how he had been treated, symbolized the dehumanization to which he had been subject:

> People of my village think I was in great happiness there. They don't under-
> stand. They think I had a nice time flying in a plane and living in a rich
> country. I cannot tell the people of my village of all the nasty things I saw in
> that place. Some of them enter the mosque smoking a cigarette. They throw
> the cigarette down on the ground for the prayer and then as soon as possible,
> start smoking again. We cannot even think of smoking in Allah's house.
> They say their prayers as quickly as possible, in three or four minutes,
> whereas we in Bangladesh take fifteen minutes. I've heard that in Saudi
> Arabia all shops are closed at the time of the *azan* [call to prayer] but that is
> far from the case in these places like Dubai. Whoever wants to pray can do so
> and others just go about as they please. From everything I have seen in that
> country, I feel our society is much better. I have seen people there who wear
> shorts and walk about outside in indecent clothes. I've seen them going
> about with their dogs. They walk their dogs in the parks near their

residences. They spend more money on their dogs than they give to us. They don't consider us human beings.

How much should I tell you? They say all Muslims are brothers. But there is no connection between what they say and what they do. I had several Arab employers. Before I started a job they might promise twenty dirham [currency unit in UAE] but then when it was time to pay, they would just give me ten dirhams. And in some cases they did not pay me at all. I cannot understand what kind of Muslim behavior that can be, to not fairly pay your workers. Before going to their country I had very high opinions about the Arabs but it was all in error. I cannot speak of these things to anyone here in the village as they will never believe me. *Apa* [elder sister], in these eight months that I have been back, I've never told anybody about these things. You are educated so I'm telling you. Please expose these frauds, these fake Muslims. Everybody should know how they torture and deprive us. This is why I'm telling you but please don't say these things to my acquaintances.

Like Matin, many of our informants offered vivid and detailed accounts of the underbelly or the negative side of the destination society that is often invisible to those of more privilege. Like him, they also often relayed this information to us as a secret—to be strictly kept away from those of their home community. Underlying these entreaties were the perceived threats of this information to their status and honor as a returned migrant. Even if Matin did not return to his village as a more prosperous man, his identity as a *Dubai-pherot* (Dubai returnee) was not entirely without benefits. He had acquired some symbolic capital, simply by virtue of going there. Quite apart from what his life had actually been like in Dubai, in the village his experience abroad had given him an aura of modernity, a modernity that was moreover shrouded with the legitimacy conferred by the destination to which he had traveled—within the Arab world. Disclosure of the often harsh realities of life abroad threatened this aura and was feared for the loss of face and honor that it could bring.

For women migrants, these fears were sharpened by the added significance of these threats for their sexual reputations. In general, Bangladeshi women who travel alone abroad, without male guardians, are already under suspicion for such violations. Under these conditions, it is not so surprising that few of the women migrants we interviewed were willing to talk about the less savory aspects of life abroad. The exception to this was Ameena, who spoke to us of these matters, however, only under the condition that we not reveal the information to those in the community around her. Ameena was a high school graduate who had worked as a nurse in a hospital in Bangladesh for two years before going to Saudi Arabia, where she worked for over twelve years. Her first job had been in a wealthy Arab household, where her duty had been to take care of a sick and elderly woman. She was later able to get a job as a nurse at a hospital in Riyadh, a situation that she much preferred. Ameena spoke with some pride about learning Arabic from her time in Saudi Arabia and also of performing *Umrah*.[5] But even as going to Saudi Arabia had given her access to these status-enhancing markers of piety, it had also made her quite skeptical of those in Bangladesh who wished to emulate Islam as practiced in the Arab states. She expressed a quiet sense of nationalist pride about Bangladesh as a good society:

> I quite honestly felt disgusted by what I saw a lot of the time. Please don't tell anyone here about what I am going to tell you as it will bring suspicion on me. I saw the young men of the home trying to force themselves on the women who worked there. And I saw a lot of drinking. Maybe it is because they have too much money, but it is a corrupt culture. What I feel is that it doesn't matter how many times you go the mosque, if your real behavior is not good then those actions have no value. In Bangladesh we are actually far more religious. Our society also treats women better. We may be poor but in comparison to them we are a good society (*bhalo shomaj*).

In their social and political impacts, the significance of critical perspectives on the receiving society such as those voiced by Ameena is clearly reduced by the shroud of silence that frequently surrounds them. If, in the most immediate sense, this silence stems from the concerns of migrants about their own reputation and status, it is also embedded in a larger set of social and political conditions. Unlike those who draw on movements of revivalist Islam to legitimate and to reinforce their acceptance of and indeed admiration for the models of Islam as observed while abroad, those who return with skepticism have fewer such supports. Indeed, they are likely to feel themselves alone, without the benefit of an ideological and institutional framework that could give meaning and significance to their experiences of life while abroad.

MEN MIGRANTS AND THE QUESTION OF WOMEN

Hasan, from the town of Gazipur, had worked in Qatar and Kuwait for a total of about seven years. He spoke of his time abroad in mixed terms, filled both with misfortunes and good experiences. In describing what he had particularly appreciated about these societies, he pointed to their authoritarian and thus orderly political systems, which stood in contrast for him to the chaos and uncertainty of politics in Bangladesh. There was, however, one point of national comparison on which Bangladesh clearly came out ahead in his mind—the position and character of women. He argued that Bangladesh gave more rights and respect to women than the Arab Gulf countries, thus affirming its status as "a good society." Like many if not most of the men who had worked in the GCC states, Hasan's direct contacts with women in the destination society had been extremely limited, confined to fleeting observations on the streets and other public spaces. Even so, he had developed quite a firm idea of what women were like there. He used a simplified notion of "American women" to refer to what he saw to be the immodest behavior and overt sexuality of women abroad. He felt that despite the fact that Arab women were more likely to cover themselves in public by using a burkha, women in Bangladesh actually displayed greater commitment to the core principles of purdah:

> We respect women more in our country. We are more advanced in this matter than them. There the men marry three to four times and make slaves of the wives. This is against Islam which gives a lot of respect to women. I do not like their system for women. The women of our country are far more decent than the women I have seen in the Arab countries. Some of the Arab women wear *burkha*. But even when they do wear burkha, underneath they dress like Americans. They behave in indecent ways. They walk and talk like men and conduct themselves in an unbecoming manner. The laws there keep them under control; otherwise, they would be like the Americans. The women of our country may not wear burkha, but they are decent, they maintain purdah.

If the literal meaning of purdah is curtain or veil, it actually refers to far more than clothing. In Bangladesh, as in many other parts of South Asia and the Middle East, purdah is better understood as an institution, a multifaceted system of gender segregation and differentiation that extends across every dimension of the social world. At its core is an often implicit, taken-for-granted code of behavior that punitively sanctions women for acting in a manner that is provocative or unseemly in its violation of the principle of men and women's separation and difference. Purdah also has powerful class meanings. Especially in rural Bangladesh, purdah can be a marker of status and privilege, a signal of the family's economic ability to effectively seclude its women.

Purdah is also far from a static institution. In fact, the late twentieth and early twenty-first centuries have also been a time of visible contest over practices of purdah in Bangladesh. As signaled by such developments as rising rates of schooling for girls and the emergence of women as a critical segment of the industrial labor force, this has been a time of important change in women's roles. These shifts have generated widespread uncertainty and debate over purdah. This is, however, not so much over the legitimacy of purdah per se but rather over what is actually required in order to maintain it. For some women, practices of intensified veiling, such as a newfound adoption of the burkha, have been a viable and meaningful response to the greater opportunities as well as demands that have arisen for their participation in activities outside the home. Intensified veiling has also been promoted by the expanding Islamic movements in the country. And so by adopting the burkha, women may feel themselves to be better equipped to move about in public spaces with greater safety and without facing accusations of violating purdah. But for other women, including those who cannot afford burkhas and other such garments, the accusations they face of being *beh-purdah* (without purdah) have been countered in other ways. These include efforts to define purdah as an internalized system of self-regulation that is best achieved not through clothing that covers the body but rather the woman's own scrupulous monitoring of her own behavior such as to maintain the highest standards of chastity and modesty (Kabeer 2000; Kibria 1995).

The institution of purdah has also been deeply enmeshed in the dynamics of male honor in Bangladesh. The honor of men has been tied to their ability to affirm and assure the sexual purity, and more generally, the conformity to purdah of their womenfolk. Thus the declarations of the migrant men about the superior conformity of Bangladeshi women to purdah may also be grounded in efforts to assert their own masculinity and honor in light of the migration experience. Here is it important to remember that many low-wage Bangladeshi migrant men find themselves in circumstances abroad that are disempowering. The sense of emasculation that can result may also be reinforced by anxiety about having left wives, daughters, and sisters behind at home, and thus out of one's direct supervision. Under these conditions, the topic of women can be an important one by which to declare honor, to reclaim it in light of the deeply felt scars of indignity that have been left behind from life while abroad.

For Bangladeshi men migrants, the potency of "women" as a discursive site of honor may also informed by its powerful relationship to ideologies of nationalism in Bangladesh (Chatterjee 1993; Mookherjee 2003). The Bangla nation has been imagined in feminized terms, as a mother who is revered and loved by her children—the Bangali people. Within this framework, women are a core symbolic site of nationalist expressions. Generalized claims about the "decency" of Bangali women in comparison to women abroad may thus be nested in nationalist sentiments. Such claims protect and affirm the sanctity of "mother Bengal" and express national pride. They may also inform the political efforts of migrant men to prevent the international labor migration of Bangladeshi women. According to observers, during the 1990s and early 2000s, organizations of migrant men gave political support to the Bangladesh government's efforts, effective until 2007, to officially ban low-wage women workers from going abroad for employment (Dannecker 2005; Siddiqui 2008). The core argument that was advanced in support of the ban was that women were especially vulnerable to exploitation abroad. And when the women of Bangladesh were compromised, so was the national image and honor of Bangladesh.

Despite such political opposition to the international labor migration of women, I found many migrant men express general support for the idea of women entering into paid employment outside the home. For those who had been to Malaysia, an especially notable feature of the gender relations observed there was the large number of women in the labor force. Malaysia as a destination was also one in which the labor migrants encountered a social environment in which cultural practices of gender segregation were far less pronounced than in Bangladesh. Javed, who had worked in Malaysia for about six years, at first on a plantation and then in manufacturing work, spoke of these practices:

> In comparison to women in Malaysia, women in Bangladesh are much better, polite. The Malaysian women wear American clothes, dresses, short skirts. And then they wear a scarf on their head. I don't see the point of that if they are showing their body. The women in our country are much more decent, they maintain purdah. They [Malaysian] are Muslim but they don't maintain purdah. They also mix freely with men. On the bus and train, men and women are sitting together. But I like that women there work. I think women should get educated and work, not sit at home. I have seen in our village, women workers from BRAC and Proshika [NGOs], riding bicycles and Hondas to do their work of teaching mothers about health matters and other things. They behave very decently. But it is different in Malaysia, the girls work but do not dress and behave decently.

Like the vast majority of our Malaysia *pherot* informants, Javed expressed approval of women working as he had seen in Malaysia, even citing it as something for women in Bangladesh to emulate. But even as he did so, he was also quite adamant that Bangladeshi women were far more chaste and modest in their behavior. Thus in describing what for him was a model working woman, he turned not to Malaysia but to an example from Bangladesh—rural NGO women workers. These are local women who travel through villages, dispensing medicine, loans, and information to other women on behalf of the many development NGOs that have mushroomed across the country since the 1980s. While these women workers have gained some degree of cultural acceptance in the country, their presence has not been without controversy, exciting the protest of Jamaat-e-Islami and other such revivalist Islamic groups. For Javed, however, the example of NGO women workers offered a means by which to affirm both the value of women's labor force participation and the morality of Bangladeshi women in comparison to the women he had seen while abroad.

Farooq, who had worked in various factory jobs in Malaysia for over eleven years, also spoke of the value of women's labor force participation. Although his time abroad had not been without trials, he expressed great satisfaction about it, given that it had allowed him to purchase land as well as to invest in a small transportation business. Based on what he had seen in Malaysia, he felt that it was beneficial for women to be employed. Not only was this a wise strategy for families in terms of their ability to make economic strides but it was also a matter of patriotism. This was because women's wage labor was important for Bangladesh, for the economic development of the country. Indeed, he felt so strongly about this matter that during his last visit home, about two years ago, he had insisted that his wife take up a job as a primary school teacher even in the face of his mother's opposition to it. Without discounting the significance of Farooq's efforts to encourage his wife to take a job as a teacher, it is also important to note the care with which he described the propriety of his wife's job. Teaching was respectable, the school was not far from home, and her children were students there. All of these conditions protected him from accusations of failing in his responsibility to ensure his wife's purdah and thereby the honor of his family and himself:

> The women there work for the economic progress of their families. Most women in our country don't work. Some women in the cities [in Bangladesh] work, but not in the villages. And the women there in Malaysia are not suspicious and fearful of relations with men, as are women in this country. Here women think that if they talk to a man, it is a love interest. But there it is just a friendship. When I was in Malaysia I talked to the women in the factory, we were friends. If I tell stories about this here, my wife gets angry. The mentality in our country needs to change. After seeing how women work in that country, I have made some changes. My wife is a high school graduate (SSC pass). Two years ago I insisted that she go to work as a teacher at the BRAC [NGO] school nearby. My mother opposed the idea. But I said, she is an educated girl, why should she sit at home? Teaching is a respectable job. The school is nearby; it takes only ten minutes to walk there. She makes three thousand taka a month and my children attend that school too.

Informed, then, by the shifting context of gender relations in Bangladesh, there were migrant men who expressed support for women's education and labor force participation, situating it within a narrative of national progress. In many cases this was so even when, as for example among those who had labored in Saudi Arabia, migration had not been accompanied by exposure to a society in which women held visible roles of power in public life. But "life while abroad" had given these men a sharp, and even embittered understanding of the weak global stature of Bangladesh as a nation, and how this trickled down in its consequences into the lives of ordinary citizens like themselves. By supporting the idea that women in Bangladesh needed to be productive economic citizens by working outside the home, the men also affirmed the possibility of change, of a not so distant future in which Bangladesh would become prosperous and assume a place of dignity in the world. At the same time, even among those who expressed these progressive ideas, there was also a strong commitment to the institution of purdah and its continued role in organizing the lives and interactions of men and women in Bangladesh.

MIGRATION AND THE MUSLIM "OTHER"

Contrary to the conventional wisdom of western social scientists ... the encounter with the Muslim "other" has been at least as important for self-definition as the confrontation with the European "other."

(Eickelman and Piscatori 1990: xv)

The movements of Bangladeshi labor migrants to the Arab Gulf states and Malaysia unfold within a world of inequality between nations. The inequality seeps through every aspect of these migrations. Dependent on remittances, the Bangladesh state is relatively powerless in its ability to ask for concessions from receiving states on behalf of its overseas workers. The inequality of nations also underlies the denigrations faced by low-wage Bangladeshi international labor migrants, who frequently find themselves stigmatized while abroad because of their national origins. These workers are, furthermore, the ones who bear the cruel brunt of the transnational labor migrant industry, specifically its underground segment, which has developed around the business of recruiting and sending Bangladeshi labor abroad. On a more uplifting note, an emerging transnational migrant worker rights sector has come to play a positive role in lobbying the sending and receiving states on behalf of low-wage overseas workers from Bangladesh.

Perhaps because of the clearly temporary nature of the overseas sojourns that are involved, research on international labor migration from Bangladesh has rarely looked beyond its purely economic impacts. My investigations suggest, however, the potentially important social and cultural consequences of these movements. As part of their personal history of living and working abroad, labor migrants reported a heightened consciousness of nationality and its significance in the world. And echoing the sentiments of Bangladeshi Americans and British Bangladeshis, as I have explored in previous chapters, they also spoke of developing a sharp and often painful awareness of the relatively unfavorable image and status of Bangladesh as a country in the world. For those who go the Arab Gulf states or to Malaysia, this cognizance of nationality is also frequently accompanied by frustration about the realities of Muslim brotherhood in the world today. There is disillusionment, born of dashed expectations about the receiving societies as models of the good Muslim society.

In the global Islamic resurgence of today, the Arab Gulf states, especially Saudi Arabia and Kuwait, are widely seen as leaders. In Bangladesh, since the 1980s, these states have extended and consolidated their field of influence by establishing and supporting Islamic institutions, including charities, banks, hospitals, and schools in the country. What has emerged is a potent transnational context, one that facilitates the transmission of ideas and resources from these countries into the religious landscape of Bangladesh. Migrant labor flows from Bangladesh to these countries are embedded in this larger transnational context. It is the fundamental inequality that runs through these contexts, between Bangladesh and the migrant receiving societies, that ultimately works to smooth over, if only by covering up, the many contradictions that I have described here in the lived experiences and sentiments of low-wage Bangladeshi labor migrants. Many of these migrants felt silenced by a world in which their labor had little value and their national background made them subject to stigma and ill treatment abroad.

CHAPTER 7

Muslim Migrants

NATIONAL ORIGINS AND REVIVALIST ISLAM

The lives of international migrants are shaped by their national origins. This is no less so for international migrants who are Muslims. Indeed, for Bangladeshi Muslim migrants, as we have seen, their country of origin exerts a powerful and multidimensional influence. Among the many ways in which it does so is through the dynamics of global national image and their effects on the reception accorded to migrants of Bangladeshi origin when they are abroad. As a result, migration tends to carry with it for them an enhanced awareness of Bangladesh in the world, specifically its relatively weak position and image in the global hierarchy of nations. The meaning and significance of being Bangladeshi becomes a central dilemma of identity that informs their strategies of affiliation and belonging.

I have used a comparative approach in this book, looking at Muslim migrant communities that hail from the same country but go to different parts of the world. I believe that the approach has offered a finely focused lens, one that has revealed both the significance of national origins as well as its varied consequences for migrants, depending on their social class backgrounds, the immigration laws of the receiving country, and many other conditions. Future studies may extend this transnational lens in a variety of ways, by including research that focuses specifically on the development of connections between migrant communities of shared national origin throughout the world. There is also the possibility of further comparison, perhaps by looking at Muslim migrants from several countries that also differ in their global stature and image. In this regard, it is important to note that by emphasizing the role of weak global national image in the Bangladeshi diaspora, I do not in any way mean to suggest that the current image of Bangladesh or of any other country for that matter is immutable or even long term in its duration. The global status and image of countries are constantly evolving matters. There have, for example, been important shifts in the early twenty-first century in popular

Western perceptions of China and India, from backward and stagnant to economically dynamic and powerful countries. Studies that look closely at such periods of national transformation and their repercussions for migrants who originate from these countries can offer important insights into the relationship of national origins to experiences of migration. This includes the dynamics of racialization for migrants or the production of ideologies of difference within the receiving society that are used to marginalize migrants, to establish their difference from those of the receiving society.

International migrants, however, are not simply subject to global national image; they are also active in molding it. They may do so in a favorable direction when they are successful in their political and economic activities abroad and are presumed to be representatives of their national group. In a more direct sense, they can foster social and economic development in the homeland through investments and other involvements, thereby also contributing to the enhancement of homeland image. In this regard, the intense concern and anxiety of Bangladeshis abroad about the unfavorable image of their homeland may be viewed as an asset rather than liability by the Bangladeshi state in its efforts to foster diaspora investments in the country. Since the 2000s, successive governments in Bangladesh have urged the diaspora to uphold the country's image abroad by refraining from public criticism of the country, especially with regard to the government's own performance. Instead, the Bangladesh government might do better to consider how it could mobilize the eagerness of its diaspora to see a strong and prosperous Bangladesh. While this desire is propelled by many different motivations, including nationalist sentiment, a powerful sense that the well-being of Bangladesh affects how they themselves are treated abroad is one of them.

In the societies of North America and Europe, there is a tendency to see Muslims in homogeneous and one-dimensional terms and concurrently to assume that identities other than that of Muslim are of no great significance to them. But just like any other identity, that of Muslim coexists with others in fluid and contingent ways. We have seen that for Bangladeshi Muslim migrants, across the varied destinations explored in this book, the dynamics of Muslim identity are deeply intertwined with those of Bangladeshi identity. Homeland politics is one arena in which this relationship is powerfully expressed. Indeed, the politics of Islam and Bangladeshi national identity are an important part of the social worlds of Bangladeshi migrants. These involvements produce the transnationalization of a central political fault line in Bangladesh, between those who see the future of Bangladesh to lie in an affirmation of Islamic identity for the country and others who believe in the continued relevance of the secular nationalist ideals on which the country was founded in 1971.

Is it correct, then, to assume, as observers in Bangladesh have done, that those who go abroad become crucial allies and proponents of the movements of revivalist Islam in Bangladesh? When placed against the rich diversity of perspectives and experiences that I have described in this book, the assessment seems simplistic. Nonetheless, revivalist Islam is, in fact, an important element of Bangladeshi migrant life. Drawing on their extensive global networks and resources, movements of revivalist Islam have been able to establish a significant presence in Bangladeshi migrant communities and spaces. But contrary to popular perception, their strength does not necessarily lie in the ability to attract large numbers of active and loyal participants. It is rather in the effectiveness with which they have shaped standards of orthodoxy, ideas of what it means to be a devout Muslim and to be engaged in the authentic practice of Islam. These claims of legitimacy seem to often silence other voices, drowning out the diversity of perspectives and practices that are a part of Muslim life.

Notes

CHAPTER 1 — MUSLIM MIGRANTS, BANGLADESHIS ABROAD

1. The GCC is a political and economic union involving six Arab states of the Persian Gulf: Kuwait, Bahrain, Saudi Arabia, Qatar, United Arab Emirates, and Oman.

2. Both "Bangla" and "Bengali" refer to the dominant language in Bangladesh and in the state of Bengal in India. The term "Bangla" is more likely to be used by native speakers of the language when speaking to each other. "Bengali" is the Anglicized term that was used by British colonists to refer to the language of the region that also remains the prevalent term in English-language writings about the region. I use both terms interchangeably throughout the book.

CHAPTER 2 — BANGLADESH

1. "Ekushe February" (21 February) or Shohid Dibosh (Martyrs' Day) is a major national holiday in Bangladesh. In 1999, UNESCO also formally designated February 21 as International Mother Language Day.

2. On March 25, 1971, before he was arrested, Sheikh Mujib signed an official declaration that read, "Today Bangladesh is an independent and sovereign country." On March 27, 1971, Major Ziaur Rahman had a radio broadcast in which he declared, "I, Major Ziaur Rahman, at the direction of Bangobondhu Sheikh Mujibur Rahman, hereby declare that the independent People's Republic of Bangladesh has been established."

3. At this time the national leaders favored "Bangalee" over the Anglicized "Bengali"—the latter being associated with British colonialism.

4. Reprinted in O'Connell (2001: 184–185).

5. Under the principle of secularism, the Constitution also mentions the elimination of "communalism in all its forms; the abuse of religion for political purposes; any discrimination against, or persecution of, persons practising a particular religion" (O'Connell 2001: 185).

6. Formed in 1992 by the writer Jahamara Imam, "Shaheed Janani" (Mother of Martyrs), the Ghatak-Dalal Nirmul Committee (Committee to exterminate the killers and collaborators) called for trial of people who committed crimes against humanity in the 1971 Bangladesh Liberation War in collaboration with the Pakistani forces.

7. In 1981, the government of Bangladesh barred low-skilled women from overseas work, with the ostensible goal of protecting them from exploitation. Siddiqui notes (2008) that the ban arose from the demands of the association of migrant workers in Kuwait. In 1988, the ban was lifted and replaced by a series of restrictive measures. In 1997, a ban was again placed on all women except professionals. In 2007, the ban was lifted.

8. A review of 1996–2001 admissions data from the U.S. Immigration and Naturalization Services showed family sponsorship accounted for 57.4 percent, the Diversity Program for 30.5 percent, and employment provisions for 10 percent of Bangladeshi admissions during this period (see Kibria 2007).

9. Census data shows 46.5 percent of the foreign-born Bangladeshi population in the United States to be college graduates, with bachelor's degree or higher (Kibria 2007).

CHAPTER 3 — BANGLADESHI AMERICAN DREAMS

1. All names have been changes to protect the identity of informants.

2. USA-Patriot Act stands for the Uniting and Strengthening America by Providing Appropriate Tools Required to Intercept and Obstruct Terrorist Act of 2001.

3. The Concert for Bangladesh took place on August 1, 1971, in Madison Square Garden. It was organized by the former Beatles star George Harrison and raised millions of dollars for the refugees pouring out of Bangladesh into India.

4. An expression that is meant to underscore the idea that there is no other homeland.

5. Zakat is the amount of money that every financially able Muslim adult is required to pay to support the poor and needy.

6. February 21, Ekushe February, honors the memory of the language martyrs—those who gave their lives in the Bengali language movement of 1952. As noted above, in 1999, February 21 was proclaimed as International Mother Language Day by UNESCO. *CloseUp* is a popular musical talent show in Bangladesh, modeled after *American Idol*.

CHAPTER 4 — BECOMING MUSLIM AMERICAN

1. Salafi teachings advocate a direct relation to the revealed text without reference to the historical contributions of the various juridical schools. In general, Salafi doctrine, with close connections to Wahhabism, seeks to revive a practice of Islam that more closely resembles the religion during the time of Prophet Muhammad. In explaining the influence of Salafi teachings in the West, Cesari (2004) notes the ease of access to theology that is provided by a perspective that emphasizes a direct relation to the revealed text.

2. Of Hamtramck residents, 41 percent are foreign-born (Muzumdar 2007).

3. The Shohid Minar is a national monument in Dhaka, established to commemorate those killed during the Bengali Language Movement demonstrations of 1952.

4. Forbidden according to Islamic rules.

5. Focusing on the children of today's immigrants—the "new second generation"— Portes and Zhou (1993) identify three possible types of adaptation for them. The first path is the traditional course of assimilation into the white middle class. The second path is of absorption into the culture of the urban underclass, which is marked by an "adversarial outlook" that rejects mainstream norms and values, including that of achievement in school. The third possible path is for the second generation to avoid this trajectory of downward mobility by continuing to identify and be involved with the immigrant community of their parents.

6. Purdah encompasses both rules of modesty and covering the body for women.

7. Wudu is a ritual washing before prayer for Muslims.

8. The Hajj is a pilgrimage to Mecca and Medina in Saudi Arabia that all Muslims are expected to perform at least once during their lifetime, if they are physically and financially able to do so.

9. Bangabandhu is the popular name ("Friend of Bengal") for Sheikh Mujibur Rahman, a pivotal figure in the history of the country and the 1971 war of independence. Rabindra Sangeet is the music of Rabindranath Tagore, literary giant of early twentieth century Bengal.

10. Maulana is the title given to Islamic scholars and leaders.

11. Iftar is the meal that breaks the fast during Ramadan.

CHAPTER 5 — BRITISH BANGLADESHIS

1. Reflecting popular usage, I use both the terms "Bengali" and "Bangladeshi" in this chapter to refer to those of Bangladeshi origin in Britain. However, for purposes of clarity, I have tried to limit my use of the term "Bengali" to refer to the community in the pre-1971 years, reserving the designation of "Bangladeshi" for after 1971 and the birth of Bangladesh.

2. The term "lascar" was used at this time to refer to sailors from South Asia who served on European ships.

3. In popular usage in Bangladesh, *bilat* refers to England, Europe, or more generally to the overseas world.

4. It is difficult to know the exact numbers of marriages to both British and Bengali women. In Gardner's (2006) research that involved twenty-three households in Britain, there were three such cases.

5. I switch to the term "Bangladeshi" to refer to the community's self-designation after 1971.

6. "Rebel Warrior" by Aniruddha Das, Steve Chandra Savale, and Josh Ashok Pandit © Warner Chappell Music Ltd (PRS) and Q.F.M. Publishing (PRS). All rights on behalf of Q.F.M. Publishing (PRS) administered by Warner Chappell Music Ltd (PRS). All rights reserved. Used by permission of Alfred Music Publishing Co., Inc.

7. "Londoni" is a term used across Sylhet to refer to those from the region who are living in Britain.

8. Among the possible reasons for this difference are the lower costs, shorter travel time, and longer holiday periods for those in Britain.

9. Originating in India in the 1860s, the Deobandi movement emphasizes knowledge of the Hadith (prescriptions based on the knowledge and life of the Prophet) and the rejection of innovation (*bida'*), including sufi practices and reverence of saints.

10. The Bangladesh Welfare Association of London was constituted in 1954 (at that time as the Pakistan Welfare Association). It offers a variety of support services for Bangladeshis in the area, including advice and assistance on housing issues, immigration and employment.

CHAPTER 6 — MUSLIM ENCOUNTERS IN THE GLOBAL ECONOMY

1. After diplomatic talks, the Malaysian government indicated that it would gradually allow the entry of the fifty-five thousand Bangladeshis who had been given contracts and also consider lifting the ban on recruitment from Bangladesh.

2. Kapiszewski (2006) emphasizes the approximate nature of these figures, given the absence of reliable statistics. For other figures, see the reports of STRATFOR, a private intelligence agency that compiles them from official government reports and the findings of the Economic Research Forum.

3. There are some signs of a loosening of citizenship restrictions for professionals. For example, as reported in the Arab News, foreign professionals who have been living in Saudi Arabia for at least ten years are now eligible to apply for citizenship (Ghafour 2004).

4. Sura Fatiha is the first chapter of the Qur'an. This chapter has a special role in daily prayers, as it is recited at the start of each unit of prayer.

5. Religious pilgrimage to Mecca that is different from the Hajj and can be performed any time of the year.

Bibliography

Abdo, Geneive. 2006. *Mecca and Main Street: Muslim Life in America after 9/11.* New York: Oxford University Press.

Abdul-Aziz, Abdul-Rashid. 2001. "Bangladeshi Migrant Workers in Malaysia's Construction Sector." *Asia-Pacific Population Journal* 16(1): 3–22. http://www.unescap .org/esid/psis/population/journal/Articles/2001/V16N1A1.pdf.

Adams, Caroline. 1987. *Across Seven Seas and Thirteen Rivers: Life Stories of Pioneer Sylheti Settlers in Britain.* London: THAP.

Ahmed, Rafiuddin. 2001. "The Emergence of the Bengali Muslims." Pp. 1–25 in *Understanding the Bengal Muslims: Interpretive Essays*, edited by Ahmed Rafiuddin. New Delhi: Oxford University Press.

Alamgir, Jalal, and Tazreena Sajjad. 2010. "Bangladesh: A Quest for Justice." *Open Democracy*, February 9. http://www.opendemocracy.net/jalal-alamgir-tazreena-sajjad/ bangladesh-quest-for-justice.

Alekry, Abdulnabi. 2005. "Demographic Changes in the GCC Countries and the Problem of Labor Rights in the Age of Globalization." Dubai, UAE: Gulf Research Center. http://www.grc.ae/index.php?frm_module=contents&frm_action=detail_ book&sec=Contents&override=Articles&PHPSESSID=dcef717f6382b42dcd1c7a8b ba06e56e%20%3E%20Demographic%20Changes%20in%20the%20GCC%20 Countries%20and%20the%20Problem%20of%20Labor%20Rights%20in%20the %20Age%20of%20Globalization&book_id=17464&op_lang=en.

Ali, A.M.M. Shawkat. 2006. *Faces of Terrorism in Bangladesh.* Dhaka: University Press.

Asian American Federation of New York Census Information Center. 2005. "Census Profile: New York City's Bangladeshi American Population." New York: Asian American Federation of New York. http://www.aafny.orgcic/briefs/bangladeshi.pdf.

AsiaPulse News. 2006. "Analysis—Flattering Aspirations of Bangladesh's Middle Class." *AsiaPulse News*, May 12. http://goliath.ecnext.com/coms2/gi_0199–5526598/ ANALYSIS-FLATERING-ASPIRATIONS-OF-BANGLADESH.html.

Bakht, Farid. 2006. "Unsung Heroes of the Economy." *Daily Star*, February 4. http:// www.thedailystar.net/suppliments/2006/15thanniv/celebrating_bd/celeb_bd11.htm.

Ballard, Roger. 1989. "Overseas Migration and Its Consequences: The Case of Pakistan." Pp. 112–120 in *The Sociology of Developing Societies: South Asia*, edited by Hamza Alavi and John Harriss. London: Macmillan.

Barrett, Raymond. 2008. "Kuwait Ramps up Deportation of Workers." *Christian Science Monitor*, August 2. http://www.csmonitor.com/2008/0802/p25s25-wome.html.

Barrowclough, Anne. 2008. "Diplomats Rescue British Teenager from Forced Marriage." *The Times* [of London], June 25. www.timesonline.co.uk/tol/news/uk/article4393909.ece.

Basch, Linda, Nina Glick Schiller, and Cristina Szanton Blanc. 2008. "Transnational Projects: A New Perspective." Pp. 261–272 in *The Transnational Studies Reader: Intersections and Innovations*, edited by Sanjeev Khagram and Peggy Levitt. New York: Routledge.

Bashi, Vilna F. 2007. *Survival of the Knitted: Immigrant Social Networks in a Stratified World*. Stanford: Stanford University Press.

Bernstein, Nina. 2005a. "Girl Called Would-Be Bomber Was Drawn to Islam." *New York Times*, April 8. http://www.nytimes.com/2005/04/08/nyregion/08suicide.html.

———. 2005b. "Questions, Bitterness, and Exile for Queens Girl in Terror Case." *New York Times*, June 17. http://www.nytimes.com/2005/06/17/ nyregion/17suicide.html.

BGMEA (Bangladesh Garment Manufacturers and Exporters Association). 2009. "BGMEA at a Glance." Dhaka: BGMEA. http://www.bgmea.com.bd/home/pages/aboutus.

Blair, Tony. 2006. "Tony Blair's Remarks on Multiculturalism and Integration as Prepared for Delivery." *Political Transcript Wire*, December 8. http://findarticles.com/p/news-articles/political-transcript-wire/mi_8167/is_20061211/tony-blairs-remarks-multiculturalism-integration/ai_n50628510/.

Blood, Archer. 2002. *The Cruel Birth of Bangladesh: Memoirs of an American Diplomat*. Dhaka: University Press.

BMET (Bureau of Manpower, Employment and Training). 2005. "Overseas Employment by Profession." http://www.bmet.org.bd/Reports/Overseas tatistics.htm.

———. 2007. "Flow of Migration by Country of Employment." http://www.bmet.org.bd/Reports/Flow_Migration.htm.

British High Commission, Dhaka. 2009. "Don't Force Me into Marriage." Dhaka: British High Commission, Dhaka. http://ukinbangladesh.fco.gov.uk/en/about-us/working-with-bangladesh/women-in-bangladesh/forced-marriage.

Brosius, Christiane. 2009. "The Gated Romance of 'India Shining.'" Pp. 174–191 in *Popular Culture in a Globalised India*, edited by K. Moti Gokulsing and Wimal Dissanayake. London: Routledge.

Buchenau, Juan. 2008. "Migration, Remittances and Poverty Alleviation in Bangladesh: Report and Proposal." Dhaka: United Nations Development Program. http://www.undp.org.bd/library/reports/UNDP%20%20BANGLADESH%20MIGRATION%20AND%20REMITTANCES%20080120.pdf.

Bunnell, Tim. 2002. "From Nation to Networks and Back Again: Transnationalism, Class, and National Identity in Malaysia." Pp. 144–160 in *State/Nation/Transnation: Perspectives on Transnationalism in the Asia-Pacific*, edited by Brenda S. A. Yeoh and Katie Willis. New York: Routledge.

Cainkar, Louise. 2004. "Islamic Revival among Second-Generation Arab-American Muslims: The American Experience and Globalization Intersect." *Bulletin of the Royal Institute for Inter-Faith Studies* 6(2): 99–120.

Cesari, Jocelyne. 2004. *When Islam and Democracy Meet: Muslims in Europe and in the United States*. New York: Palgrave Macmillan.

Chatterjee, Partha. 1993. *The Nation and Its Fragments: Colonial and Postcolonial Histories.* Princeton: Princeton University Press.

Choudhury, Yousuf. 1993. *The Roots and Tales of Bangladeshi Settlers.* Birmingham, U.K.: Sylhet Social History Group.

Chowdhury-Sengupta, Indira. 1995. "The Effeminate and the Masculine: Nationalism and the Concept of Race in Colonial Bengal." Pp. 282–292 in *The Concept of Race in South Asia,* edited by Peter Robb. Delhi: Oxford University Press.

Cohen, Jeffrey H. 2005. "Remittance Outcomes and Migration: Theoretical Contests, Real Opportunities." *Studies in Comparative International Development* 40(1): 88–112.

Council on American-Islamic Relations. 2008. "Without Fear of Discrimination: The Status of Muslim Civil Rights 2008." Washington, D.C.: Council on American-Islamic Relations. http://www.cair.com/Portals/o/pdf/civilrights2008.pdf.

Cowell, Alan. 2006. "Blair Criticizes Full Islamic Veil as 'Marks of Separation.'" *New York Times,* October 18. http://www.nytimes.com/2006/10/18/world/ europe/18britain.html.

Daily Star. 2008. "Kuwait Won't Renew Residency Visas." *Daily Star,* August 1. http://www.thedailystar.net/newDesign/news-details.php?nid=48413.

———. 2009b. "Malaysia Cancels 55,000 Visas for Bangladeshis." *Daily Star,* March 12. http://www.thedailystar.net/story.php?nid=79336.

———. 2009c. "New Bahrain Rule May End Labour Exploitation." *Daily Star,* May 9. http://www.thedailystar.net/story.php?nid=87402.

———. 2009d. "Employment in Middle East." *Daily Star,* May 12. http://www .thedailystar.net/story.php?nid=87785.

———. 2009e. "Bangladesh Fights back Fallout Good." *Daily Star,* December 13. http://www.thedailystar.net/newDesign/news-details.php?nid=117533.

———. 2010. "Agents Push up Costs of Migration." *Daily Star,* May 13. http:// www.thedailystar.net/newDesign/news-details.php?nid=138221.

Dale, Angela. Nusrat Shaheen, Virinder Kalra, and Edward Fieldhouse. 2002. "Routes into Education and Employment for Young Pakistani and Bangladeshi Women in the U.K." *Ethnic and Racial Studies* 25(6): 942–968.

Dannecker, Petra. 2005. "Bangladeshi Migrant Workers in Malaysia: The Construction of the 'Others' in a Multi-Ethnic Context." *Asian Journal of Social Science* 33(2): 246–267.

Das, Savele, Pandit. 1995. "Rebel Warrior." London: Asian Dub Foundation. http://www.lyricsdownload.com/asian-dub-foundation-rebel-warrior-lyrics.html.

Dinnie, Keith. 2007. *Nation Branding: Concepts, Issues, Practice.* Oxford: Butterworth Heinemann

Drishtipat Worldwide. 2007. "About Us." Astoria, N.Y.: Drishtipat Worldwide. http://www.drishtipat.org/aboutus.html.

Eade, John. 1989. *The Politics of Community: The Bangladeshi Community in East London.* Aldershot, U.K.: Avebury.

Eade, John, and David Garbin. 2002. "Changing Narratives of Violence, Struggle, and Resistance: Bangladeshis and the Competition for Resources in the Global City." *Oxford Development Studies* 30(2): 137–149.

———. 2006. "Competing Visions of Identity and Space: Bangladeshi Muslims in Britain." *Contemporary South Asia* 15(2): 181–193.

Eaton, Richard. 2001. "Who Are the Bengal Muslims?" Pp. 26–52 in *Understanding the Bengal Muslims: Interpretive Essays,* edited by Rafiuddin Ahmed. New Delhi: Oxford University Press.

Eickelman, Dale F., and James Piscatori. 1990. *Muslim Travellers: Pilgrimage, Migration, and the Religious Imagination*. Berkeley: University of California Press.

Espiritu, Yen Le. 1993. *Asian American Panethnicity: Bridging Institutions and Identities.* Philadelphia: Temple University Press

———. 2003. *Homebound: Filipino American Lives across Cultures, Communities, and Countries.* Berkeley: University of California Press.

Fernandes, Leela. 2006. *India's New Middle Class: Democratic Politics in an Era of Economic Reform*. Minneapolis: University of Minnesota Press.

Fetzer, Joel S., and J. Christopher Soper. 2005. *Muslims and the State in Britain, France, and Germany*. Cambridge: Cambridge University Press.

FOBANA (Federation of Bangladeshi Associations of North America). N.d. "About FOBANA." Washington, D.C.: Federation of Bangladeshi Associations of North America. http://www.fobanaonline.com.

Garbin, David. 2005. "Bangladeshi Diaspora in the UK: Some Observations on Socio-cultural Dynamics, Religious Trends, and Transnational Politics." London: University of London. http://www.surrey.ac.uk/Arts/CRONEM/SOASBangladeshi%20diaspora%20PaperDRAFT-7June2005.pdf.

Gardner, Katy. 1995. *Global Migrants, Local Lives: Migration and Transformation in Rural Bangladesh*. Oxford: Oxford University Press.

———. 2006. "The Transnational Work of Kinship and Caring: Bengali British Marriages in Historical Perspective." *Global Networks* 6(4): 373–387.

Gardner, Katy, and Filippo Osella. 2004. "Migration, Modernity, and Social Transformation in South Asia: An Introduction." Pp. xi–xlviii in *Migration, Modernity, and Social Transformation in South Asia*, edited by Filippo Osella and Katy Gardner. New Delhi: Sage.

Ghafour, P. K. Abdul. 2004. "A Million Expatriates to Benefit from New Citizenship Law." *Arab News*, October 21. http://www.arabnews.com/?article=53213.

Giddens, Anthony. 1991. *Modernity and Self-Identity: Self and Society in the Late Modern Age*. Stanford: Stanford University Press.

Gillian, Audrey. 2002. "From Bangladesh to Brick Lane." *The Guardian*, June 21. http://www.guardian.co.uk/uk/2002/jun/21/religion.bangladesh.

Glynn, Sarah. 2002. "Bengali Muslims: The New East End Radicals." *Ethnic and Racial Studies*. 25(6): 969–988.

———. 2006. "The Spirit of '71: How the Bangladeshi War of Independence Has Haunted Tower Hamlets." Edinburgh: Institute of Geography, University of Edinburgh. http://www.geos.ed.ac.uk/homes/rgroves/glynnpub1.pdf.

Grewal, Zareena A. 2009. "Marriage in Colour: Race, Religion, and Spouse Selection in Four American Mosques." *Ethnic and Racial Studies* 32(2): 323–345.

Guzder, Deena. 2008. "The Best Way to Curb Forced Marriages." *Time*, December 26. http://www.time.com/time/world/article/0,8599,1868757,00.html#ixzz0bkvswoLQ.

Hagan, Jaqueline, Karl Eschbach, and Nestor Rodriguez. 2008. "U.S. Deportation Policy, Family Separation, and Circular Migration." *International Migration Review* 42(1): 64–88.

Hefner, Robert W. 2001. "Introduction: Multiculturalism and Citizenship in Malaysia, Singapore, and Indonesia." Pp. 1–58 in *Politics of Multiculturalism: Pluralism and Citizenship in Malaysia, Singapore and Indonesia*, edited by Robert W. Hefner. Honolulu: University of Hawaii Press.

————. 2005. "Introduction: Modernity and the Remaking of Muslim Politics." Pp. 1–36 in *Remaking Muslim Politics: Pluralism, Contestation, and Democratization*, edited by Robert W. Hefner. Princeton: Princeton University Press.

Herberg, Will. 1955. *Protestant—Catholic—Jew: An Essay in American Religious Sociology*. Chicago: University of Chicago.

Hitchens, Christopher. 2001. *The Trial of Henry Kissinger*. London: Verso.

Hossain, Maneeza. 2007. *Broken Pendulum: Bangladesh's Swing to Radicalism*. Washington, D.C.: Hudson Institute.

Hossain, Naomi. 2005. "Productivity and Virtue: Elite Categories of the Poor in Bangladesh." *World Development* 33(6): 965–977.

Human Rights Watch. 2006. "Building Towers, Cheating Workers: Exploitation of Migrant Construction Workers in the United Arab Emirates." *Human Rights Watch*, November 11. http://www.hrw.org/en/node/11123/section/1.

————. 2009. "The Island of Happiness." *Human Rights Watch*, May 19. http://www.hrw.org/en/node/83110/section/4.

Huq, Saleemul, and M. Asaduzzaman. 2007. "Overview." Pp. 1–13 in *Vulnerability and Adaptation to Climate Change for Bangladesh*, edited by Saleemul Huq, Zahurul Karim, M. Asaduzzaman, and F. Mahtab. Boston: Kluwer Academic Publishers.

Hussain, Delwar. 2006. "Bangladeshis in East London: From Secular Politics to Islam." *Open Democracy*, July 7. http://www.opendemocracy.net/democracyprotest/bangladeshi_3715.jsp.

International Organization for Migration (IOM). 2002a. "Are Migrants Chasing after the 'Golden Deer'? A Study on Cost-Benefit Analysis of Overseas Migration." Dhaka: International Organization for Migration (IOM) Regional Office for South Asia.

————. 2002b. "A Study on Remittance Inflows and Utilization." Dhaka: International Organization for Migration (IOM) Regional Office for South Asia.

————. 2002c. "Contribution of Returnees: An Analytical Survey of Post-return Experience." Dhaka: International Organization for Migration (IOM) Regional Office for South Asia.

Islam, Aminul S. 2004. "Is the Candle Still Burning? Weber and the Crisis of Democratic Transition in Bangladesh." *Bangladesh e-Journal of Sociology* 1(1): 1–14. www.bangladeshsociology.org/Max%20Weber%20%20Aminul%20Islam%20PDF.pdf.

Ito, Sanae. 2004. "Globalization and Agrarian Change: A Case of Freshwater Prawn Farming in Bangladesh." *Journal of International Development* 16(7): 1003–1013.

Jacobsen, Jessica. 1997. "Religion and Ethnicity: Dual and Alternative Sources of Identity among Young British Pakistanis." *Ethnic and Racial Studies* 20(2): 238–256.

Jaffe, Eugene, and Israel Nebenzahl. 2006. *National Image and Competitive Advantage: The Theory and Practice of Place Branding*. Frederiksberg, Denmark: Copenhagen Business School Press.

Jones, Aidan. 2009. "British Warning: Summer Is Forced Marriage Season." *Christian Science Monitor*, July 2. http://www.csmonitor.com/World/Europe/2009/0702/p06s06-woeu.html.

Kabeer, Naila. 2000. *The Power to Choose: Bangladeshi Women and Labour Market Decisions in London and Dhaka*. London: Verso.

Kamrava, Mehran. 2006. "Introduction: Reformist Islam in Comparative Perspective." Pp. 1–28 in *The New Voices of Islam: Rethinking Politics and Modernity*, edited by Mehran Kamrava. Berkeley: University of California Press.

Kapiszewski, Andrzej. 2001. *Nationals and Expatriates: Population and Labor Dilemmas of the Gulf Cooperation Council States*. New York: Ithaca Press.

————. 2006. "Arab versus Asian Migrant Workers in the GCC Countries." United Nations Expert Group Meeting on International Migration and Development in the Arab Region. Beirut: Population Division, Department of Economic and Social Affairs, UN Secretariat.

Kapur, Devesh. 2005. "Remittances: The New Development Mantra?" Pp. 331–360 in *Remittances: Development Impact and Future Prospects*, edited by Samuel Munzele and Dilip Ratha. Washington, D.C.: World Bank.

Karim, Lamia. 2008. "Demystifying Micro-credit: The Grameen Bank, NGOs, and Neoliberalism in Bangladesh." *Cultural Dynamics* 20(1): 5–29.

Kershaw, Sarah. 2001. "Queens to Detroit: A Bangladeshi Passage." *New York Times*, March 8. http://www.nytimes.com/2001/03/08/nyregion/queens-to-detroit-a-bangladeshi-passage.html.

Khondker, Habibul H. 2010. "'Wanted but Not Welcome': Social Determinants of Labor Migration in the UAE." *Encounters* 1 (1): 1–27.

Kibria, Nazli. 1995. "Culture, Social Class, and Income Control in the Lives of Women Garment Workers in Bangladesh." *Gender and Society* 9(3): 289–309.

————. 2002. *Becoming Asian American: Second-Generation Chinese and Korean American Identities*. Baltimore: Johns Hopkins University Press.

————. 2004. "Returning International Labor Migrants from Bangladesh: The Experience and Effects of Deportation." Working Paper 28, Inter-University Committee on International Migration. Cambridge: Massachusetts Institute of Technology.

————. 2007. "South Asia: Pakistan, Bangladesh, Sri Lanka, Nepal." Pp. 612–623 in *The New Americans: A Guide to Immigration since 1965*, edited by Mary C. Waters and Reed Ueda. Cambridge: Harvard University Press.

Kim, Nadia. 2008. *Imperial Citizens: Koreans and Race from Seoul to LA*. Stanford: Stanford University Press.

Kurien, Prema A. 2002. *Kaleidoscopic Ethnicity: International Migration and the Reconstruction of Community Identities in India*. New Brunswick: Rutgers University Press.

Kuwait Times. 2008. "Warning against Strike Action." *Kuwait Times*, August 4. http://www.kuwaittimes.net/read_news.php?newsid=Njg3MDIyNDkw.

Lamont, Michèle, and Virág Molnár. 2002. "The Study of Boundaries in the Social Sciences." *Annual Review of Sociology* 28: 167–195.

Leland, John. 2004. "Tension in a Michigan City over Muslims' Call to Prayer." *New York Times*, May 5. http://query.nytimes.com/gst/fullpage.html?res=9501E5D8113DF936A35756C0A9629C8B63&sec=&spon=&pagewanted=all.

Levitt, Peggy, and B. Nadya Jaworsky. 2007. "Transnational Migration Studies: Past Developments and Future Trends." *Annual Review of Sociology* 33: 129–156.

Mamdani, Mahmood. 2002. "Good Muslim, Bad Muslim: A Political Perspective on Culture and Terrorism." *American Anthropologist* 104(3): 766–775.

Mandaville, Peter. 2001. *Transnational Muslim Politics: Reimagining the Umma*. London: Routledge.

Mascarenhas, Anthony. 1971. *The Rape of Bangla Desh*. New Delhi: Vikas.

Masood, Ehsan. 2005. "A Muslim Journey." *Prospect*, August 28. (http://www
.prspectmagazine.co.uk/2005/08/amuslimjourney.

Migration News. 2008. "Southeast Asia." *Migration News* 15:(4). http://migration
.ucdavis.edu/mn/more.php?id=3445_0_3_0.

Modood, Tariq. 2005. *Multicultural Politics: Racism, Ethnicity, and Muslims in Britain.*
Minneapolis: University of Minnesota Press and Edinburgh: Edinburgh University Press.

Mookherjee, Nayanika. 2003. "Gendered Embodiments: Mapping the Body-Politic of
the Raped Woman and the Nation in Bangladesh." Pp. 157–177 in *South Asian Women
in the Diaspora*, edited by Nirmal Puwar and Parvati Raghuram. Oxford: Berg.

Murshid K., Kazi Iqbal, and Meherun Ahmed. 2002. "A Study on Remittance Inflows
and Utilization." Dhaka, Bangladesh: International Organization for Migration
(IOM) Regional Office for South Asia. Mimeograph.

Muzumdar, Tanya. 2007. "The Nations of Michigan." *Metromode*, May 10. http://www
.metromodemedia.com/features/Nations0018b.aspx.

NABIC (North American Bangladesh Islamic Community). 1990. "NABIC." Oak Ridge,
Tenn.: North American Bangladeshi Islamic Community. http://www.nabic.org.

National Web Portal of Bangladesh. N.d. "National Statistics." Dhaka, Bangladesh:
National Web Portal of Bangladesh. http://www.bangladesh.gov.bd/index.php?
option=com_content&task=view&id=126&Itemid=197.

Nirmul Committee. 2006. *Tales of Three Generations of Bengalis in Britain*, edited by
John Eade, Ansar Ahmed Ullah, Jamil Iqbal, and Marissa Hey. London: Nirmul
Committee.

O'Connell, Joseph. 2001. "The Bengali Muslims and the State." Pp. 179–208 in
Understanding the Bengal Muslims: Interpretive Essays, edited by Rafiuddin Ahmed.
New Delhi: Oxford University Press.

———. 2009. "Resident Population Estimates by Ethnic Group, All Persons."
Newport, UK: Crown. http://www.neighbourhood.statistics.gov.uk/dissemination/
LeadTrendView.do?a=3&b=276772&c=tower+hamlets&d=13&e=13&f=21810&g=
346968&i=1001x1003x1004x1005&l=1809&o=198&m=0&r=1&s=1218827780554&enc=
1&adminCompId=21810&variableFamilyIds=6286&xW=1014.

Office for National Statistics. 2006. "Ethnicity and Identity: Employment Patterns."
Newport, UK: *Annual Population Survey, January 2004* to December 2004. http://
www.statistics.gov.uk/CCI/nugget.asp?ID=463.

Ong, Aihwa. 1995. "State versus Islam: Malay Families, Women's Bodies and the Body
Politic in Malaysia." Pp. 159–194 in *Bewitching Women, Pious Men: Gender and Body
Politics in Southeast Asia*, edited by Michael G. Peletz. Berkeley: University of
California Press.

Osella, Filippo, and Osella, Caroline. 2008. "Introduction: Islamic Reformism in South
Asia." *Modern Asian Studies* 42(2/3): 247–257.

———. 2009. "Muslim Entrepreneurs in Public Life between India and the Gulf:
Making Good and Doing Good." *Journal of the Royal Anthropological Institute* 15(S1):
S202–S221.

Palma, Porimol. 2009a. "Workers Returning in Alarming Numbers." *Daily Star*, March
14. http://www.thedailystar.net/story.php?nid=79611.

———. 2009b. "Overseas Jobs on the Wane." *Daily Star*, February 1. http://www
.thedailystar.net/story.php?nid=73813.

Patterson, Rubin. 2006. "Transnationalism: Diaspora-Homeland Development." *Social Forces* 84(4): 1891–1907.

Paul, Ruma. 2008. "Bangladesh Expat Remittances Hit Record in July." *Reuters India*, August 7. http://in.reuters.com/article/asiaCompanyAndMarkets/idINDHA32640 820080807.

Peach, Ceri. 2006. "South Asian Migration and Settlement in Great Britain." *Contemporary South Asia* 15(2): 133–146.

Peek, Lori. 2005. "Becoming Muslim: The Development of a Religious Identity." *Sociology of Religion* 66(3): 215–242.

Peletz, Michael G. 2005. "Islam and the Cultural Politics of Legitimacy in Malaysia in the Aftermath of September 11th." Pp. 240–272 in *Remaking Muslim Politics: Pluralism, Contestation, Democratization,* edited by Robert Hefner. Princeton: Princeton University Press.

PEW Research Center. 2007. Muslim Americans: Middle-Class and Mostly Mainstream. Washington, D.C.: PEW Research Center. http://pewresearch.org/pubs/483/muslim-americans.

Piper, Nicola. 2004. "Rights of Foreign Workers and the Politics of Migration in South-East and East Asia." *International Migration* 42(5): 71–98.

———. 2005. "Transnational Politics and Organizing of Migrant Labour in South-East Asia–NGO and Trade Union Perspectives." *Asia-Pacific Population Journal* 20(3): 87–110.

Portes, Alejandro, and Min Zhou. 1993. "The New Second Generation: Segmented Assimilation and Its Variants among Post-1965 Immigrant Youth." *Annals of the American Academy of Political and Social Sciences* 530 (1): 74–96.

Portes, Alejandro, and Ruben Rumbaut. 2006. *Immigrant America: A Portrait,* 3rd edition. Berkeley: University of California Press.

Pradeep, Begena P. 2008. "Ban on Workers Will Spell Misery." *Gulf Daily News,* May 26. http://www.gulf-daily-news.com/NewsDetails.aspx?storyid=218474.

Rahman, Md Mizanur. 2000. "Emigration and Development: The Case of a Bangladeshi Village." *International Migration* 38(4): 109–130.

Raymond, Barrett. 2008. "Kuwait Ramps up Deportation of Workers." *Christian Science Monitor,* August 2. http://www.csmonitor.com/2008/0802/ p25s25-wome.html.

Riaz, Ali. 2004. *God Willing: The Politics of Islamism in Bangladesh.* Lanham, Md.: Rowman and Littlefield.

Roy, Olivier. 2004. *Globalized Islam: The Search for a New Ummah.* New York: Columbia University Press.

Rummel, Rudy J. 1997. *Death by Government.* New Brunswick: Transaction.

Salway, Sarah. 2008. "Young Bangladeshi Men in the UK Labour Market: Inclusion, Exclusion, and Identity." *Ethnic and Racial Studies* 31(6): 1126–1152.

Samad, Yunus, and John Eade. 2002. "Community Perceptions of Forced Marriage." London: Foreign and Commonwealth Office. http://www.fco.gov.uk/resources/en/pdf/pdf1/fco_forcedmarriagereport121102.

Schaller Consulting. 2004. "The Changing Face of Taxi and Limousine Drivers." Schaller Consulting Archive. http://www.schallerconsult.com/taxi taxidriverreport.htm.

Sercombe, Charles, and Nargis Hakim, 2008. "Hamtramck's Bangladesh Community Had Plenty to Celebrate on Saturday 11/8/08." *New Michigan Media,* November 15.

http://www.newmichiganmedia.com/articles/34/1/Hamtramcks-Bangladesh-community-had-plenty-to-celebrate-on-Saturday-11808/Page1.html.

Shaham, Dahlia. 2008. "Foreign Labor in the Arab Gulf: Challenges to Nationalization." *Al Nakhlah: The Fletcher Online Journal of Southwest Asia and Islamic Civilization* (Fall 2008). http://fletcher.tufts.edu/al_nakhlah/Fa112008/DhaliaShaham ANformat.pdf.

Shehabuddin, Elora. 2008. *Reshaping the Holy: Democracy, Development and Muslim Women in Bangladesh.* New York: Columbia University Press.

Siddiqui, Tasneem. 2007. "Ratifying the UN Convention on Migrant Worker Rights." *New Daily Star,* December 18. www.thedailystar.net/story.php?nid=15843.

———. 2008. "Migration and Gender in Asia." Bangkok: United Nations Economic and Social Council for Asia and the Pacific. http://www.un.org/esa/population/meetings/EGM_Ittmig_Asia/P06_Siddiqui.pdf.

Siddiqui, Tasneem, and C. R. Abrar. 2001. "Migrant Workers' Remittances and Micro-finance Institutions." Geneva: International Labour Organization. Mimeograph.

Simon, Stephanie. 2004. "Muslim Call to Prayer Stirs a Midwest Town." *Los Angeles Times,* May 6. http://articles.latimes.com/2004/may/06/nation/na-mosque6.

Simpson, Edward. 2004. "Migration and Islamic Reform in a Port Town of Western India." Pp. 83–108 in *Migration, Modernity, and Social Transformation in South Asia,* edited by Filippo Osella and Katy Gardner. New Delhi: Sage.

Smith, Robert C. 2006. *Mexican New York: Transnational Lives of New Immigrants.* Berkeley: University of California Press.

Smith, Timothy. 1978. "Religion and Ethnicity in America." *American Historical Review* 83(12): 1155–1185.

STRATFOR. 2009. "Gulf States: Labor Policies, Financial Crisis and Security Concerns." http://www.stratfor.com/analysis/20090224_gulf_states_labor_policies_financial_crisis_and_security_concerns.

Sutton, Philip, and Stephen Vertigans. 2005. *Resurgent Islam: A Sociological Approach.* Cambridge: Polity.

Swadhinata Trust. 2010. "Home." http://www.swadhinata.org.uk.

Taboh, Julie. 2009. "Arab Women Gaining Rights in Gulf States." *VOA News,* March 6. http://www.voanews.com/english/archive/2009-03/2009-03-06-voa52.cfm.

Thai, Hung Cam. 2008. *For Better or for Worse: Vietnamese International Marriages in the New Global Economy.* New Brunswick: Rutgers University Press.

Turner, Bryan. 2004. "Fundamentalisms, Spiritual Markets and Modernity." *Sociology* 38(1): 195–202.

Twomey, Breda. 2001. "Labour Market Participation of Minority Ethnic Groups." *Labour Market Trends,* January: 29–41.

U.S. Bureau of the Census. 2000. "Foreign-Born Profiles (STP-159)." Washington, D.C.: U.S. Census Bureau, Population Division. http://www.census.gov/population/www/socdemo/foreign/STP-159-2000tl.html.

Wadud, Amina. 2006. "Aishah's Legacy: The Struggle for Women's Rights within Islam." Pp. 201–204 in *The New Voices of Islam: Rethinking Politics and Modernity,* edited by Mehran Kamrava. Berkeley: University of California Press.

Waldinger, Roger, and Michael Lichter. 2003. *How the Other Half Works: Immigration and the Social Organization of Labor.* Berkeley: University of California Press.

Waldinger, Roger, Eric Popkin, and Hector A. Magana. 2008. "Conflict and Contestation in the Cross-Border Community: Hometown Associations Reassessed." *Ethnic and Racial Studies* 31(5): 843–870.

Waters, Mary. 1999. *Black Identities: West Indian Immigrant Dreams and Immigrant Realities.* New York: Russell Sage Foundation.

Webb, Suhaib. 2007. "Imam Suhaib Webb's Eid Sermon." Boston: Islamic Society of Boston Cultural Center. http://www.masboston.org/index.php?action=view&id=61&module=newsmodule&src=%40random41940a897e943.

Williams, Raymond B. 1988. *Religions of Immigrants from India and Pakistan: New Threads in the American Tapestry.* New York: Cambridge University Press.

Willoughby, John. 2008. "Segmented Feminization and the Decline of Neopatriarchy in GCC Countries of the Persian Gulf." *Comparative Studies of South Asia, Africa, and the Middle East* 28(1): 184–199.

Winant, Howard. 2008. "The Historical Sociology of Race." Pp. 196–202 in *The Transnational Studies Reader: Intersections and Innovations,* edited by Sanjeev Khagram and Peggy Levitt. New York: Routledge.

Index

About the Author

Nazli Kibria is an associate professor of sociology at Boston University where she teaches courses on the sociology of international migration, family, and childhood as well as on contemporary South Asia. She grew up in Bangladesh and in other parts of the world, and received her undergraduate degree from Wellesley College and her doctorate in sociology from the University of Pennsylvania. A renowned scholar of migration and family, her publications include *Family Tightrope: The Changing Lives of Vietnamese Americans* and *Becoming Asian American: Second-Generation Chinese and Korean Americans.*

CPSIA information can be obtained at www.ICGtesting.com
Printed in the USA
BVOW01s1418190115

383957BV00001B/56/P